EFFECTIVE PERSONAL LETTERS
SECOND EDITION, REVISED AND ENLARGED

BY THE SAME AUTHOR

THE BUSINESS LETTER IN MODERN FORM

SUCCESSFUL COLLECTION LETTERS

TWELVE WAYS TO WRITE BETTER LETTERS

PRACTICAL PROBLEMS IN BUSINESS CORRESPONDENCE

GOODWILL LETTERS THAT BUILD BUSINESS

CREDIT LETTERS THAT WIN FRIENDS

BUSINESS-BUILDING LETTERS FOR HOTELS

HOW TO USE LETTERS IN COLLEGE PUBLIC RELATIONS

PRACTICAL BUSINESS LETTER PROBLEMS

BETTER CUSTOMER RELATIONS BY LETTER (with others)

BANK LETTERS: HOW TO USE THEM IN PUBLIC RELATIONS

HOW TO WRITE GOOD CREDIT LETTERS

PROBLEMS IN BUSINESS LETTER WRITING

TESTED CREDIT AND COLLECTION LETTERS

LETTERS THAT BUILD BANK BUSINESS

COMMON SENSE IN LETTER WRITING

EFFECTIVE PERSONAL LETTERS

By

WILLIAM H. BUTTERFIELD

Executive Director, University of Illinois Foundation; Formerly Chairman, Department of Business Communication, University of Oklahoma; Formerly Educational Director and Editor of Better Letters Service, National Retail Credit Association

SECOND EDITION, REVISED AND ENLARGED

Englewood Cliffs, N. J.

PRENTICE-HALL, INC.

FIFTEENTH PRINTING . . . JANUARY, 1967

PRINTED IN THE UNITED STATES OF AMERICA

24430–MO

Preface

The Amenities of Business

AMONG the oft-neglected contacts of business are many that would build stronger personal relationships between individuals. In the pressure of everyday events, most of us become so absorbed in the *necessities* of our work that the little courtesies—the *amenities* of business—are crowded out of our daily programs.

Many of the potential courtesies of business are splendidly adapted to expression through personal letters. A few words of appreciation for the help or kindness of an associate, a note of congratulation upon the achievement of a friend, an expression of sympathy for one who has met grief, a holiday note of good wishes to a friend—all these are opportunities for thoughtfulness. The person who takes time to practice the amenities enriches both his business associations and his personal experiences. Friendliness begets friendship.

Many who neglect the little courtesies of business do so because of procrastination rather than thoughtlessness. All of us can recall situations in which we "fully intended" to write that congratulatory note to Jim, or to send a word of sympathy to Mr. Jones on the death of his brother, or to thank Paul Roberts for his helpful suggestion. But too often our good intentions yield to the urgency of other things, and we do not translate them into written words. We postpone the correspondence amenities of business, sometimes with momentary relief, because such letters will be "hard to write," and should be set aside for a day when more time can be devoted to them. That day never comes!

The primary purpose of this book, therefore, is to provide a variety of specimen letters for ready reference in simplifying the preparation of personal letters in business. Some of these letter examples can be used for specific purposes with very little alteration or adaptation. Others will serve to suggest an appropriate approach to a situation, and to provide the general framework of a suitable letter.

In addition to the several types of letters motivated entirely by "voluntary courtesy" rather than by necessity—such as messages of congratulation and seasonal good wishes—the following chapters consider also many forms of correspondence required in conformity with business etiquette. Among them are letters of acceptance and declination, letters of introduction and recommendation, letters of apology, letters explaining delayed action, letters of regret, and letters granting and declining requests.

True enough, one's business would still go on if none of these types of letters were written, but it would be seriously handicapped through a needless loss of good will. Moreover, any person content to ignore the dictates of accepted business etiquette would eventually find himself with very few friends.

"The amenities of business," then, defines the scope and purpose of this book. The 855 complete letter specimens presented in the following pages have been carefully selected —and, in many cases, actually formulated—to illustrate the effective handling of everyday personal situations in business. To anyone who would make the most of friendship in business, the many opportunities for cordial personal contacts by letter cannot be overemphasized.

W. H. B.

Introductory Acknowledgment

THE AUTHOR acknowledges with gratitude the assistance of the numerous persons, business concerns, and noncommercial organizations whose letters are presented in this book. So that each contributor of specimen examples may be identified with the type or types of letters he has made available, a brief acknowledgment section precedes each of the ten chapters. In each case the acknowledgment mentions the names of all persons and organizations whose letters, in original or revised form, appear in that chapter.

WILLIAM H. BUTTERFIELD

Contents

CHAPTER   PAGE

PREFACE . . . . **v**

INTRODUCTORY ACKNOWLEDGMENT . . . . **vii**

CHECK LIST OF REQUIREMENTS FOR EFFECTIVE PERSONAL
LETTERS . . . . **xv**

I.   LETTERS OF CONGRATULATION AND GOOD WISHES .   **1**

    Letters to Business and Professional Associates . . .   **2**
      Upon professional or civic honor **2**
      Upon new business or professional connection . .   **9**
      Upon promotion **12**
      Upon retirement from business **17**
      Upon speech, article, pamphlet, or book **19**
      Upon outstanding community service **25**
      Upon accomplishment of son or daughter . . .   **28**
      Upon business anniversary or special business achieve-
        ment **30**

    Letters to Employees **34**
      Upon promotion or other business advancement . .   **34**
      Upon significant personal occasion **37**
      Upon outstanding work for firm **39**
      Upon professional honor or achievement **43**

II.   LETTERS OF APPRECIATION **46**
    Letters to Business and Professional Associates . . .   **48**
      For personal favor or service **48**
      For assistance to firm, club, or association . . .   **54**
      For luncheon or dinner at home or club **59**
      For overnight visit at home or club **62**
      For theater, sports event, or other entertainment . .   **64**
      For message of congratulation **66**
      For message of condolence or sympathy **71**
      For speaking before club or association **73**
      For favorable mention in speech, article, or book . .   **77**

CHAPTER   PAGE

II.   LETTERS OF APPRECIATION (*cont.*)

      Letters to Employees 79
        For loyal or outstanding service 79
        For valuable suggestion 82

      Letters to Dealers 85
        For loyal patronage over period of years 85
        For outstanding success in sale of product . . . 87
        For promptness in meeting obligations 90
        For act of special service or courtesy 93

      Letters to Consumers 96
        For opening charge account 96
        For first use of charge account 99
        For regular patronage 102
        For prompt payment of bills 107
        For co-operation in correcting error 111
        For recommending firm to others 112
        For renewed patronage 115

III.   LETTERS OF SEASONAL GOOD WISHES 118
      Letters to Business and Professional Associates . . . 119
      Letters to Employees 122
      Letters to Dealers 124
      Letters to Consumers 128

IV.   LETTERS OF WELCOME 131
      Letters to Business and Professional Associates . . . 132
      Letters to Employees 134
      Letters to Dealers 138
      Letters to Consumers 142
      Letters to Prospective Consumers 145

V.   LETTERS OF CONDOLENCE AND SYMPATHY . . . 150
      Letters to Business and Professional Associates . . . 151
        Upon a death in family 151
        Upon personal injury or illness 155
        Upon injury or illness of a member of family . . . 159
        Upon death of a company officer 161
        Upon material loss or damage 163

      Letters to Employees 167
        Upon a death in family 167
        Upon personal injury or illness 169

CHAPTER   PAGE

V. LETTERS OF CONDOLENCE AND SYMPATHY (*cont.*)
   Letters to Relatives of Business Associates Taken by Death 173
   Letters to Relatives of Employees Taken by Death . . 177

VI. LETTERS OF RECOMMENDATION 180
   Letters Recommending a Personal Friend 181
   Letters Recommending a Business or Professional Associate 185
   Letters Recommending an Employee or Former Employee 189

VII. LETTERS OF INTRODUCTION 195
   Letters Introducing a Personal Friend 196
   Letters Introducing a Business or Professional Associate . 199
   Letters Introducing a New Sales Representative . . . 203

VIII. LETTERS OF INVITATION 207
   Letters to Business and Professional Associates . . . 208
     To attend banquet, club luncheon, lecture, or entertainment 208
     To be luncheon or dinner guest 211
     To be overnight guest at home or club 214
     To give address or informal talk 217
   Letters to Employees 220
     To attend company social event 220
   Letters to Consumers 224
     To open charge account 224
     To renew use of account 228
     To attend special event 232

IX. MISCELLANEOUS COURTESY LETTERS 236
   Letters of Acceptance 236
     Of invitation to banquet, club luncheon, lecture, or entertainment 237
     Of luncheon or dinner invitation 238
     Of hospitality of home or club on overnight visit . . 239
     Of speaking invitation 241
     Of invitation to attend meeting or convention . . . 243
     Of membership in professional or civic organization . 244

CHAPTER   PAGE

IX. MISCELLANEOUS COURTESY LETTERS (*cont.*)

Of invitation to serve on civic or professional commit-
tee or board 245
Of resignation from position, board, or committee . . 246
Of resignation from club or association 248

Letters of Declination 249
Of invitation to banquet, club luncheon, lecture, or en-
tertainment 250
Of luncheon or dinner invitation 251
Of hospitality of home or club on overnight visit . . 253
Of speaking invitation 254
Of invitation to attend meeting or convention . . . 257
Of membership in professional or civic organization . 258
Of invitation to serve on civic or professional commit-
tee or board 259

Letters of Apology 261
For delay in returning borrowed property . . . 261
For delay in acknowledging favor or courtesy . . 262
For delay in sending promised material 264
For absence from meeting 266
For inability to keep appointment 267

Letters of Regret 268
For absence during call of out-of-town visitor . . 269
For inability to call upon associate during visit to his
city 270
For inability of associate to call at office as planned . 271
For absence of associate from meeting or convention . 272

Letters Explaining Delayed Action 273
Requesting additional time in which to make final reply 274
Acknowledgment by secretary in absence of addressee 276

Letters Granting Requests 277
For information 278
For booklet, pamphlet, or magazine 280
For business appointment 282
For permission to reprint material in book or article . 284
For charge account 285

Letters Declining Requests 288
For information or material 288
For business appointment 290
For charge account 291

CONTENTS

CHAPTER   PAGE

IX.   MISCELLANEOUS COURTESY LETTERS (*cont.*)

      For support of charitable organization, public-welfare
        institution, co-operative-advertising campaign, etc. . 292

X.   LETTERS SOLICITING CONTRIBUTIONS TO CHARITY ORGANIZATIONS 296

Appendices

A. TRITE EXPRESSIONS TO BE AVOIDED IN LETTERS . . 311

B. COMMON ERRORS IN ENGLISH USAGE 314

C. GUIDES TO CORRECT PUNCTUATION 343

D. GUIDES TO CORRECT CAPITALIZATION 348

E. TITLES COMMONLY USED IN ADDRESSING INDIVIDUALS . 351

F. FORMS OF ADDRESS FOR PERSONS OF RANK 356

G. CORRECT FORM IN WRITING TO ARMY AND NAVAL OF-FICERS 371

H. STANDARD FORMS OF LETTER LAYOUT 373

I. MECHANICS OF ENVELOPE ADDRESS 377

J. PROPER FOLDING AND INSERTION OF LETTERS IN EN-VELOPES 379

INDEX 383

Check List of Requirements for Effective Personal Letters [1]

1. Be sure your letter is opportunely timed. A note of congratulation, a message of condolence, or a letter of appreciation, for example, will be far more effective if it is written promptly—that is, immediately after the occurrence that occasions it.

2. Be sure your letter is neat and attractive in appearance. Clean-cut typing, balanced layout, and freedom from mechanical errors are important factors in creating a favorable impression. Standard forms of letter arrangement are shown on pages 373-376. The mechanics of envelope address are discussed on pages 377-378.

3. Make your letter as brief as its purpose permits. A short message will convey most thoughts just as well as a long one, and it will make a far better impression. Brevity saves the reader's time; wordiness wastes it.

4. Choose your words carefully. Use your own vocabulary. Avoid the trite, "rubber-stamp" expressions that make many of the personal letters in business sound stilted and unnatural. An alphabetical list of objectionable expressions appears on pages 311-313.

5. Make the tone of your letter personal, so that the message is "tailor-made" for the *individual* reader.

6. Be cordial and friendly, but not gushy. An effusive letter suggests a lack of sincerity. Such a letter may even irritate a reader who prefers conservatism.

---

[1] Several items included in this section are reprinted, with adaptations, from summaries of good letter practice that appear in *How to Use Letters in College Public Relations*, by William H. Butterfield (Harper & Brothers, New York), and *Credit Letters That Win Friends*, by William H. Butterfield (University of Oklahoma Press, Norman). Material reprinted from these books is presented by permission of their publishers.

7. Select a salutation and complimentary close that harmonize with the friendly tone of the message. Use the reader's name in the greeting [2] (*My dear Mr. Smith, Dear Mr. Smith, My dear Smith, Dear Smith, My dear John, Dear John*).[3] Close your letter with *Very sincerely yours, Yours very sincerely, Sincerely yours, Yours sincerely, Sincerely, Very cordially yours, Yours very cordially, Cordially yours, Yours cordially,* or *Cordially*.[4] (Special forms of address for persons of rank are shown on pages 356-370.)

8. Express your thoughts clearly and concisely. Avoid the use of redundant expressions and involved sentences that obscure meaning.

9. Avoid violations of correct English usage. These faults jeopardize the reader's respect for one who commits them, since they are obviously the result of ignorance or carelessness. They also distract the reader's attention from the message. A review of common errors in English usage appears on pages 314-342.

10. Say what you mean and mean what you say. Write with genuine sincerity that lends conviction to your message.

11. Inject a spirit of enthusiasm into your letter. Make the reader feel that you enjoyed writing to him.

12. Be sure your letter is punctuated correctly. Punctuation marks serve either to clarify or to obscure what one writes. Correct punctuation helps to make one's meaning unmistakably clear at a glance. Faulty punctuation often creates a misunderstanding. A list of guides to correct punctuation appears on pages 343-347.

13. Capitalize the right words. The indiscriminate use of

---

[2] The letter addressed to a business house or other organization is an exception; for it the plural salutation *Gentlemen* is customary.

[3] For correct use of titles commonly employed in addressing individuals, see pages 351-355.

[4] Exceptions are (1) the letter addressed to a business house or other organization, and (2) the letter written by a secretary in the absence of her employer. In these instances *Very truly yours* or *Yours very truly* is often preferable. Either of these complimentary closes is also permissible in personal letters in general, although a form including *sincerely* or *cordially* carries a warmth of tone more consistent with the friendly informality of most personal letters.

capital letters denotes slovenliness. A list of guides to correct capitalization appears on pages 348-350.

14. When the same message will go to several persons, have the letter individually typed for each recipient. An obvious form letter kills the reader's interest and enthusiasm.

15. Sign the letter yourself. The recipient will value the personal touch of your own handwriting, not that of your secretary.

16. Be sure your letter is properly folded and inserted in its envelope. Correct methods of folding and insertion are outlined and illustrated on pages 379-381.

ONE

Letters of Congratulation and Good Wishes

This chapter includes letter specimens made available through the courtesy of the following persons and organizations: Crocker-McElwain Company, Holyoke, Massachusetts; Mr. J. Gordon Dakins, New York City; Mr. Whitman Daniels, Ithaca, New York; Davison-Paxon Company, Atlanta, Georgia; Deltox Rug Company, Oshkosh, Wisconsin; Mr. Richard P. Ettinger, New York City; Mr. Lloyd H. Geil, Chicago, Illinois; Harper & Brothers, New York City; Professor Edward J. Kilduff, New York University, New York City; Marquardt & Company, Inc., New York City; Norcross, New York City; Professor Herbert H. Palmer, Rhode Island State College, Kingston, Rhode Island; Professor C. C. Parkhurst, Boston University, Boston, Massachusetts; Prentice-Hall, Inc., New York City; The Roosevelt, New Orleans, Louisiana; Miss Bernice C. Turner, New York City; Mrs. Pieter C. Vosburgh, Northampton, Massachusetts; Mr. Clarence E. Wolfinger, Philadelphia, Pennsylvania; Mr. Herbert E. Wrinkle, Norman, Oklahoma.

THE NORMAL COURSE of business presents many excellent opportunities for the writing of congratulatory letters. The progress and good fortune of one's friends, business associates, and employees provide many occasions on which notes of congratulation are appropriate and fully justified. But this type of letter often falls victim to the pressure of more urgent correspondence. Because even a short congratulatory note is difficult for many persons to formulate, it is frequently postponed until the occasion has lost its timeliness, and is then forgotten.

In the expression of congratulations and good wishes, brevity is a cardinal virtue. Direct, concise language adds vigor to the message. Naturalness of expression is also essential to give one's words the ring of sincerity. Trite, stereotyped phrases [1] should be carefully avoided; they destroy the personality of the letter and indicate a lack of genuineness on the part of the writer.

[1] A list of trite expressions appears on pages 311-313.

1

Finally, the contagious quality of enthusiasm adds zest and animation to the message. The letter of congratulation should be written with relish or not written at all. If the sender has enjoyed writing it, this fact will communicate itself to the recipient through the tone of the message.

The following pages present examples of congratulatory letters suitable for various occasions that occur frequently in business. The tone of these illustrations ranges all the way from the conservatism appropriate in addressing an elderly executive to the colloquial informality permissible in writing to a former college roommate.

Letters to Business and Professional Associates [2]

Upon professional or civic honor:

Dear Mr. Larimer:

Hearty congratulations upon your election as President of the Indiana Bankers Association.

You bring to this important office a fine record of experience and achievement in the banking profession. We feel sure the Association will make great progress under your leadership.

As an Evansville firm with a real interest in this community, we take pride in the recognition that has come to you.

Sincerely yours,

———

Dear Allen:

I have just learned of your election to the post of Treasurer of the Salmagundi Club.

Congratulations! This shows that the Club is really progressive and knows how to pick the right man for the job.

With your hand on the financial helm, I feel sure the Club will enjoy one of its most successful years.

Cordial regards to you.

Sincerely,

———

[2] Letters marked with an asterisk (*) are especially appropriate for mailing by manufacturing concerns or wholesale houses to their retail dealers.

* Dear Mr. Bennett:

It is a genuine pleasure to congratulate you upon your election as President of the Sheridan Merchants Association. Such a vote of confidence by your fellow businessmen is a high personal tribute to you.

The other members of Gilmer & Company join me in this expression of hearty congratulations and good wishes.

Sincerely yours,

———

Dear Mr. Bradley:

We feel sure that every business house in this community shares our enthusiasm over your re-election as President of the Better Business Association.

The fine progress of the Association during your first term of office proves the wisdom of your re-election.

Congratulations on receiving for the second time an honor that no other man has held more than once. The Association is fortunate in having such excellent leadership for another year.

Sincerely yours,

———

* Dear Bob:

Congratulations! Dick Simmons just told me that you have been named Chairman of the Arlington Community Fund.

This adds still another to the long list of honors accorded you by your fellow townsmen. You have done much for Arlington, and your reward is the trust and respect of all who know you.

Your other friends in this office join me in wishing you every success with the Community Fund drive.

Sincerely,

———

Dear Miss Samuels:

In this morning's paper we read of your election as President of the Midwest Association of Business and Professional Women's Clubs.

Congratulations upon this fine recognition of your leadership. It gives us a feeling of genuine pride when an Omahan receives such a high honor.

Sincerely yours,

Dear Emerson:

That the handsome fellow whose picture I saw in last night's paper has been elected President of the American Arbitration Association is certainly good news. Congratulations! But it is really the A.A.A. that should be congratulated on its good fortune.

I know that, with your enthusiasm for arbitration, the Association will accomplish a great deal under your leadership. Unquestionably, arbitration is about to embark on its greatest mission, both domestically and on a world-wide basis. It seems that the peace of the world rests upon the successful application of its principles through the U. N.

Cordial regards to you.

Sincerely,

---

* Dear Mr. Greenough:

Upon his return from Hillsboro yesterday, Jim Turner told me that you had been elected President of the Chamber of Commerce there.

Congratulations on this fine recognition and honor!

Because of our close business relationship with you for almost fifteen years, we know that you are ideally qualified for this important work. We are sure your term of office will be one of real accomplishment.

Sincerely yours,

Dear Mr. Munson:

Hearty congratulations upon your election as President of the Missouri Society of Certified Public Accountants.

As a firm now in its forty-third business year in Kansas City, Davis & Company has a deep interest in this community . . . and in the achievement of Kansas Citians.

It is a high honor to be named President of your statewide professional organization. Best wishes for every success as you assume this important office.

Sincerely yours,

---

* Dear Mr. Forbes:

We learned this morning of your election as President of the Greater Des Moines Club.

Congratulations upon this splendid recognition of your ability. It shows the high esteem in which you are held by your fellow merchants.

If there is any way that we can co-operate during your term of office, it will be a pleasure to do so.

Sincerely yours,

Dear Everett:

Warmest congratulations to you upon your election as President of the Wisconsin Bar Association.

All of us in this community have good reason to be proud of the honor you have brought to Waupun.

Sincere best wishes to you for a successful administration.

Cordially,

---

* Dear Mr. Gurney:

I have just read in today's paper of your election as Mayor of Billings Center, and I congratulate both you and the community you represent. I am sure that you will bring to your job the same ability that has made your business such a success.

Sincerely yours,

Dear Bill:

I have just noted in the October *Bulletin* that you were duly elected President of the American Business Writing Association.

Congratulations!

If I can ever be of help to you during your term of office, please feel free to write to me.

Sincerely yours,

___

Dear Mr. Berry:

I was very glad to see your name mentioned as one of the three prize winners in the Better Letter Contest recently conducted by *The Credit World.*

Among the credit men who are working toward higher standards of business correspondence, your contributions are already well known. I have read several of your articles myself, and have seen some of your letters reproduced in books on letter writing.

So the announcement of your success in a nationwide business letter contest strikes me as most appropriate recognition of the fine work you are doing. Hearty congratulations on the blue ribbon award!

Cordially yours,

___

Dear Leonard:

Your election the other day as District Governor of Rotary pleased me so much that I wanted to send you this word of congratulations and best wishes.

By every standard of measurement you have earned this honor, and I am delighted that it has come to you. I know you will continue your outstanding work for the greater effectiveness of Rotary and its high purposes.

Sincerely yours,

___

Dear Mr. Hammond:

I feel that all of us in Fort Wayne can be proud of your election as President of the Indiana State Educational Association. You are to be congratulated upon this recognition of your high standing among the educators of this state.

Sincerely yours,

___

Dear Ralph:

I was delighted to learn of your election as President of the Chamber of Commerce, and I am sure my reaction is typical of every businessman in this community.

You have earned this honor through years of unselfish work for the betterment of Middletown, and you are eminently qualified to fulfill the responsibility which it carries.

Congratulations and best wishes for every success!

Sincerely,

My dear McNees:

I find before me an article from the *Legal Intelligencer* of Philadelphia, dated from Bedford Springs, which carries the good news that Sterling G. McNees has been elected President of the State Bar Association. My congratulations and best wishes for a successful administration.

I shall be looking for your picture in the American Bar Association *Journal*.

Cordially,

Dear Wayne:

This is just a note to congratulate you upon your election as Congressman from the Fifth District. Your friends share with you the satisfaction of your smashing victory.

Personally, my only regret is that your election will take you away from this community the greater part of the year. You will be doing an important job, however, and I know you will do it exceptionally well.

Feeling as I do that your election is a big step toward better government, I wanted to send you these words of congratulations and best wishes.

Sincerely yours,

---

* Dear Mr. Graham:

Word reached me this morning that you have been elected Mayor of Cameron, and I extend to you my hearty congratulations.

Such an honor proves that, in addition to being a top-notcher in the furniture business, you are also an acknowledged leader in the civic affairs of your community.

From my ten years of business dealings with you, I am in a position to know that your honesty, fairness, and sound judgment make you an ideal man for the office to which you have been elected. In fact, my congratulations might well be addressed to the citizens of Cameron for having made such a wise choice.

Sincerely yours,

Dear Dean Adams:

Congratulations on your election as President of the American Association of Collegiate Schools of Business. I learned of it this morning.

This recognition is most appropriate in view of your many contributions to the progress of the Association and to the teaching of business administration on the undergraduate level.

Cordially yours,

Dear Mr. Townsend:

Congratulations on the splendid recognition recently accorded your editorial column in the *Daily News*. I was much pleased to see that you had won the state award for editorial excellence during 195-.

The people of Milburn have profited much, I am sure, from the thoughtful interpretation of news events in your daily column. I know many who will share my feeling of satisfaction that your outstanding newspaper work has received statewide recognition.

Sincerely yours,

Dear Mr. Kauffman:

I read in the Sunday paper that you have been inducted into the Oklahoma Hall of Fame in recognition of your many contributions to the intellectual growth of the state.

This is just a word to congratulate you upon an honor well earned, and to tell you how glad I am to see this tribute paid you.

Sincerely,

Dear Mr. Summers:

C O N G R A T U L A T I O N S ! ! !

May I add my felicitations to the many you have already received on your election to the Presidency of the New Orleans Rotary Club.

I think the members of your club should also be congratulated upon their choice.

Sincerely yours,

Upon new business or professional connection:

Dear Paul:

Arthur Connor told me this morning that you will soon be leaving your present connection to become Director of Publicity for J. A. Reimer & Company.

I wanted to send you this word of congratulations and best wishes, for I am happy to learn of your advancement to a position of greater responsibility and opportunity. The best of luck to you in your new work.

Cordially,

Dear Mr. Grund:

I was delighted to receive the announcement of your becoming a member of the firm of Seidman & Seidman.

Congratulations to you and congratulations to the firm. I am sure that your partnership has been well earned and that your addition to the firm will add strength to it.

Sincerely yours,

Dear Fred:

The other day I heard of your fine new position with General Electric, and I was thoroughly pleased to learn of it.

I shall always remember with admiration the way you worked your way through college and earned your engineering degree entirely on your own power.

Surely you have "made" the break that has just come your way, and I know that your spirit of determination and enthusiasm will carry you on to further accomplishments.

Sincere congratulations on your new position, and the best of luck to you.

Cordially yours,

Dear Mr. Herrick:

I was very glad to learn that you are the new Secretary of the Omaha Chamber of Commerce. I can think of no one better qualified for this important work, and I know you will make an outstanding success of it.

Whenever I can be of assistance in any way, you will find me glad to co-operate.

Cordially yours,

Dear Jim:

Congratulations on your appointment to a top-notch faculty post at Northwestern University.

Many of your old Rotary friends here were happy to read the announcement that you had re-entered the field of higher education. No doubt you were most successful in the commercial field, but we need your influence in educational circles.

Please accept my best wishes for the greatest of happiness and success in your new position. Whenever you are back in Oklahoma, remember that we shall be very glad to see you.

Sincerely,

Dear Dick:

When I was in Cleveland for a few days recently, I stopped at the Peerless Products office hoping to have a visit with you.

I was surprised to discover that you were no longer with that firm, and disappointed at not seeing you. But recalling your enthusiastic interest in public relations work and your belief in its future, I was delighted to learn that you are now doing that type of work with such a fine organization as John Thomas & Sons.

Hearty congratulations to you on making a business connection of such bright promise for the future. I hope your new work will bring you a full measure of satisfaction and success.

Sincerely,

Dear Mr. Wheaton:

This is just a word to wish you the best of success in your new position.

I am certain that you will do a good job. In the form of experience and practice, you have a keen-edged set of tools with which to work. By no means do you have a raw product on which to use these tools, since the name Woolf Brothers has meant quality and satisfaction for a great many years.

The master craftsman, however, has a manner of smoothing rough spots that the layman cannot see. I feel that your ability will help to create an even smoother running organization than before.

Sincerely,

Dear Dr. Dodge:

I read with mixed feelings the announcement of your election as President of Norwich University. I am delighted, of course, at this splendid tribute to your ability and achievements; but I am also keenly regretful that it will take you away from Norman. The place you hold in the life of this community will be hard to fill.

The purpose of this letter, however, is to congratulate you upon the high honor which has come to you, and which is so well deserved. You have my best wishes for success and happiness in your new work.

Sincerely yours,

Dear Hugh:

I was happy to learn this morning of your appointment as Controller of J. L. Benning & Company. This note brings you my hearty congratulations!

The Benning organization should be congratulated, too. They certainly picked the right man for this important job. Your qualifications for the position are ideal, and I know you will be highly successful in it.

Best wishes for many years of happiness in Pittsburgh.

Sincerely,

Dear Bill:

It was with very special interest, derived from our pleasant past association at the University of Oklahoma and our common experience in the publishing business, that I noted the news of your appointment at DePauw University. Congratulations!

It happens that I am carrying a corresponding responsibility in public relations at Cornell, so we continue to have a mutual interest.

If you should make a trip into this part of the country which might offer the possibility of a reunion, I hope you will let me know. It would be great to see you again and to hear what you have been doing in these intervening years. There is no immediate prospect of my traveling to Indiana, but if I should get out that way I shall certainly look you up.

Sincerely,

Dear Gordon:

Please consider this little note from me as a volume of good wishes to greet you in your new office. I feel sure you will like your new surroundings, and I know your new surroundings will like you.

Congratulations on your appointment as Educational Director of the N.R.C.A. You have my best wishes for many years of success and happiness in your new position.

Sincerely,

Upon promotion:

Dear John:

I have just learned of your promotion to the top spot in your department. Congratulations!

You are ideally qualified to direct the public-relations program of Baker & Keating, and I know you will add new achievements to those which have earned you this fine promotion.

Cordial regards and best wishes to you.

Sincerely,

---

* Dear Mr. Whitcomb:

It was a pleasure to read in this morning's *Globe* that you have been made Vice President of Warren & Company.

Such a promotion is a fitting recognition of your ability and your valuable service to your firm. The other members of the Byers-Kinley organization join me in this expression of hearty congratulations.

Sincerely yours,

Dear Don:

A letter this morning from Paul Miller gave me the latest chapter of your success story.

Congratulations on your fine promotion. You will do your usual outstanding job as Manager of the College Book Department.

I know how hard you have worked, Don, and it delights me to see you receive the recognition you so well deserve.

Sincerely,

Dear Ralph:

I always like to see advancement reward a man who is so well qualified for it. Congratulations on your promotion to the Vice Presidency of your firm.

You have made remarkable strides during the past ten years, and I have followed your progress with a deep sense of interest and satisfaction.

Best wishes for still greater success in your new position.

Sincerely,

Dear Mr. Hartwick:

We read with much interest of your appointment as Secretary-Manager of the Madison Chamber of Commerce.

Congratulations upon this splendid promotion. We know from your previous work that you will do an outstanding job.

You can depend on our co-operation whenever we can be of assistance. Please feel free to call on us.

Sincerely yours,

Dear Eric:

The news that you have been made General Manager of The Mills Company has just reached me, and I am happy to learn of your promotion. It is a recognition of the splendid work you have done.

I know you will be highly successful in your new capacity with the firm, and that it will bring you even further opportunities for advancement.

My congratulations and best wishes to you!

Cordially,

Dear Mr. McGugin:

I have just learned of your appointment as Division Superintendent of the Santa Fe Railroad.

At a time when you have such good reason to be proud and happy, may I add my sincere congratulations? I was very glad to hear of your promotion, and I wish you every success in your new position.

Cordially yours,

Dear Mr. Glenroy:

I was glad to see in the March *Publicity Journal* that you have been made Director of Public Relations at The Phillips Company.

From watching your record as Assistant Director, I know that you will do a splendid job. In fact, your promotion to a post of such responsibility proves that you have been doing just that in the past.

Hearty congratulations and best wishes for your continued success.

Sincerely yours,

Dear Jim:

I'm sure that nobody is more delighted than I am over your appointment as Sales Manager of your firm. I have never known a harder worker than you, and you surely deserve this fine advancement.

I know you will go on to further achievements, and my best wishes go with you in your new job.

Sincerely yours,

Dear Mr. Randall:

I congratulate you most sincerely on your recent advancement to the Presidency of your company. And I congratulate your firm on having a new chief who knows thoroughly every department of the business, and who is eminently fitted to cope with the problems of today and the future.

Looking back, the twenty-five years you have been associated with Holmes & Sampson seem to me only a few short summers. Our work for your company all this time has been so interesting and pleasant that a quarter of a century has gone by very fast indeed.

By the very nature of the service we have rendered your company, we know how well you have filled every position you have occupied on your way to the top. Your steady advancement from shipping room to the President's chair has been won by hard work and by the exercise of keen foresight and business intelligence.

These words of felicitation are not from me alone. Mr. Reynolds and Mr. Stevens are figuratively looking over my shoulder. They ask personally to be remembered to you.

Sincerely yours,

Dear Bob:

I was delighted to learn this morning that you have been made Associate Editor of *The Journal of Retailing.* Congratulations on this fine promotion.

Your ability and hard work have carried you to one of the top positions on the editorial staff. I have no doubt that you will do an excellent job in your new capacity, and that you will go on to still greater achievements in the years ahead.

Sincerely,

Dear Mr. Parker:

This is just a word to tell you how glad I was to learn that you have been made Manager of Courtland's.

Your promotion is the best possible recognition of long and efficient service to your organization. I am happy for you in your success.

Sincerely yours,

Dear Mr. Dollman:

News of your advancement in the publishing field gives me genuine pleasure. You have all the requisites for success in the college textbook field—teaching experience, authorship of several books, knowledge of the mechanics of publishing, and a fine personality.

Congratulations to both you and your firm, and every good wish for your success and happiness in your new job.

Sincerely yours,

Dear Jack:

As I browsed through the Sunday paper, my eyes fell upon an item headed: "Carson New Chief of WJY Staff."

Your appointment as Chief Announcer of WJY is a splendid recognition of your ability and a fine opportunity for still greater achievement.

Congratulations and more power to you!

Sincerely,

Dear Bob:

Congratulations! I have just learned that the firm of Miles & Lindley has become Miles, Lindley & Snow.

It is no small honor to become a partner in this highly-respected firm; and doing so before your thirtieth birthday is indeed an achievement.

You have my sincere best wishes for every success in your new capacity.

Cordially,

Dear Mr. Sanford:

Davison's wishes to congratulate you on your appointment as Assistant Manager of Hotel Georgian, which we find mentioned in today's press.

When we hear of the advancement of one of our young citizens, we are especially interested, because the young men of today are the leaders of tomorrow. The progress of Atlanta depends upon the young people of today—and what Atlanta becomes in the future interests Davison's immensely, since we are a part of it and are eager to see it progress.

We wish you great success in your new position. Our relationship with you in the past has been a pleasure, and we hope it will continue through the years.

Cordially yours,

Nice Work, Stan!

I mean, of course, your fine promotion to the position of Personnel Director of Harvey & Sons.

You are very well qualified for this responsible post, and I know you will fill it with complete success.

Sincerely,

Dear Raymond:

It always does me good to see a friend rewarded for ability and hard work, so I was very much pleased to learn of your advancement to Manager of the Montgomery Ward store.

I know you will do an excellent job, and I congratulate you on this fine promotion.

Cordially,

Upon retirement from business:

Dear Mr. Kingston:

Word of your retirement from business, which reached me today, occasions this letter of congratulations and best wishes.

I doubt if any man has contributed more to the progress of the textile industry than you have. I am sure no man has ever left behind him a finer record of loyalty and devotion to the highest type of business ideals.

Please add my best wishes to those you have already received from the many who wish you well.

Sincerely,

Dear Mr. Williamson:

I have just learned of your resignation from the Board of Directors of Hartman & Company.

Upon the occasion of your retirement, I congratulate you upon your long and honorable business career. Many have found inspiration in your leadership; many more will find a worthy example in your fine record.

Sincerely,

Dear Mr. Cassidy:

Last night I saw your picture in the June issue of *Modern Retailing*, accompanied by the announcement of your retirement from active business.

Yours has been a splendid career of service to your firm and to the whole field of retailing. I send you my warm congratulations upon the place of honor you have earned among American retail executives.

I know that hundreds of others share my wishes for your continued good health and happiness.

Sincerely yours,

Dear George:

Thirty successful years in a position of great responsibility is an accomplishment to be proud of, and I want to add my word of congratulation on your splendid record of service.

I am sure that no man, upon retiring from business, ever took with him the good wishes of a larger group of friends and associates.

Sincerely,

Dear Mr. Gardner:

No words of mine can do justice to your record of achievement as President of Wharton, Jones & Company. As you retire from

active business, I congratulate you upon your many y[
standing service to your firm and to the hardware in[
whole.

Sincerely

Dear Mr. Baker:

Twenty-eight years of helpful counsel to your associates and wise leadership of your community is a record of service that few men achieve. It is also a record that deserves a sincere word of gratitude from those whom you have helped so generously during all these years.

We shall miss your steady hand, but we know how fully you have earned the first leisure time of your entire twenty-eight years in Mansfield.

Congratulations on your outstanding record of service, and best wishes for many happy years ahead.

Sincerely yours,

Dear Mr. Henshaw:

In last night's *Star* we read of your retirement as President of Denton, Black & Company.

No words of ours could pay you a finer tribute than the record of achievement you have made during your thirty years in Morrisville.

We congratulate you upon your splendid service to your firm and to the life of this entire community.

Best wishes for many more years of good health and happiness.

Sincerely yours,

Upon speech, article, pamphlet, or book:

Dear Mr. Mason:

This note brings you my hearty congratulations.

For years I have been attending A.R.A. conventions, but no speaker within my recollection has ever made such a "hit" as you did yesterday.

Your address was excellent, and I enjoyed every minute of it. Judging from the prolonged applause, so did everyone else who heard you.

Sincerely yours,

Dear Mr. Meadows:

Your publishers were good enough to send me a copy of your new book, *Making Advertising Pay*. Though I have not yet had a chance to read it thoroughly, I have progressed far enough to realize that you have written a most practical and worth-while book.

All of us in advertising will profit from your contribution. You have certainly earned the satisfaction that comes from a job well done.

Sincerely yours,

Dear Mr. Conwell:

Last night I read your excellent article in the June issue of *The American Banker*. You have presented the soundest treatment of bank credit problems that I've ever seen.

I congratulate you on this fine article. Many others, I am sure, have learned as much from your constructive analysis as I have.

Cordially yours,

Dear Harold:

When there is a job to be done, it is given to the busiest man, who secures the best results.

The National Association must have realized this when they selected you to edit "A Guide to Better Consumer Relations." You have done an excellent job, and the booklet will benefit thousands of retailers. Congratulations!

Cordially,

My dear Morrison:

You certainly rang the bell at the Advertising Club luncheon yesterday, and I congratulate you on giving one of the best talks we've had in years.

Your subject was one of intense interest to every man present, and you handled it masterfully.

Yours cordially,

Dear Mr. Walker:

Your article on "Collecting Accounts by Mail," in the March issue of *Credit Management,* was one of the best I have ever read on this subject. I liked particularly your suggestions for protecting consumer good will while applying increased pressure upon delinquent accounts.

Having profited materially from your article, I wanted to compliment you on it. You have made a real contribution to the development of higher standards in credit correspondence.

Cordially yours,

Dear Joe:

I'm dead on my feet today, and it's all your fault.

Last night I picked up your little book, "They Called Him a Dreamer," intending to read a few minutes before bed. It was after two when I finished it, and I haven't been up at that hour for years.

But I'm going to forgive you for the way I feel today because you gave me three hours of the best reading I've enjoyed in months. Congratulations on a most remarkable book. My copy is already on loan to a friend.

Sincerely,

Dear Dean Adams:

I have just finished reading, with deep gratification, your article entitled "Importance of Business English in Business Training," which appeared in the March issue of the *ABWA Bulletin*—and I send you my congratulations.

What many undergraduates do not realize is that, when they get into business and begin to advance in it, they are called upon more and more to dictate memoranda, letters, and reports. It is only when they are actively engaged in business that they appreciate the importance of the ability to write and talk effectively.

It was, therefore, most gratifying to read your article in which you emphasize the value of knowing how to write effectively in business.

I extend to you my personal best wishes for your good health and continued success.

Cordially yours,

———

Dear Mr. Carlile:

Congratulations on your splendid address last night before the Men's Dinner Club. I liked your approach, your delivery, and your conclusions so much that I wanted to let you know.

After the banquet I rode home with several other members of the Club, and all shared my enthusiasm about your fine address.

Sincerely yours,

———

Dear Mr. Sweeney:

Your new book, *Better Public Relations for Business*, is so interesting that I read it from cover to cover in one sitting—and right in the middle of the morning, at that!

I should like to congratulate you on the book and say that I am sure it will meet a need. I hope it will enjoy great success.

Sincerely yours,

———

Dear Mr. Wheeler:

I have just read your pamphlet called "Take an Hour to Say 'No.'" Though I am not given to writing letters when I can avoid doing so, I can't resist telling you how much I like your folder.

You have certainly hit the nail on the head. Congratulations!

Cordially yours,

———

My dear Mr. Crawford:

Your article on the late James M. Beck, in the *Law Journal* for April 27, is worthy of the subject and of the profession which he adorned.

For a number of years I have taught constitutional law in one of the law schools of this city. Until I read your article I had not realized the large part Mr. Beck played in our recent constitutional history, though I knew it was by no means a small one. I had heard him argue several cases when he was Solicitor General, and I heard him in several occasional and after-dinner speeches. Your description of his ability and charm does not exaggerate.

But the Bar of this city, I believe, is as proud today of your eulogy as of his accomplishments.

Congratulations and thanks for a quarter hour of most enjoyable reading.

Sincerely yours,

Dear Mr. Brown:

Your talk on "Collection Methods" at yesterday's Rotary Club meeting was instructive and interesting to everyone present. I congratulate you on your command of the subject and the manner in which you presented it.

Sincerely yours,

Dear Mr. Flynn:

Your book arrived yesterday, and I spent most of last evening browsing through it. I think you have done a very fine job, and one that needed doing.

I like not only the contents of the book, but the breezy, chatty style in which it is written. It ought to be as fascinating to the business man whose contacts are directly with the public as the latest thriller is to the mystery story fan.

Best wishes, and my congratulations on an excellent piece of work. I hope you sell a million copies!

Sincerely,

Dear Mr. Du Teau:

Your recent article on the importance of effective public relations struck me as so timely and so sound that I wanted to write you this expression of congratulations about it.

The ideas you have so well expressed make it clear to me that you are planning carefully and wisely for the future of the Alumni

Association and for that of the University as a whole. I feel that Nebraska is fortunate to have a man so well qualified, by both intellect and experience, to direct what is sure to be an increasingly important phase of its activity.

Cordially yours,

Dear Dr. Rister:

I was delighted to read last night that your latest book, *Oil: Titan of the Southwest,* has received the Book-of-the-Month Club recommendation.

It took real courage for you to dive into such a tremendous project, involving so much research, checking of records, and sifting of details, not to mention the many miles of travel necessary to collect your material.

I knew at the outset that your finished product would be another fine book. You always combine scholarship and thoroughness of research with a style that makes excellent reading. It's a great achievement to give readers well-documented history in a way that entertains them. And you have done it time after time.

Hearty congratulations on the new book—and on the good things the reviewers are saying about it.

Sincerely,

Dear Mr. Cummings:

I have heard so many enthusiastic comments about your fine address in this city last week that I wanted to write you these words.

All of us who were fortunate enough to hear you benefited from your penetrating analysis of the responsibilities of business to higher education in America.

I knew at the time that I had never listened to a more thought-provoking address, and the longer I think about your words, the more I appreciate their significance.

Sincerely yours,

My dear Miss Turner:

I simply want to add my note of congratulations to the many which you must be receiving on the publication of your book, *The Federal Fund Market.*

It always requires a great deal of courage to be the first to commit one's self in writing on any subject, but I feel sure yours is the fore-runner of many other books on Federal Funds which will be much more voluminous and complicated, and not nearly so direct and practical as yours.

Yours sincerely,

Upon outstanding community service:

My dear Mayor Dudley:

As a citizen of Oakland, I want to express my sincere apprecia-tion of the many things you have done to make it a better city in which to live.

Probably yours has seemed like a thankless task at times, but the satisfaction of a big job well done is no small reward in itself.

Certainly that satisfaction is yours in abundant measure, and also the pleasure of knowing that you have the gratitude of every citizen who stands for honest and efficient city government.

Sincerely yours,

Dear Mr. Blackmer:

As you complete your term of office as President of the Marion Chamber of Commerce, we send you this word of sincere congratu-lations.

Under your leadership the Chamber of Commerce has made ex-cellent progress. You have performed a fine service to this com-munity, and every business concern in town owes you a debt of gratitude.

Sincerely yours,

Dear Mr. Hartley:

In last night's *Courier* I read with great interest that the fund campaign for the Recreational Center has exceeded its goal.

Your hard work in planning and carrying out this campaign has made possible a splendid forward step for Danville. I want to join other members of this community in congratulating you on a job well done.

Sincerely yours,

Dear Mr. Cartwright:

I was genuinely sorry to read in last night's paper that you are retiring as President of the Board of Education.

The mothers and fathers in this community owe you a big debt of gratitude for the progress of our schools these past two years.

As the father of two boys in our public schools, I want to congratulate you and thank you for all you have done. I hope you will continue your valuable service to the Board even though you no longer act as its President.

Sincerely yours,

Dear Ted:

This year's Community Forum was the best within my memory, and I've been attending them for ten years.

Congratulations on your fine work in organizing such an excellent program. I know it took a lot of work, but the results were well worth it.

All of us enjoyed the sessions and profited from them.

Sincerely,

Dear Harry:

Last night, when I read the summary of Chamber of Commerce activities for 195-, I was particularly impressed with the wide range of accomplishments realized within the past year.

All of us who are interested in the Chamber of Commerce are aware that its fine record has been due largely to your work as Secretary-Manager. Your energetic driving power, efficient management, and enthusiasm have combined to give the Chamber of Commerce its best year since I have lived in Madison.

I congratulate you and wish you continued success during 195-.

Sincerely,

Dear Major Lohr:

All of us here were delighted at the fine tribute paid you by the *Tribune* the other day when the Chicago Railroad Fair completed its second year.

You have contributed to the pleasure and the education of millions, and I can think of no form of achievement that would be more gratifying.

Sincerely yours,

———

Dear Mr. Kennedy:

I want to compliment you on the splendid way you handled the Civic Improvement Forum. I think you did a fine piece of work, and everyone with whom I have talked feels the same way. Without a doubt it was one of the best programs we have ever had.

Cordially,

———

Dear Mr. Askew:

The annual report of the Y.M.C.A., as reviewed in last night's *Times,* is a record of progress and service that all of us in this community can be proud of.

You are doing a splendid job, and I want to add my sincere congratulations to the many that you must be receiving today.

Cordially yours,

———

My dear Mayor Thornton:

Last night, as I listened to your analysis of the problems of this community and the plans for solving them, I realized how fortunate we are to have you as our Mayor. I know that you are giving generously of your energy and ability in making Norman a better city.

In addition to giving an excellent talk last night, you showed clearly your insight into civic problems and your capacity for efficient management. Because of my admiration for both your ideas and your methods, I wanted to send you this note of congratulations.

If there is any way in which I can co-operate with you, I shall do so gladly.

Sincerely yours,

———

Dear Frank:

Though I know the customary time for congratulations is one's election to office, I feel that you deserve them even more right now. Your fine work as President of the Milton Chamber of Commerce during the past year has been a great service to this community.

The progress of the Chamber of Commerce these past twelve months has taken a heavy toll of your time, I know, and I congratulate you on a job very well done.

Cordially yours,

Dear Mr. McHenry:

"Greater Columbus Week" was a very fine thing for this community. We are sure that every firm in town will want to support it next year.

The Elkins Company is proud to have had a small part in this program. We congratulate you upon your able leadership in making it an outstanding success.

Sincerely yours,

Upon accomplishment of son or daughter:

Dear Jim:

I read in last night's *News* that Jim, Jr. has been elected President of the Senior Class at the University of Illinois. Of the many undergraduate honors that have come to him, I believe this one is the most outstanding.

You have every reason to be proud of his fine record. Mrs. Gleason joins me in this word of hearty congratulations.

Cordially,

---

* Dear Mr. McQuiston:

I met a fine young fellow the other day when I stopped at the offices of Clapham & Company in Omaha. Learning that his name was McQuiston, I mentioned having had years of pleasant business dealings with McQuiston Brothers of Cedar Rapids. It was then that I learned I was talking with your son.

During the day I saw quite a lot of him in the course of conferences with the advertising department, and I want to congratulate you on his many fine qualities. He has a keen mind, a thorough understanding of his work, and a splendid personality.

I have no doubt that he will be heard from in the advertising field. You must be very proud of him.

Cordially yours,

Dear Mr. Spaulding:

If anyone had asked me how old your daughter was, I'd probably have guessed from ten to twelve years. You can imagine my astonishment, then, when I read in last night's paper that she had just been graduated from high school, and with top scholastic honors thrown in for good measure.

Now that I have caught up with the calendar, I want to compliment you upon her splendid achievement. The record that she climaxed this week must make you very proud of her.

I note from the newspaper account that she plans to enter the University of Michigan next September. Please convey to her my congratulations and my best wishes for her continued success in college.

Sincerely yours,

Dear John:

In glancing through the morning paper a few minutes ago, I read with much interest that your son has been elected Captain of the 195- Dartmouth football team. He is surely following in the footsteps of his dad.

This vote of confidence by his fellow students is a real honor—one that speaks volumes for his character, personality, and capacity as a leader. I know he could have won no distinction that would give you more pleasure.

Cordially yours,

Dear Burt:

I read in last night's paper that Dorothy won three of the top awards this week at the Cheley Colorado Camp.

As she goes on adding new honors to those she has earned in the past, you must be tremendously proud of her. I am sure I would burst my vest buttons if I were in your place.

Cordially,

---

* Dear Clint:

Ken Pearson told me this morning that your son has received an appointment to West Point, and that he will be leaving soon for the East.

You are very proud of him, I know, and you have every right to be. Please give him my congratulations and best wishes.

Ken said he met your boy during a visit to your office last week, and that he's a fine-looking "six footer"—a real chip off the old block. Knowing the "old block" as we do, we are betting on Clint, Jr. to make a name for himself at West Point.

Sincerely,

Dear Stan:

Last night I read in the *Evening News* that Paul had carried off top scholastic honors in this year's graduating class at the University.

I can well imagine your pride in Paul and in his great accomplishment. My congratulations and best wishes to both of you.

Sincerely,

Upon business anniversary or special business achievement:

* Dear Mr. Gregory:

Jim Rasmussen told me this morning that your new building will be ready for its Grand Opening on the twenty-fifth anniversary of your business.

I write to congratulate you on both the new building and the anniversary. You have accomplished a great deal in the past twenty-five years, and every step forward has been made possible by good judgment and honest hard work.

Best wishes for the Grand Opening and for many more years of success.

Sincerely yours,

---

* Gentlemen:

We send you our warmest congratulations on the occasion of your Fiftieth Anniversary. You can well be proud of your half century of progress, during which you have won public confidence through consistent service and fair dealing.

Accept our best wishes for your continued success and prosperity.

Yours sincerely,

Dear Mr. Shields:

I heard today that your son, Paul, has just become a partner in your business.

On this happy occasion I send you my warmest congratulations. I know the new partnership fulfills one of your fondest dreams, and offers your son a fine opportunity to follow in the footsteps of his father.

My best wishes to Shields & Son.

Cordially yours,

---

* Dear Mr. Hendricks:

This is the day of days for you—the one toward which you have worked and looked forward for so long. And these few words are just to tell you that all of us here are happy for you.

The new home of the Hendricks Dry Goods Company is a real credit to your organization and to your community. To you, whose foresight and leadership have made this day possible, go our congratulations and good wishes.

Sincerely yours,

---

* Dear Mr. Hensley:

What a thrill it must give you to look back over your many years in the retail furniture business. Each year testifies that you treated your customers fairly and squarely, and gave them full value for the money spent in your store.

Fifty years in business is a long time. And we'll gamble your records show that the children and grandchildren of your original purchasers have bought from you.

There's something very satisfying in a long record of service to the public. And we know you are going to find, on the day your business is fifty years *young,* that the good will you have earned is particularly heart warming.

As a comparative youngster, with only thirty-seven years of business life behind us, we congratulate you.

Sincerely yours,

Dear Walter:

I learned today that you will shortly open a branch office in Milwaukee. Congratulations on the expansion of your business, and best wishes for continued success.

Cordially,

Dear Mr. Grimes:

On the eve of your Fortieth Business Anniversary, I want to extend to you my congratulations on your record of achievement and my sincere best wishes for the future.

Your forty years in business represent not only a career of the highest ethical standards, but also one of genuine service to this community. You have won the respect, confidence, and admiration of the people of Clinton; and you have every right to be proud of the reputation you have earned.

Yours sincerely,

Dear Mr. Hilliard:

As one department store man to another, I wish to pay homage to your genius for dramatizing your window displays. The way you have worked out the selling idea for party gowns in your southeast window is masterly.

Congratulations!

Sincerely,

---

* Dear Mr. Ray:

It is a privilege to extend our congratulations and best wishes to your organization on the occasion of its fiftieth year in business.

We read with great interest your Golden Anniversary section of The Owensboro *Messenger*. Only a business built on a solid foundation of loyalty, fair dealing, and fine quality could have made the outstanding advancement that you have accomplished.

We are proud to be numbered among the suppliers to such a splendid enterprise, and all of us at Deltox join in wishing you many more years of progress and success.

Yours sincerely,

Dear Mr. Leland:

In last night's paper I saw the announcement of your Tenth Anniversary Sale. As I glanced at it, I realized how much you have accomplished during your first decade in this community.

From a little frame building to a modern, air-conditioned store in ten years is a remarkable achievement—one that can be built only on service, confidence, and friendship.

I hope that your Tenth Anniversary Sale is an outstanding success and that your next decade in business will bring you as much to celebrate as the first one has.

Sincerely yours,

---

* Gentlemen:

As you complete your first year as authorized Charnley dealers in Sioux City, we wish to congratulate you upon your excellent record in the sale of our products.

We consider ourselves most fortunate to be represented in Sioux City by such an alert, progressive firm, and we look forward to the long continuance of a mutually pleasant and profitable association with you.

Sincerely yours,

Dear Mr. Makowsky:

Congratulations and many happy returns of the day are my wishes for you on your Fiftieth Anniversary. It is not the years a man has lived, but how much he has accomplished, that indicates his usefulness to society.

You are blessed with an irrepressible spirit and a dynamic energy, transmitting your power to others. This is proved by the organization you have built since coming to this country and establishing the J. Makowsky Corporation, whose reputation is enviable and growing daily.

May you continue to enjoy the splendid health and the spirit of optimism you radiate, and may your firm continue to grow so that it may render still greater service in its field.

Sincerely yours,

---

* Dear Mr. Sutherland:

C-o-n-g-r-a-t-u-l-a-t-i-o-n-s!!!

Your fine new store is not only a splendid personal accomplishment, but a real credit to your city.

It has taken years of sound planning to make possible this achievement, and we salute you upon this milestone of your progress.

Cordially yours,

Letters to Employees [3]

Upon promotion or other business advancement:

Dear Burt:

I am sure that everyone in our entire organization shares my satisfaction in your appointment as Assistant Sales Manager.

During your five years with the Company you have won the friendship and respect of everyone because of your ability, your desire to co-operate with others, and your square shooting.

Your appointment to this position of increased responsibility and greater opportunity has been well earned. I know you will make a success of your new work, and I send you my congratulations and best wishes.

Cordially,

---

[3] A number of the letters presented in earlier sections of this chapter are also appropriate for mailing to employees.

Dear Joe:

Heartiest congratulations on your promotion to Chief Clerk of the Glen Ridge office. I know how very happy you and your family must be.

You should consider this promotion a well-deserved reward for your many years of conscientious and untiring efforts in behalf of the Company.

My very best wishes to you as you begin your new duties.

Sincerely,

Dear Charles:

I regret very much that you will soon be leaving Finch & Company, for your record here has been outstanding. At the same time, I congratulate you on the splendid opportunity that has come to you in a field of work for which you are exceptionally well qualified.

Though we shall miss you here, I extend to you sincere best wishes for every success and happiness in your new work.

Cordially yours,

Dear Jack:

It gives me a lot of pleasure to write this letter. Its purpose is to tell you that the Board has voted unanimously to increase your annual salary to $4,800, effective July 1.

You have earned this substantial increase by doing an outstanding job during your three years in the field. Congratulations and best wishes for still greater accomplishments during the coming year. You have a bright future.

Cordially yours,

Dear Ralph:

This note brings you my warm congratulations upon your appointment as Manager of the College Department.

During your nine years with the firm you have made an enviable record—a record that shows initiative, dependability, and a real capacity for leadership. You have steadily increased the volume of sales in your territory, and you have shown a thorough understanding of the college market.

Your promotion to a key position in the Douglas organization is well deserved. We feel that the College Department, under your direction, will be in very capable hands.

Sincerely yours,

Dear Bruce:

It is only natural that I should be sorry to see you leave us. No sales manager likes to lose a man of outstanding ability.

You are going, however, to a position of great promise and opportunity for the right man. That you will prove to be the right man I have no doubt.

My best wishes go with you.

Sincerely,

Dear Frank:

Congratulations upon your promotion to the rank of Assistant Vice President. Your fine work in managing the Denver office has earned you this important advancement.

All of us are proud of your record with Fink & Avery, and we are confident of your further success in your new capacity.

Sincerely,

Dear Mr. Rogers:

As you leave our organization to accept your new responsibilities, the executive officers of the Dearborn Bennett Company want you to know that you carry with you our sincere wishes for your continued success.

I need not reiterate our disappointment over your leaving us; yet we are satisfied that this change of positions is but another step in your rise to a place of prominence in the automobile industry. The creditable record you leave behind more than substantiates this belief.

The best of luck to you!

Very sincerely yours,

Dear John:

I am much pleased over your promotion to the managership of the Des Moines branch, and I want to add my congratulations to the many you have doubtless received already.

Your fine record of achievement with the Company has earned this advancement for you, and I know you will realize new accomplishments in the position which you will assume next month. You have my every good wish for continued success.

Sincerely,

Dear Vincent:

I learned with genuine regret that you will leave us shortly to go into college publicity work. I have watched your record here with a great deal of satisfaction; it proves you to be energetic, adaptable, and extremely capable.

A young man with these qualities will go far in his chosen field. Since you have decided upon college publicity work as a career, I congratulate you upon the excellent opportunity that has come to you.

You have my very best wishes for every success in your new work. I know you will do it exceptionally well.

Sincerely yours,

Upon significant personal occasion:

Dear Henry:

This is just a word to convey to you my hearty congratulations upon your marriage. May it bring to you and your lovely wife happiness in abundance for many years to come.

Sincerely,

Dear Frank:

I was very happy to learn that you have a fine young son. I could wish for him no finer future than that he follow in the footsteps of his father.

My very best regards to you and Mrs. Roberts, and to the young gentleman just arrived my sincere wishes for a long and happy life.

Sincerely,

Dear Miss Warfield:

I was told today that you have completed work for your master's degree at Columbia, and that you will receive the degree this week.

Congratulations on this splendid achievement. I know that it requires a lot of spirit and determination to attend night classes over a period of three years, and I have the greatest admiration for you in this accomplishment.

Cordially yours,

Dear Miss Elliott:

I was much pleased to learn of your engagement and approaching marriage to Mr. John Schuyler.

Please accept my sincere best wishes for every happiness.

Cordially,

Dear Mr. Fernald:

On the occasion of your seventieth birthday, I want to send you this brief message of congratulation and my sincere wish that you may enjoy the best of health for years to come.

I hope that your seventieth milestone will be a happy day, and since friendship is the real measure of happiness, I know it will be.

Sincerely yours,

Dear Jim:

I've just this minute heard about the son and heir, and I'm delighted for both you and Mary.

I know how happy you both are to have a boy. Congratulations, and to Jim, Jr. my best wishes for ninety years of health and happiness.

Sincerely,

Dear Alex:

How does it feel to be a celebrity? Today, no doubt, you have noticed that members of your office staff are approaching you with a respect bordering on awe.

After all, few business houses can boast of a state tennis champion within their ranks, and who would ever expect to find one in a cosmetics firm? Isn't it natural that we're all much impressed and fairly bursting with pride?

Cordially,

Dear Vernon:

I was happy to read in yesterday's *Tribune* of your approaching marriage.

Congratulations and best wishes for many years of happiness.

Sincerely,

Dear Frank:

I have just learned of the safe arrival on this earth of Mary Frances Barton, and I know how happy you and Eleanor must be.

For one so young and inexperienced in the ways of this world, Mary Frances has exercised remarkably fine judgment in the selection of her parents. May she fulfill all the high hopes her parents hold for her!

Sincerely,

Upon outstanding work for firm:

Dear Jack:

Well, you've done it again!

The report placed on my desk this morning shows that you brought in a larger number of new accounts last year than any other man on the sales staff.

When you come to New York next month for the regional meeting, I'll have an opportunity to congratulate you personally on your record. In the meantime, this is just a note to tell you that all of us here are proud of the fine work you are doing.

Sincerely yours,

Dear Ray:

I have just seen the series of promotional letters you prepared for the fall campaign. My enthusiasm about them prompts the writing of this note.

Your letters have zest, variety, curiosity appeal, excellent continuity—all the qualities that should make them the most effective series we've ever used.

Congratulations on a very fine piece of work!

Sincerely,

Dear Cliff:

It's a real pleasure to write you these words of congratulation on winning first prize for the best sales record of 195-.

The hard work you have done so willingly and so constantly throughout the past year has surely produced excellent results, and you have every right to be proud of your record.

I know that the fine recognition you have just won will provide the incentive for another year of achievement, and I wish you continued success during 195-.

Sincerely,

Dear Van:

This is just a word to congratulate you on landing the Davis & Wilson contract. I know it was a tough assignment, but you handled it like a veteran.

Cordially,

Dear Phil:

This morning I have been going over proofs of the 195- catalog. In every respect it strikes me as the equal of any catalog we have ever issued, and in many ways I think it superior to any previous one.

I like especially the organization plan you have worked out and the changes you have made in type faces.

You have done such a superb job that I wanted to write you a few words of personal commendation and congratulations.

Cordially,

Dear Homer:

Congratulations! You have just been awarded the $100 prize for the largest volume of trade sales during the past year.

This newest feather in your cap helps to round out a record of which you can be justly proud. Your future with Beck & Woodson looks very bright indeed. Keep up the good work!

Sincerely yours,

My dear Jackson:

When you took over on the Stark & Robbins negotiations, with only a few hours' notice, you were working under a great handicap.

And yet, less than a week later, we have received the signed contract from Mr. Whiting. It came in this morning, accompanied by a letter in which he praised your work highly.

This is just a note to congratulate you on a job very well done. Though the odds were all against you, you certainly "came through" in a big way.

Cordially yours,

Dear Gene:

Just ten years ago today you joined Myers and Milford.

During the past decade everyone in the firm has come to admire your energy, respect your judgment, and marvel at your capacity to get things done.

I congratulate you on a truly fine record and a reputation, very well earned, for absolute dependability. All of us take pride in your accomplishments.

Sincerely,

Dear Sam:

When a salesman breaks his own record for the size of an order, it may be something for the sales manager to talk about, but—

When a salesman breaks all the records in his company—that's news!

You know perfectly well that I am talking about the Wales Company order.

Great work, Sam!

Sincerely,

Dear Lynn:

I have just been checking over the sales figures for the past year. While I knew you had been doing outstanding work in your territory, your record looks even more impressive in black and white.

Congratulations on the fine year you have had, and every good wish for 195-.

Sincerely,

Dear Miss Langdon:

Years ago, in my early days with the Company, I prepared copy for the annual catalog. So I know how much real work goes into this job.

This morning I saw the new 195- catalog. Its layout is excellent, and the finished product is unusually attractive. You and your associates have done an excellent piece of work, and I extend to you my hearty congratulations.

Sincerely yours,

Dear Phil:

Perhaps you thought I expected you to land the Pembroke order all along.

But I didn't—so I was both surprised and delighted when it came in a little while ago.

No salesman on the B & J staff ever tackled a tougher assignment during his first six months with the Company. And nobody could have handled it more effectively than you did. Congratulations!

Sincerely,

Upon professional honor or achievement:

Dear Roy:

Your election as President of the Junior Chamber of Commerce pleased me immensely, and I congratulate you on it.

You have worked hard in the organization, and I can think of no way in which its members could tell you more clearly what they think of your ability.

Sincerely,

Dear Neil:

I feel that your being invited to address the state meeting of the Wholesale Grocers' Association is a high personal tribute to you, and incidentally, a very fine thing for Watson Brothers.

Your part in the state convention program will climax your rapid rise to a position of prominence in the Association. Congratulations on this very real honor.

Sincerely,

Dear Harold:

Last night I spent a most pleasant and profitable evening reading *Bigger Profits from Better Advertising*. Often, as I turned the pages, I paused to reflect upon the good fortune of this firm in having you at the head of its advertising department.

You have written a fine book, and I know its completion has given you a great deal of satisfaction. Warmest congratulations!

Cordially,

Dear Ralph:

Your election as President of the Altoona Retail Credit Association is an honor upon which you deserve most hearty congratulations.

This recognition of your leadership in the retail credit field is also a vote of confidence on the part of your fellow credit men. I am happy for you in your achievement, and I am naturally pleased at the "reflected glory" which your fine record brings to this firm.

I know the Association will continue to grow and prosper under your leadership.

Sincerely,

Dear George:

As I read your "Cutting Correspondence Costs," in the current issue of *Mail Order Journal*, I stopped between paragraphs to marvel at the regularity with which your fine articles appear in the leading business magazines.

I don't know how you do it, but my hat's off to you! Whenever I see your name heading an article, I know there is an interesting and profitable half hour ahead for me. Keep up the good work, and sometime please tell me what kind of vitamins you take.

Cordially,

Dear Roger:

It pleased me very much indeed to learn this morning that you have been elected President of the A.B.C. Club for the coming year. Congratulations upon this fine honor.

Your record of accomplishment in civic affairs is keeping pace with your rapid progress in the Company. All of us are proud of you.

Sincerely,

Dear Mr. Fenmore:

It was fine of you to give me an autographed copy of your book, and I shall value it highly.

Last night I took it home with me, and spent a most enjoyable evening reading it. Today I know a lot more about the printing industry than I knew yesterday.

You are to be congratulated upon packing so much factual information into your account and still making every page intensely interesting. I hope the sale of the book is commensurate with its excellence. In this case you will receive a handsome royalty.

Cordially,

Dear Paul:

Mr. Oliver told me this morning that you have completed the course in Retail Credit Management, and have received your certificate from the National Retail Credit Association.

Congratulations on this fine accomplishment. I know you have devoted many hours of your own time to the N.R.C.A. study program. I am sure you will find your time and effort well spent.

Sincerely,

Dear Bill:

I am delighted at your election as Vice President of the Denver Advertising Club. You are one of the youngest men ever elected to an office in the Club, and I feel that this fact is significant in itself.

You are rapidly making a name for yourself, and I congratulate you on the honor that has just come to you.

Cordially,

TWO

Letters of Appreciation

This chapter includes letter specimens made available through the courtesy of the following persons and organizations: The Alms & Doepke Company, Cincinnati, Ohio; Mr. Charles D. Anderson, New York City; L. Bamberger & Company, Newark, New Jersey; Joseph Bancroft & Sons Co., Wilmington, Delaware; Mr. Leonard Berry, St. Louis, Missouri; J. L. Brandeis & Sons, Omaha, Nebraska; Bromberg & Company, Birmingham, Alabama; The Brooklyn Association for Improving the Condition of the Poor, Brooklyn, New York; Brown-Trueblood, Inc., Marion, Indiana; Frank T. Budge Company, Miami, Florida; Burdine's, Inc., Miami, Florida; Burger-Phillips, Birmingham, Alabama; *The Burroughs Clearing House*, Detroit, Michigan; The Cain-Sloan Company, Nashville, Tennessee; Professor Walter S. Campbell, University of Oklahoma, Norman, Oklahoma; Capper & Capper, Chicago, Illinois; The H. C. Capwell Company, Oakland, California; Carson Pirie Scott & Company, Chicago, Illinois; The Dartnell Corporation, Chicago, Illinois; Davison-Paxon Company, Atlanta, Georgia; Dreyfuss & Son, Dallas, Texas; Duff & Repp Furniture Company, Kansas City, Missouri; Mr. E. F. Du Teau, Lincoln, Nebraska; Eagle Pencil Company, Inc., New York City; Mr. Charles A. Emley, Philadelphia, Pennsylvania; Marshall Field & Company, Chicago, Illinois; Mr. F. J. Fitzpatrick, Buffalo, New York; J. A. Folger & Company, Kansas City, Missouri; Mr. L. E. Frailey, Columbus, Ohio; John Geyer Company, New York City; Gimbel Brothers, Milwaukee, Wisconsin; Harper & Brothers, New York City; Mr. Stewart Harral, Norman, Oklahoma; J. F. Hink & Son, Berkeley, California; Howse Company, Wichita, Kansas; Illinois Central Railroad, Chicago, Illinois; Professor E. A. J. Johnson, New York University, New York City; Mr. F. William Johnson, Dallas, Texas; Kline's, St. Louis, Missouri; The LaSalle & Koch Company, Toledo, Ohio; Lit Brothers, Philadelphia, Pennsylvania; Mr. Savoie Lottinville, Norman, Oklahoma; Loveman, Berger & Teitlebaum, Inc., Nashville, Tennessee; Mandel Brothers, Chicago, Illinois; Mayo Furniture Company, Inc., Tulsa, Oklahoma; McGraw-Hill Book Company, Inc., New York City; Mr. A. Mitchell, Chicago, Illinois; Mr. H. Hamilton Morse, Cedar Rapids, Iowa; National Retail Credit Association, St. Louis, Missouri; National Retail Dry Goods Association, New York City; *Nation's Business*, Washington, D. C.; M. L. Parker Company, Davenport, Iowa; Professor C. C.

46

Parkhurst, Boston University, Boston, Massachusetts; Peck & Peck, New York City; The H. & S. Pogue Company, Cincinnati, Ohio; Prentice-Hall, Inc., New York City; *Printers' Ink*, New York City; Puget Sound Power & Light Company, Seattle, Washington; Mr. T. J. Ross, New York City; Maurice L. Rothschild, Minneapolis, Minnesota; Russeks, Detroit, Michigan; Scruggs-Vandervoort-Barney, Inc., St. Louis, Missouri; W. & J. Sloane, Beverly Hills, California; J. J. Stangel Hardware Company, Manitowoc, Wisconsin; The Wm. Taylor Son & Company, Cleveland, Ohio; Miss Bernice C. Turner, New York City; The Union, Columbus, Ohio; United Autographic Register Company, Chicago, Illinois; University of Nebraska Alumni Association, Lincoln, Nebraska; University of Oklahoma Press, Norman, Oklahoma; Van Winkle's, Ponca City, Oklahoma; Mr. Clarence E. Wolfinger, Philadelphia, Pennsylvania; The Young-Quinlan Company, Minneapolis, Minnesota.

APPRECIATION LETTERS are of many types, as evidenced by the diversity of examples shown on the following pages. All of them, however, are based upon such pleasant circumstances that writing the letter should be an enjoyable and relatively simple task. Sometimes the situation definitely calls for an expression of thanks in conformity with business etiquette. In other instances the note of appreciation is not actually necessary; in fact, it may not even be expected by its recipient.

But the unexpected letter is often the one that is most happily received and longest remembered. Mere conformity with the rules of etiquette is an unreliable standard and a false motive upon which to base the writing of the appreciation message. Above all else, such a letter should reflect genuine sincerity and honest gratitude; it should not represent merely one's desire to be "on record" as having observed the requirements of propriety.

In general, the tone of friendly informality is most appropriate for a note of thanks. Although the writer should avoid effusiveness, he should feel free to express himself with complete naturalness—and ease of expression can best be achieved through an informal style. There are, of course, several factors that should be weighed in determining the degree of informality most suitable for the occasion. One is the extent to which the favor, service, or courtesy performed is a personal one; another is the degree of friendship existing between the two persons concerned; still a third is the age and temperament of the reader.

As in other types of letters, brevity adds strength and conviction to the appreciation message. Conversely, undue length is sure to weaken its statements through tiresome repetition.

The letter of appreciation is easiest to write and is most enthusiastically received when it is written promptly. Delay takes the edge off the reactions of both writer and reader; it destroys the element of spontaneity that so often adds warmth to a friendly relationship.

The numerous letter specimens, presented in the following pages illustrate many situations and occasions upon which the writing of an appreciation message is a thoughtful gesture. No letter that one can write in business is more effective in maintaining and strengthening friendship.

Letters to Business and Professional Associates [1]

For personal favor or service:

Dear Mr. Edwards:

The letter you wrote in my behalf has been submitted to the State Department. It is a hopeless understatement for me to say that I am deeply grateful.

If anything comes of my application, no doubt I shall pay dearly for your kindness. For how can I ever vindicate your most generous appraisal of my ability?

Very sincerely yours,

———

Dear Frank:

Yesterday, when I sent the manuscript of the new book off to the publishers, I was reminded again of all you have done to help me gather material for it.

It was generous of you to take so much interest in my work and to extend such wholehearted co-operation. I hope the autographed book which I shall send you upon publication will indicate, in some

[1] Several of the letters of seasonal good wishes to business and professional associates (pages 119-121) contain an expression of appreciation for past co-operation and friendship.

small measure, my gratitude for your kindness and for the friendship that prompted it.

Sincerely,

Dear Mr. Miller:

Stops in Chicago and Kansas City delayed my return to the office until yesterday. During the past two weeks, however, I have thought many times of that fine visit with you on my recent trip to Boston.

It was very generous of you to give me such a liberal portion of your day, and I thank you most sincerely for your kindness.

Cordially,

Dear Tom:

I regretted very much that you had left Oklahoma City before my return from the North, for I had wanted to see you again and thank you for the generous assistance you have given me.

Please accept this note as grateful acknowledgment of your help. I shall await the chance to thank you personally when you next visit Oklahoma, which I hope will be soon.

Sincerely,

Dear Mr. Pitkins:

Walter Phillips telephoned this morning to tell me of your kindness to him recently in Dayton. He says he is indebted to you for one of the most enjoyable evenings he has spent in many months.

I, too, want to thank you most sincerely for getting in touch with Walter, and for contributing so much to the pleasure of his visit in Dayton.

Cordially yours,

Dear Mr. Cunningham:

It was generous of you to speak to Mr. Deming about my qualifications for the position I am seeking with his firm. If I am fortunate enough to be selected for it, I'll do my best to live up to the good things you said about me.

I surely appreciate your giving me such a fine boost.

Sincerely yours,

Dear Mr. Albertson:

I want to thank you for having given so freely of your time yesterday in talking with Warren Sloan, the young man whom I recommended to you for a sales position with your firm.

I talked with him again this morning, and he is enthusiastic over the prospect of joining your organization. He was particularly impressed by what you told him, and he appears eager to tackle the job.

Though I have grown extremely wary of recommending people, still I cannot help feeling that in this particular case I was justified in suggesting that you meet the young man.

Sincerely yours,

Dear Mr. Cummings:

Thank you for your letter of September 7. Your book will be welcomed and very much appreciated.

Will you be good enough to autograph the copy which you send me? It has been a privilege to have a part in this book, and I feel grateful for such an opportunity.

Cordially yours,

Dear Howard:

It was fine to see you again, and I want to thank you for all you did to make my visit to the Burgess & Parker offices so enjoyable.

The conferences with you and the members of your staff will aid me materially in developing my plans. Thanks again for doing so much to make my New York trip pleasant and resultful.

Sincerely,

Dear Roy:

What a pity it is that Diogenes isn't alive today to meet you! He could throw his lantern in the air and rejoice.

An inveterate pipe smoker who returns a zipper tobacco pouch—in these zipperless days—surely passes the acid test of integrity.

I do thank you for retrieving my pouch from the conference table this afternoon and returning it to me. At the moment it reached my office, I was already searching through suit and overcoat pockets for it.

Your thoughtfulness also exonerates two innocent persons from the shadow of suspicion for life. My only two callers during the early afternoon were a minister and an Army major. But for your assistance, I should have spent my remaining years wondering which one of them got off with my tobacco pouch.

Cordially,

Dear Paul:

This is just a note to thank you again for your kindness to me recently, and to tell you how much I enjoyed the visit with you in your office.

It was certainly good to see you, and I wish the factors of time and distance made it possible to do so more often.

I hope something will bring you to the Southwest one of these days, and that I'll have an opportunity to return your cordiality.

Sincerely,

Dear Bill:

Thanks a billion (millions are chicken feed these days).

I value highly both the new book and the friendship which prompted you to send it.

When I think of the imposing list of books you have written, it recalls the old days when you were just spreading your wings—and my own humble prediction that you would fly high and far.

I shall read the new book with a lot of pleasure—and through the smoke rings will picture the author, a college professor who knows his stuff and has managed to remain *human*.

Sincerely,

Dear John:

It was thoughtful of you to send me a ticket for the Retailers' Forum. I enjoyed attending the sessions, and I learned a lot by doing so.

My sincere thanks to you for doing me a very real favor.

Cordially,

Dear Mr. Forbes:

The help you gave me last week was all that made it possible to meet the publisher's deadline.

I realize that you went out of your way to do me a favor, and at the busiest possible time for you. I want you to know how much I appreciate it.

Sincerely,

Dear Mr. Clifton:

It was good to see you last week, and I want to thank you again for a thoroughly enjoyable day in Atlanta.

I hope your activities during the next few months will bring you to Washington, and that you will let me try to repay you in kind for your many courtesies.

Cordially yours,

Dear Mr. Lottinville:

You have done a superb production job on *Credit Letters That Win Friends,* and I thank you for making of it a most attractive book. In fact, every book I have seen bearing your imprint has been representative of the highest standards of craftsmanship.

In the present instance, however, I have noticed the uniform excellence of your work with particular interest, and I appreciate the care and precision that have produced such a handsome book.

Sincerely yours,

Dear Mr. Meikle:

I want to send you this further word of thanks for your kindness last Friday morning when I called at your office. No one could have been more generous and helpful than you were.

It is easy to see why the Purdue University Research Foundation has made great strides under your direction. You are doing a splendid job.

I hope we shall have many further contacts in the years ahead. Whenever there is an opportunity for me to return your kindness in any way, please be sure to let me know.

Sincerely yours,

Dear Miss Smythe:

Years ago I was teaching—just as you are now. It was interesting work. I knew that young lives had been placed in my hands, and that I had something to say about how those lives were going to turn out.

But the work was always a challenge. Some of the parents were hard to please. There was plenty of worry in the job, and at times the youngsters did get on my nerves.

I think it is the memory of those days that prompts me to write this note to you. I want you to know that Mrs. Frailey and I are grateful for the splendid leadership and training you are giving our boy.

Your inspiration is leading him in the right direction, and we thank you for it.

Sincerely,

Dear Mr. Long:

It was fine of you to send me so much useful material in connection with the study I am making of "Hotel Promotional Methods by Mail."

I realize that gathering this information from your files required a considerable amount of time, and I want you to know that your co-operation is much appreciated.

When my report has been completed, I shall be happy to send you a copy. You will recognize much of the material included in it, but I hope there will be a few items that will supplement your files and prove useful to you.

Sincerely yours,

Dear Paul:

Unexpected stops for business calls in Cleveland and Pittsburgh delayed my return to New York, and this is my first day back in the office.

Along the way, I have thought many times of your kindness to me last week. The visit with you was the best tonic I've had in a long time, and I surely appreciate your making my stay in Omaha so pleasant and profitable.

Whenever there is an opportunity for me to reciprocate in some measure, you know I'll jump at the chance.

Sincerely,

My dear Miss Turner:

I wish to express my sincere thanks for the autographed copy of *The Federal Fund Market,* received today.

Although I have not yet had time to look through the book very searchingly, I am sure that you, as its author, have done yourself proud, and I extend my felicitations. I trust that the treatise will be fruitful of the sort of results you desire. At any rate, it should be decidedly helpful to the large and growing class of readers who are interested in the subject.

Thank you again for remembering me with a copy.

Yours sincerely,

Dear Dave:

I want to thank you for your courtesy to John Kinsey when he called at your office last week.

Upon his return to Buffalo the other day, John told me of the many things you did to help him. He feels that he benefited a great deal from the trip through your plant, and he thoroughly enjoyed the visit with you. Moreover, he described talking with you about production problems as "an education in itself."

It was fine of you to give John so much of your time and to make his call at your office so profitable to him. He appreciates it very much, and so do I.

Sincerely,

For assistance to firm, club, or association:

Dear Mr. Sandifer:

It has seldom been my privilege to receive such a courteous letter as yours of September 22. I appreciate very much your kindness in sending me a copy of your booklet on "Improving Direct-Mail Methods."

One of the functions of our business is to furnish advertisers with enclosures that will boost the returns from their sales letters and circulars. So we are naturally interested in your evaluation of direct-mail methods. I am sure it will prove helpful to us.

Again many thanks for your great courtesy. We shall welcome an opportunity to return it.

Yours sincerely,

Dear Mr. Ball:

It was generous of you to give me so much of your time yesterday, and I appreciate your fine co-operation.

You have made a number of suggestions that will help us materially in improving the organization of our sales promotion department, and you will find us eager to reciprocate in any way possible.

Thank you again for your help.

Sincerely yours,

Dear Mr. Kenny:

Looking back on last week's convention, I feel that its success was due very largely to the consistent excellence, as well as the variety, of the program.

I want to tell you how much I appreciate your tireless efforts in developing this outstanding program. Your splendid work vastly simplified my job as general convention chairman, and I owe you a real vote of thanks for your co-operation and support. You also deserve the gratitude of members of the Association for contributing so much of interest and value to them.

It was good to see you again, and the visit with you was one of my most enjoyable convention experiences.

Sincerely yours,

Dear Mr. Millis:

Thank you for your helpful letter of May 20, suggesting a number of books on business correspondence which will serve as a nucleus for our departmental library.

You have given us exactly the information we wanted, and we appreciate your co-operation in sending it.

Sincerely yours,

Dear Mr. Hitchcock:

Your co-operation and thoughtfulness in offering us warehouse space is sincerely appreciated.

Fortunately, we shall be able to shift merchandise from the fire-damaged area to a wing of the new building which is not yet in use because of the delayed arrival of fixtures.

Your kindness is none the less appreciated, however, and we thank you for the generous spirit of co-operation which prompted your offer of assistance.

Sincerely yours,

Dear Mr. Yelkin:

I should like to acknowledge, with my warmest personal thanks, your recent handsome contribution to the work of our Association.

The past few years have been lean years for private welfare organizations such as ours. Owing to many factors our income has decreased; yet the demand for the specialized welfare work which we do shows no abatement.

It is, therefore, with a special gratitude that we salute the understanding and generous friends, like yourself, who are standing by.

Yours sincerely,

Dear Mr. Gilchrist:

It was generous of you to send me a copy of the new correspondence manual recently compiled for the use of your secretaries and stenographers.

I looked it over this afternoon, and was amazed at the completeness with which the manual covers its subject. You and your staff have done a superb job, and I appreciate your kindness in making this useful volume available to us. I shall pass it along to my secretary for reference whenever she encounters a question of usage or correct form.

Thanks again for a very real favor.

Cordially yours,

___

Dear Mr. Sherman:

I wish to express to you my personal appreciation for your contribution to the Loyalty Fund. You may be sure that your interest in helping the Association to carry out its objectives in a comprehensive and effective manner is an important morale factor and active support.

As a formal acknowledgment of your contribution, we are enclosing your Loyalty Fund certificate, which we believe will return to you deep satisfaction as a reminder of your loyalty and devotion to the University of Nebraska and to the greater service of its Alumni Association.

Cordially yours,

___

Dear Mr. Haines:

In the middle of a busy morning yesterday it was generous of you to take the time for our conference. This is just a note to tell you how much I appreciate it.

You gave me some excellent ideas, and your suggestions will be of great value as we tackle our public-relations problem.

Again my thanks for your fine co-operation.

Sincerely yours,

___

Dear Mr. Bradbury:

At the close of another year of pleasant business dealings with your firm, we should like to convey to you our appreciation of the splendid co-operation you have given us during the past twelve months. The understanding and help of your firm and your representatives have been of immeasurable assistance to us.

We look forward to a continuation of the same close relationship that we have had with you for many years. Sincere best wishes to you and your associates.

Cordially yours,

___

Dear Paul:

You were certainly a good fellow to send me copies of the dealer-relations letters you have used with so much success.

I read your letters with a great deal of interest, and I discovered several methods of approach that can be used with propriety and effectiveness by such a business as ours. They will require some adaptation, of course, and I shall begin work on it shortly. When our new series is complete, I shall gladly send you a copy. Meanwhile, I am returning your letters in case you should need to refer to them.

Your generosity has helped us a lot, and all of us in this office appreciate it immensely. If there is anything in our series that contains a suggestion useful to you, I shall be delighted.

Sincerely yours,

Dear Mr. Whalen:

Throughout the year you have worked hard to interest the merchants of your community in becoming members of the National Association of Retailers. You have done a splendid job.

Thanks to your efforts, twenty-two of your local merchants have joined the Association. It has been a pleasure to welcome them, and every effort will be made to serve them well.

We deeply appreciate your loyal interest in the N.A.R., as well as your large part in making its work more effective. The other officers join me in this expression of sincere thanks.

Cordially yours,

Dear Mr. Whitaker: [2]

Your decision to retire as a director of the Illinois Central has been received with keen regret by the directors and also by the officers of the railroad. For myself, I regard your retirement as a deep personal loss.

The ties of nearly half a century are not easily broken in any

[2] The following letter was written by the late Lawrence A. Downs, former President of the Illinois Central Railroad, to a member of his board of directors who was retiring after many years of service. The message combines the elements of appreciation (both official and personal), regret, congratulation, and good wishes.

case, and in the case of a man of your accustomed vigor and devotion to duty, I know this decision was a hard one to make.

As compensation for the sacrifice, however, you have the knowledge of an extraordinary length of responsibility ably and conscientiously performed. Your service as a director has covered more than half the history of our railroad, and you have participated in decisions which have more than doubled its mileage and have multiplied its capacity and efficiency many times.

Your faithfulness in attendance upon the annual inspection trips has endeared you to many members of our organization, few of whom have ever rendered longer service than your own. They, too, will regret your retirement.

My own work as officer and director has benefited from the example and counsel derived from your seniority in years and experience. For that I thank you. It is my earnest wish that the relinquishment of the cares which you have borne so faithfully will result in your improved health.

Sincerely,

For luncheon or dinner at home or club:

Dear Mr. Courtney:

Since I returned to Dallas only last night, this is my first opportunity to write you a word of thanks for your great kindness to me recently in Philadelphia.

The dinner at the Athletic Club I shall long remember for its excellence, and the visit with you gave me one of the most enjoyable evenings I have spent in many months.

I owe you a big debt of gratitude for your hospitality, and I shall hope for an opportunity to return your kindness before many months have passed.

Very sincerely yours,

Dear Ed:

The leisurely visit we had over a luncheon table last week was something I had been counting on for a long time. Needless to say, I enjoyed it thoroughly.

It was good to see you again, and very fine of you to give me such a large slice out of the middle of your day.

Thank you, too, for an excellent meal in one of the most unusual and interesting restaurants I have seen in years.

Sincerely,

Dear Ken:

It was certainly fine of you to take me along to your Rotary Club luncheon when I was in Des Moines last week, and I had a thoroughly good time. It is seldom that one has a chance to enjoy—at a single meal—the best of company, food, and entertainment.

Please be sure to let me know the next time you are coming through Duluth, and I'll do my best to return your kindness, though I can't promise the variety of attractions to which you treated me.

Cordially,

My dear Warren:

My work in St. Louis took several days longer than had been expected, and I returned home only last night.

I wish to thank you again for all the time you gave me to make my visit to your city such an enjoyable one; and I thank your wife especially for the delicious luncheon she served.

It was a pleasure to see New Orleans, which I had never visited, and doubly pleasurable to see it in the company of old friends. I was certainly shown around and treated as if I were visiting royalty.

You and your wife, singly or together, must certainly give us the chance to return your kindness when you come this way.

Sincerely,

Dear Mr. Greenough:

This is my first day back in the office after my long northern trip.

Everything considered, it was an extremely pleasant trip, and the luncheon visit with you in Buffalo was one of its most enjoyable features. Thank you again for rearranging your plans on such short notice so as to include me in your day.

I hope something will bring you through the South before the year is over, and that you will be sure to plan for a day in Birmingham.

Sincerely yours,

Dear Mr. Burkett:

It was a pleasure indeed to have such a fine visit with you during my eastern trip last week.

The luncheon with you at the University Club was most enjoyable, and I thank you again for adding so much to the pleasure of my stay in New York.

I hope you will come to St. Louis soon, for I shall welcome the opportunity to reciprocate your kindness.

Cordially yours,

Dear Walter:

It was good of you to spend so much time with me last Friday. I thoroughly enjoyed our visit and the luncheon at the Electric Club.

The next time you are in the East, I hope you can arrange to stop off here for a day. You will receive a warm welcome, and I'll be delighted at the chance for another visit with you.

Again my thanks for a most enjoyable day in Chicago.

Sincerely,

Dear Leroy:

This is just a note to thank you for an excellent dinner and a fine visit with you last week in New York.

I appreciate your kindness very much indeed, and I enjoyed every minute of the time spent with you.

Now all I ask is that you give me an opportunity to reciprocate. Best regards to you.

Sincerely,

Dear Frank:

It was certainly good to see you on my recent visit to Pittsburgh, and to find you looking so well.

Your thoughtfulness in inviting me to attend the University Club luncheon will be long appreciated. I enjoyed it thoroughly.

Whenever you come this way, remember that a warm welcome awaits you in Indianapolis.

Sincerely,

For overnight visit at home or club:

Dear Mr. Stone:

The gracious hospitality of your home was the most memorable feature of my recent business trip through the Southwest. I want you and Mrs. Stone to know how much I appreciate your kindness.

You were certainly good Samaritans to take in a totally unexpected traveler, and to make him feel so thoroughly welcome in your home. I hope the course of events will bring you to Hartford before too many months, so that I'll have an opportunity to reciprocate. Please keep in mind that you have a standing invitation at 410 Circle Drive whenever your New England trip materializes.

Again my thanks to you and Mrs. Stone for all you did to make my visit in your home so enjoyable. The recollection of Mrs. Stone's delicious fried chicken, by the way, is stamped indelibly on my memory.

Sincerely,

Dear Paul:

My overnight stay with you at the Professional Men's Club was by far the most enjoyable experience of my three-week trip to the West Coast. It was certainly fine of you to treat me so royally.

The remainder of my trip went according to schedule except for an unexpected stop of ten hours in St. Louis, which resulted from missing my train connection by twenty minutes.

Thank you again for your kindness and for one of the most enjoyable evenings I have spent in years.

Sincerely,

Dear Mr. and Mrs. Whitman:

I have at last returned to New York from my trip through the Midwest, and wish belatedly to thank you for your kindness on the occasion of my visit to Indianapolis in early April.

It was a pleasure to see you and to be in your home. You left nothing undone to make me both welcome and comfortable. I hope you will give me an opportunity to repay your kindness when you come to New York again.

Very best wishes to you for an enjoyable summer.

Cordially yours,

Dear Mr. Wescott:

Thanks to you and Mrs. Wescott, my stay in Akron proved a most delightful one.

May I add this further word of appreciation to you both for your generous hospitality. I shall long remember the friendly atmosphere of your home and the charm of the people who live in it.

Sincerely yours,

My dear Charles:

I don't know when I've had such a delightful weekend as the one spent at your lodge recently. It was an experience I shall long remember and which I shall relive many times.

So I want to tell you once again of my appreciation for all you did to make the occasion such an enjoyable one for me.

Please let me try to do as much for you when you next come to Rochester.

Sincerely,

Dear Mr. and Mrs. Lewis:

Your gracious hospitality made my visit to Nashville a most memorable one, and I thank you for all you did for me. I have never been treated so royally.

All I ask now is that you include a visit to Wichita on the itinerary of your western trip next summer. You have a cordial invitation to visit in our home for just as long a time as your plans will permit. It will be difficult to repay your great kindness in full, but we shall certainly do our best.

Sincerely,

Dear Mr. Beck:

It was fine of you to provide so completely for my comfort at the Athletic Club when I spent a night in your city last week. My stay was most enjoyable, and I am grateful for your hospitality.

It will be a genuine pleasure to return your kindness when you come to Chicago, and I do hope you will give me an opportunity.

Sincerely yours,

Dear Mr. and Mrs. Fairbanks:

Your meeting me at the station in Grand Rapids last Monday evening was the most pleasant surprise I have had in a long time.

Even when I saw you waiting on the platform, I had no idea what a delightful evening was in store for me. The visit in your home, after a procession of hotels across the country, was more of a treat than you can possibly realize.

My warm thanks to both of you for making my stay in Grand Rapids so enjoyable.

Sincerely,

For theater, sports event, or other entertainment:

Dear Mr. Kennedy:

Attending the Municipal Opera with you and Mr. Clark last Thursday evening was a perfect climax for my visit to St. Louis. This is just a further word to thank you for including me in your plans.

The Opera deserves all the fame it has gained over the country, and I certainly saw it in ideal company. The evening was a memorable one for me, and I appreciate your kindness very much indeed.

Sincerely yours,

Dear Dick:

It was good to see you last week, and I appreciate all you did to make my day in Casper such a pleasant one.

The afternoon at the rodeo was one I shall remember for a long time. You have no idea how much I enjoyed it. Having grown up right here in Boston, I had never seen a real, honest-to-goodness rodeo. You were generous to save a place for me in your box—and to put up with my innumerable questions.

Again my thanks for a delightful day.

Sincerely,

My dear Major Lohr:

The evening of July 26 was one of the most enjoyable I have spent in many months. My sincere thanks to you for making it so.

Though I had heard many enthusiastic reports about the Railroad Fair, it exceeded my highest expectations. "Wheels a-Rolling" is wonderful!

Very sincerely yours,

Dear Roger:

Last Saturday was a banner day for me in every way. Excellent company, fine food, a thrilling football game for the conference championship—how could anyone ask for more?

This is just a word to thank you again for a delightful day. It was one I shall long remember.

Sincerely,

Dear Mr. Huntington:

Last week, thanks to you, a routine business day was followed by one of the most delightful evenings I have spent in a long time.

I surely appreciate your kindness during my visit to Champaign. The twilight drive around the University campus was extremely interesting, and the Van Doren lecture was one of the finest it has ever been my privilege to hear.

Please remember your promise to let me know when the dates of your New York trip become definite. I'll be looking forward to your visit with a great deal of pleasure.

Sincerely yours,

Dear Jack:

I haven't laughed as hard in years as I did last night. Even the all-night ride on a train with square wheels hasn't affected my gay mood.

Thanks again for a really wonderful evening. The theater and the visit with you over doughnuts and coffee gave me just the lift I needed after several hectic days in New York.

Sincerely,

Dear Mr. Wallace:

The evening spent with you in St. Louis last week was one of the most enjoyable I have had in a long time. Thanks again for inviting me to stay over for the game.

For years I have heard that the Cardinals and the Dodgers are at their best when they meet each other. Now I know it's a fact. I never expect to see a better ball game.

Your thoughtfulness gave me a lot of pleasure, and I surely appreciate it.

Cordially,

For message of congratulation:

Dear Ronald:

I appreciate your kind words about my efforts to guide the recent Credit Management Conference. It was a lot of fun, and I only hope that all the participants in our discussion enjoyed this exchange of ideas as much as I did.

Your making a special effort to attend, despite adverse circumstances, will linger long in my memory. I was very glad you were able to be there, for it is likely that we shall be working together on similar programs for a long time to come. I hope so.

Thanks again for your thoughtful note.

Cordially,

Dear Ralph:

Your note of congratulations a few weeks ago was appreciated far more than the speed of this acknowledgment would seem to indicate. I have just returned, however, from an extended northern trip, and this is my first opportunity to thank you.

As one who has served Rotary with distinction in many capacities, you were thoughtful and generous to send me those words of encouragement. Doubtless I shall need the benefit of your experience many times during the coming year. Thank you for making me feel that I may ask your co-operation without reluctance.

Sincerely yours,

Dear Miss Jensen:

Your letter of May 10 gave me a lot of pleasure, and I thank you for writing it.

It is gratifying to know that you like the little book on "Better Letters." Writing it was more of a pastime and diversion than a task, but of course I'll be delighted if it meets a need.

I have thought of you often in recent months, and I hope that all is going extremely well with you.

Yours sincerely,

Dear Andy:

That was a fine letter you wrote me about my talk in Milwaukee last week, and I appreciate it ever so much.

Speaking to the members of your organization was a most enjoyable experience, and I am very glad if my remarks contributed in some small way to the success of your meeting.

Cordially,

Dear Jack:

You have no idea how much I appreciate your generous letter of February 17. It was the first piece of mail that reached me in my new office.

Having been on the job only two days, I am still in the process of locating the light switches and trying to figure out the telephone buzzer system. But I know already that both the work and the people are going to be thoroughly congenial.

Your good wishes mean a lot to me, and your letter is one I shall long remember. My warm thanks to you for writing it.

Sincerely,

Dear Mr. Emley:

That was a bully letter you wrote me.

If I can't get my hat on when I'm ready to leave the office this afternoon, you will be to blame.

Cordially yours,

Dear Mr. Balfour:

Thank you indeed for your thoughtful letter of good wishes. It was, of course, quite a thrill to me to have my letter selected as the prize winner in the contest.

Letter writing is an important factor in improving the standards of credit management, and I think the efforts of the national association are helping to improve the general tone of letters written by credit men.

Thanks again for your congratulations. It is always good to hear from you.

Cordially yours,

Dear Mr. Vaughan:

Your kind letter of July 12 has just reached me. I am very glad if my talk before the Kiwanis Club last week proved interesting to your members. It was a real pleasure to see you again and to meet your fellow Kiwanians.

Thanks for the invitation to visit your club, and also for the thoughtful note which arrived this morning.

Cordially yours,

Dear Bill:

Your letter bringing me good wishes is much appreciated. From your friendship I have gained both strength and inspiration. How true it is that no man walks alone when he takes with him the encouragement of good fellows like you.

Today I am completing the first week of my new work. Already I have discovered that real estate is a lot more fun to practice than to preach. It is indeed a fascinating business.

I shall not forget your kindness. Until we meet again—the best of life to you!

Sincerely,

Gentlemen:

On behalf of Rogers & Sons I wish to thank you for your congratulations and good wishes upon the occasion of our Fortieth Anniversary.

Your letter symbolizes the fine spirit of friendship and co-operation between our two firms, and it is most sincerely appreciated.

Cordially yours,

Dear Don:

Your letter of March 5 has given me a lot of pleasure, and I thank you sincerely for it.

I don't know of anyone whose kind words about my recent article would mean more to me than yours. I am very glad you agree with the point of view expressed in the article, and I do appreciate your taking the time to tell me so.

It has been a long time since we have had a chance for a good visit. I hope that something will soon bring you to Cleveland, or that I may find myself heading toward Denver one of these days.

Thanks again for your letter and for the pleasure it has brought me.

Cordially,

Dear Herb:

Your note of good wishes reached me this morning, and it certainly started the day off right.

My sincere thanks for your thoughtfulness, and also for your generous remarks about my new assignment. It was fine of you to write me.

One of these days I may be coming east on business. If so, I'll be counting on a good visit with you. Best regards.

Sincerely,

———

Gentlemen:

We acknowledge with gratitude your message of good wishes, and thank you for the high tribute you have paid J. D. Williams & Company.

Your friendly sentiments are heartily reciprocated. We look forward to the long continuance of the co-operation and mutual respect between our two organizations.

Very sincerely yours,

———

Dear Mr. Fitzgerald:

It was nice of you to write me as you did. I thoroughly enjoyed being with you at your convention, and I am highly complimented indeed if my small participation in your discussions contributed anything that you think worth while.

It was a pleasure to meet you, and I hope our paths will cross frequently.

Sincerely yours,

———

Dear Mr. Newkirk:

Thank you very much for your letter of April 12. I appreciate both your good wishes and your generous comments on my work with the Association.

You may be sure that your letter will be among the records of these seven years that I shall take with me into the new field, and which I shall cherish in the years to follow.

Sincerely yours,

———

For message of condolence or sympathy:

Dear John:

Your words of sympathy are deeply appreciated, and I thank you for them.

Kindness such as yours helps to carry one through, and I shall long remember it with gratitude.

Sincerely,

Dear Lyle:

Your fine letter certainly helped to brighten up my days in the hospital. Thanks a lot for writing it.

I am back in the office again on a half-time program, and in another week or two I'll get back to the old schedule. The operation really wasn't so bad, and I did get a good rest. The only really distressing experience was discovering how well the business can get along without me.

The next time you plan a trip to Minneapolis, please keep a couple of hours open to have lunch with me. I hope you will be coming this way soon.

Sincerely,

Dear Harold:

Your kind expression of sympathy helped me a lot, and it is much appreciated. I know that you meant every word of it.

I have found that there is no greater solace in an hour of personal sorrow than the kind wishes of one's good friends. Thank you for both your sympathy and your thoughtfulness in expressing it.

Sincerely,

Dear Mr. Ames:

Your message of good wishes could not have been more timely, and it gave me a lot of pleasure.

Though I have not previously had an opportunity to acknowledge your thoughtful note, I want you to know that it is much appreciated.

This is my first week back at my desk, and it seems very good indeed to be getting into the swing of things again. Just as soon as my physician will let me venture forth entirely on my own power, I plan to be off on a business trip through New England. If possible, I shall stop at your office to say hello on my way through Chicago.

Sincerely yours,

Gentlemen:

The members of this organization appreciate your kind expression of sympathy upon the sudden death of our Treasurer, Mr. Thomas Thornhill.

We feel keenly the loss of one whose ability and sterling personal qualities have meant so much in the growth of this firm.

Please accept our sincere thanks for both your sympathetic message and your splendid tribute to Mr. Thornhill.

Yours sincerely,

Dear Mr. Gates:

Thank you for your note of good wishes, which reached me shortly after I entered the hospital. The kind thoughts of friends do a lot for one's morale at such a time, and I appreciate your thoughtfulness in writing.

I expect to return to my desk the first of next week, and I shall hope to see you at the University Club meeting on Wednesday.

My thanks again for your cheering note.

Yours sincerely,

Dear Bob:

Your note—so characteristic of you—is the kind of thing that has done much to sustain my family and me during a period of sore trial. I want you to know that it is appreciated.

Sincerely,

Dear Henry:

Your words of encouragement did me a lot of good, and I appreciate them far more than the speed of this reply would indicate.

It will still be a few weeks before I shall be able to return to the office, but my secretary comes out to the house for an hour or two each morning. This keeps me in touch with developments at the office, and makes me feel that I am once more a part of it.

By the time you plan to visit South Bend again I shall no doubt be back in the office, and I want you to allow time for a good visit if you can arrange to do so. Meanwhile, thank you again for your fine message of sympathy and good wishes.

Sincerely yours,

Gentlemen:

On behalf of the personnel of Barton & Company, I wish to thank you for your kind letter of sympathy upon the death of our President, Mr. Albert S. White.

It is true that this organization has sustained a shock and a great loss in the sudden passing of Mr. White. But by holding to the high standards he represented, we believe we shall be paying him the most appropriate tribute.

Your friendship, as manifested in your letter, gives us encouragement as we undertake this task.

Very sincerely yours,

Dear Myron:

Your cheerful letter gave me a lift just when I needed it most. Thanks a million!

I am coming along nicely, and will soon be going full tilt again. There are several items about which I plan to write you soon; but I did want to tell you, without further delay, how much I appreciated your good wishes.

Sincerely,

For speaking before club or association:

Dear Mr. Hogan:

No program given at the Lions Club this year has brought more enthusiastic comments than your talk a few days ago. It was enjoyed by all who were privileged to hear you.

During such busy days it was especially generous of you to accept our invitation, and to devote your personal time to the preparation of such an excellent analysis of current banking problems.

As Program Chairman I took a lot of pride in your appearance before the Club, and I thank you for giving us one of the finest talks we have had in many months.

Sincerely yours,

Dear Mr. Leroy:

I want to thank you again for everything you did to make this year's meeting of the Retailers' Association such an outstanding success.

Your name on the program was a big factor in attracting the largest attendance we have ever had, and your fine address proved the wisdom of those who attended the meeting primarily to hear you speak.

I can assure you that my gratitude for your contribution is shared by the entire membership of the Association.

Cordially yours,

Dear Mr. Collins:

This is just a note to tell you again how much we appreciated the fine address you gave at the weekly meeting of the Prosperity Club last Wednesday noon.

You really rang the bell; in fact, our members are already asking if we can get you back for a return engagement. So we are hoping that it may be our pleasure to hear you again on some future occasion.

Both officially and personally, thank you for providing for us a program that was outstanding in every respect.

Sincerely yours,

Dear Mr. Talbot:

It was gracious of you to share with our members your interesting experiences in foreign lands. In thanking you for your splendid talk last night, I speak for the entire membership of the Professional Women's Club.

Because of your generosity last night's meeting was one of the most enjoyable of the entire year. We owe you a real debt of gratitude for a most entertaining and informative talk.

Very sincerely yours,

Dear Mr. Garnett:

This note brings you a sincere "Thank you" for your splendid contribution to our recent state meeting in Cedar Rapids.

Your address was outstanding, and I have heard nothing but praise of it from all sides.

The other officers of the Association join me in this expression of appreciation for your large part in making the meeting so successful.

Sincerely yours,

Dear Mr. Trumbull:

As we complete the series of talks on civic improvement, I want to thank you again for your participation last month. It added a great deal to both the value and the prestige of the series, and I am grateful to you for accepting my invitation.

No talk in the entire series brought us more expressions of approval than yours. All of us appreciate your contributing so much to the success of the series.

Sincerely yours,

Dear Jim:

That was a crackerjack talk you gave the Advertising Club last Tuesday. I know you did it as a favor to me, and I appreciate it ever so much.

Your subject would have been timely for any business group, and it was especially so for a crowd of advertising men. Surely the response to your question-and-answer session demonstrated the keen interest of your audience.

Thanks again for giving us such an enjoyable and worth-while hour.

Cordially,

Dear Mr. Harral:

On behalf of members of our staff and also of persons in attendance at our Public Relations Short Course held at Nashville last week, I want to say thank you for the fine contribution you made to our program.

Your address on "Colleges and the Press" and the copy clinic which you conducted were both exceptionally well done. In fact, we have received a number of letters praising your participation in the program.

I hope you had a pleasant trip back to Oklahoma, and that our paths will be crossing frequently in the future.

Yours sincerely,

———

Dear Mr. Jergens:

I am sure you could tell, from the attentive silence of your listeners, how much they enjoyed your talk yesterday.

Having heard you speak at the Y.M.C.A. conclave in Topeka several weeks ago, I knew that members of the Rotary Club would be intensely interested in your European experiences. I believe I enjoyed your talk yesterday even more than the previous one, which is saying a great deal.

Thank you again for your kindness in accepting my invitation, and for giving one of the finest talks that the Rotary Club has been privileged to enjoy.

Cordially yours,

———

Dear Mr. Sturgeon:

Many favorable comments have been made about your address yesterday before the Association of Retail Advertisers. You played a large part in making the convention such an outstanding success.

After the program I had hoped for an opportunity to thank you again, personally, for your excellent speech and for the time you gave us in coming to Cleveland.

You provided one of the highlights of the entire program. The other members of the committee join me in this expression of sincere thanks.

Cordially yours,

———

Dear Mr. Bell:

Your talk before the Kiwanis Club yesterday gave me so much enjoyment that I think a few words of appreciation are in order.

During my twenty-two years as a member of the Club we have had few speakers who succeeded in packing so much entertainment and information into a thirty-minute talk. It was a real privilege to hear you speak, and I thank you for giving us a most outstanding program.

Sincerely yours,

Dear Paul:

Needless to say, I was proud to be the program chairman of this week's meeting of the Business Men's Club.

The talk you gave us was exceptional in many ways. It was straightforward and crystal clear; it was well planned and equally well presented; it supported every basic point with the solid proof of facts.

No program in months has met such an attentive reception or produced so much enthusiastic comment on the part of our members. I thank you again for giving us the benefit of your experience and your thorough understanding of a very timely subject.

Sincerely yours,

For favorable mention in speech, article, or book:

Dear Mr. Gillette:

I hope these lines will reflect my deep appreciation of the enthusiastic review you gave *Successful Radio Advertising* in your October issue.

It is most gratifying to know that you think so well of the book, for there is no one whose opinion I value more highly than yours. I hope the test of time will vindicate your generous appraisal.

Very sincerely yours,

Dear Mr. Gunnison:

We wish to thank you for your complimentary reference to this organization in your article on "Personalizing Dealer Relations," which appears in the July issue of *Better Business*.

The subject so ably discussed in your article is one of special interest to several of us in this firm, and we appreciate your high evaluation of our efforts to improve dealer relations through personal contact.

Cordially yours,

Dear Mr. Needham:

I appreciate the generous words in your house magazine about my booklet, "Courtesy Keeps Customers." It was fine of you to mention it, and I thank you also for sending me the marked copy of your magazine. I read the entire issue with much interest.

The association with you by letter these past several weeks has been most enjoyable, and I shall long remember the courtesy on your part which brought it about. I hope that our paths will cross one of these days, and that I shall have the pleasure of knowing you personally.

Sincerely yours,

Dear Mr. Gates:

In your speech before the state convention of the Dry Goods Association the other day, you made a most generous reference to my efforts in behalf of that organization.

I thank you for your kind remark about my part in the activities of the Association. Coming from one of your high standing among the businessmen of this state, this compliment pleased me very much.

Yours sincerely,

My dear Harral:

I have read your glowing account of my book, *Writing Non-Fiction*, which appeared in the October number of *Publicity Problems*, and I am naturally delighted with it. It was fine of you to give me such a boost, and I appreciate it.

I am sending a copy of your review to the publisher. I hope it will cheer him on. So far the advance sales of the book have been good. What they will be after people have seen it, I cannot predict.

Cordially yours,

Dear Mr. Hallock:

All of us here were gratified to see the John Kingsley Company listed among the fifty firms whose business letters received your superior rating. I refer, of course, to page 26 of your recently published book, *New Methods in Business Correspondence.*

We consider it quite an honor to be mentioned in a list that includes so many leading concerns throughout the nation, especially when the selection was made by an acknowledged authority on the subject of business letters.

Cordially yours,

Dear Mr. Alford:

Thank you for your letter of July 21, telling us that you are quoting several statements from *The Burroughs Clearing House* in your forthcoming article.

We appreciate very much the credit you are giving to our publication in your article, which we shall look forward to seeing when it is released.

Sincerely yours,

Dear Mr. Connelly:

It was fine of you to mention my little book in the August issue of *Better English,* and I was delighted that you thought well of it.

Thank you also for sending me a marked copy of the magazine. Your courtesy is very much appreciated.

Sincerely yours,

Letters to Employees [3]

For loyal or outstanding service:

Dear Fred:

Tomorrow you will complete your tenth year with Breyer & Company.

This is just a word to tell you of my deep personal appreciation for your decade of dependable and loyal service to the firm.

[3] Several of the letters of seasonal good wishes to employees (pages 122-124) contain an expression of appreciation for loyal or outstanding service.

As you begin your eleventh year with the Company, I send you my sincere best wishes for your continued accomplishment and advancement.

Cordially yours,

Dear Tom:

Of the Wilburton Company's many accomplishments during 195-, one of the most outstanding has been the development of our direct-mail program.

You have made great strides in your first year in the promotion department, and the results are already apparent. I know that your work has extended far beyond the actual duties of your position, and that you have devoted a lot of your own time to Company interests.

I should like to express to you, both personally and in behalf of the Company, sincere appreciation for the splendid interest and enthusiasm on your part which is already being reflected in the work of the promotion department.

Cordially yours,

Dear Miss Mills:

The purpose of this note is to express my deep appreciation of your fine spirit in helping us through the difficult month just ended.

I don't know when the "flu" or any other disease has ever laid low so many members of our office staff; and I am frank to admit that, without your willingness to work many extra hours, we should have been in a desperate plight.

I want you to know that this fine manifestation of your loyalty is deeply appreciated, and that it will not be forgotten.

Cordially yours,

Dear Grover:

Some fine things were said about you last night at the Company dinner in your honor. You deserved every one of them.

Under your direction the mail order department has made great progress, and has earned a reputation as one of the finest units of its kind in this part of the country. You have been a real inspiration to others in the department, always setting an example worthy of their respect and confidence.

As you begin your twenty-sixth year with Wheeler & Sims, I want to express my deep personal thanks for your splendid record of service and loyalty to the firm.

Sincerely,

Dear Al:

For several months I have noticed the help and encouragement you are giving the two new men, Webster and Simpson. Though I have said nothing about it, I want you to know that I appreciate your generosity in helping them along and giving them a boost now and then.

Thanks to your assistance, both of these men are progressing more rapidly than if they had not received the benefit of your experience and suggestions. You have given them confidence and self-assurance; you have also taught them many things that they would otherwise have had to learn the hard way. I think it is very fine of you.

Cordially,

Dear Miss Hooper:

As you know, we have done more laundry and dry cleaning for the people of Marion during the past year than ever before. That's understandable. People have been taking better care of their clothes.

Because of the personnel shortage, we have had to handle this increased volume with a smaller staff than we had back in 194-, when our business was only two-thirds as large. And yet, we've insisted on keeping our quality right up there where it belongs.

This has meant that you have had to plug hard to turn out the work for our customers. It hasn't been easy, I know.

But you have done a splendid job. The way you have turned out quality work under pressure is something to be proud of. The Company appreciates it; and I am sure our customers do, too.

The work you have done during the past year has made friends for our outfit, and those friendships will unquestionably help to assure your prosperity in the future.

Sincerely yours,

———

Dear Carl:

On the thirty-fifth anniversary of your service to Niles & Company, I wish to express to you my deep appreciation of your loyalty to the firm.

You have been a part of this organization through more than half of its business history, and throughout your long years of service you have done your work with the utmost efficiency and dependability.

Please accept the enclosed little gift as a token of sincere gratitude for your faithful service. With it go my best wishes for your continued success and happiness for many years to come.

Yours sincerely,

———

My dear Conroy:

When you took over our public-relations work some five months ago, I would not have believed it possible that so much could be accomplished before the end of the year.

I realize that these things didn't just happen, but that your energy and ability supplied the drive to make them happen. You may be sure that I appreciate the untiring efforts on your part which have produced such excellent results. It is good to know that an increasingly important phase of our work is in such capable hands.

Sincerely yours,

———

For valuable suggestion:

Dear Kenneth:

I am very enthusiastic about your idea for the new company letterheads, and I sent your sketch off to the engravers this afternoon.

If they are able to develop the design you have suggested—and I feel sure they will be—your idea will soon become a reality, and a very worth-while one for the firm.

Thank you for your clever idea and for your co-operation in passing it on to me.

Cordially yours,

Dear Eric:

The "Letter of the Month" contest has produced such excellent results that it will be continued indefinitely—at least throughout the remaining months of this year.

I want to thank you for contributing this splendid idea and for working out the details of the contest. It is one of the best employee-participation methods we have ever used, and I appreciate the interest and initiative on your part which made it possible.

Cordially,

Dear John:

Some time ago you suggested that the James A. Davis Company might be interested in our Business Letter Service.

We wrote to this firm immediately, and today we received their three-year subscription to the Service.

I wish to thank you for giving the Sales Promotion Department a valuable lead. Your loyalty to the firm and your interest in its future are very much appreciated.

Sincerely yours,

Dear Henry:

The recent Efficiency Contest among our eight departments benefited the firm in many ways. The contest worked out so well that we shall have another next year.

In suggesting this idea, and in planning a sound basis for friendly competition among departments, you made a contribution of real value to the Kearney-Davis organization.

Mr. Clark and Mr. Stevens join me in this expression of sincere thanks.

Cordially,

Dear Frank:

I have just finished reading, for the second time, your report on proposed improvements in the setup of our Mail Order Department.

Your report shows many hours devoted to careful study of this problem, and I am looking forward to discussing it with you shortly after my return from Philadelphia next week.

Meanwhile, I wish to express my appreciation of the thoroughness with which you have tackled this big job. You have done some excellent research work, and I have no doubt that your suggestions will lead to worth-while changes.

Sincerely,

Dear Rex:

Thank you for submitting your idea for a leaflet of "Facts and Figures" about Williams & Company, to be used as an envelope stuffer in our promotional mailings. I have just discussed the proposed folder with Mr. Kenyon and Mr. Miles, and both agree with me that your plan is entirely practical.

Your sketch of such a leaflet and your suggestions as to pertinent items show a good deal of thought on your part. I appreciate your interest and your progressive spirit in developing this novel and promising idea.

Sincerely yours,

My dear Whitney:

Mr. Jones told me today that you are the man responsible for the much-improved floor plan of the Shipping Department.

This is just a word to thank you for making a real contribution to our operating efficiency. Your suggestion proves that you are on your toes.

Cordially yours,

Dear Fred:

Your "Thrift Week" plan has worked out so well that it will undoubtedly become a regular annual feature.

I appreciate your suggestion of a really fine promotional idea, and I shall not forget who deserves the credit for it.

Cordially,

Letters to Dealers [4]

For loyal patronage over period of years:

Gentlemen:

As we pause to observe the Fiftieth Anniversary of Wallace Brothers, it is only natural for us to think of those whose friendship and patronage have made possible the growth of our business.

To you, as one of our loyal customers over a long period, we express our sincere thanks for your confidence and co-operation. We hope that the business relationship between our two organizations has been as pleasant to you as it has been to us.

In beginning our second half century in business, we assure you of our best efforts to maintain the highest standards of quality and service. Your confidence in us is sincerely appreciated, and we shall do all within our power to merit its continuance.

Cordially yours,

Gentlemen:

This letter has only one purpose—to tell you how much we appreciate the business you have given us during the past five years.

As our association with you enters its sixth year, we pledge to you our continued efforts to provide for you the best of merchandise, service, and prices.

It is a pleasure to deal with a concern of your high business standards, and we take pride in the fact that you represent Durotex Products in Fort Wayne.

Very sincerely yours,

---

[4] Letters of seasonal good wishes to dealers (pages 124-128) contain an expression of appreciation for their confidence and patronage. Letters of welcome to new retail dealers (pages 138-142) include an expression of appreciation for the confidence implied in the new business relationship.

Dear Mr. Kingsley:

At this time of year most business concerns, like ourselves, are taking inventory. The general practice entails taking stock of tangible and physical assets.

But there remains in our accounting an item of immeasurable value—the good will of our friends, among whom we are pleased to number you.

In 195-, as in other years, your loyal patronage has played a vital part in whatever measure of success we have achieved.

And with the arrival of the New Year we pause, before setting our sights for 195-, to express our appreciation to you for your friendship.

                                        Very sincerely yours,

---

Dear Mr. Burnett:

It was exactly ten years ago that we received your first order for Standard Typewriters.

This is just a personal note to thank you for your confidence and for the business you have given us during the past decade.

We value the spirit of co-operation and mutual trust that has developed between your firm and ours. In all your dealings with us, you can depend on our earnest efforts to maintain this fine relationship.

                                        Sincerely yours,

Dear Mr. Burnham:

Today is our birthday, and the members of our organization have just come from the annual anniversary luncheon. During that very enjoyable affair we reviewed the progress of the past twenty-six years and outlined plans for adding several new services in the future.

It seems especially appropriate, on such a happy occasion for us, to tell you how much we appreciate the part you have played in making this day possible. Your friendship, your confidence, and your patronage have been a material factor in the development of our business.

We have tried to serve you well, and we sincerely hope we have succeeded. In the future we pledge our continued efforts to give you the best of merchandise and service. You have helped to build this organization, and we want it to serve you to the full measure of its possibilities.

Cordially yours,

Dear Mr. Whiting:

Every day we write letters asking for this and for that, but this letter asks only that you accept our thanks for the privilege of serving you.

We hope that we have satisfied you in the three primary functions which we perform—service, quality, and price. We shall welcome your suggestions, and we assure you that they will receive interested attention.

Thank you again for your confidence and friendship.

Sincerely yours,

Dear Mr. Quigley:

Twenty years is a long time! When two firms do business together for so many years—in a spirit of co-operation and mutual confidence—there develops a real bond of friendship.

That's why we are writing you today. Just twenty years ago you sent us your first order for Milton Hosiery. Since that day you have sent us many more.

This seems an appropriate time to tell you how much we value your confidence and appreciate the business you have given us. For many more years we shall try to deserve your reliance upon us for top-quality merchandise.

It's a pleasure to do business with you—and we thank you for your friendship.

Sincerely yours,

For outstanding success in sale of product:

Dear Mr. Newburn:

Thank you for the splendid order that we received from you this morning.

Ever since you became our Springfield distributor, the size of your orders has shown a consistent increase. This can only mean that the volume of your Flintex sales is increasing proportionately.

All of us here appreciate the fine work you are doing in expanding the market for our merchandise in your community. We are eager to give you every possible assistance, and hope you will let us know of any special service we can render in support of your efforts.

Best wishes for the continued growth of your Flintex business.

Cordially yours,

Dear Mr. Frederick:

When a Mellotone dealer chalks up as fine a record as you have made during your first year of business dealings with us, we feel that it calls for a great big THANK YOU on our part.

We take a lot of pride in the outstanding success you are making of your Mellotone sales, and we appreciate the increasing size of your orders.

Sincerely yours,

Gentlemen:

When a house increases its purchases from us as considerably as you did last year, we are happy for many reasons.

Our first reaction is that business has been exceptionally good with you, which pleases us immensely, for you are a valued friend as well as a good customer, and your success gives us real pleasure.

Our next reaction is that your trade must like Eagle merchandise, that they buy it eagerly and come back for more. That makes us proud of Eagle quality and inspires us to make it still better.

Then we like to think that your approval of our products extends to us personally, that a growing good will for our policies and our people is reflected in the increased business you place with us.

Whatever the reasons, the record is there. Your purchases from us have increased markedly during each of the past four years, and we are sincerely grateful to you.

Here's hoping that all business will go ahead in 195-, that yours will be better than ever, and that you will still find us deserving of your confidence. We pledge our very best efforts to be worthy of it.

Sincerely yours,

Dear Mr. Fleming:

January is an ideal time to review the past year . . . and express thanks where they are due.

The steady increase in your sale of Keating Products during the past year has meant much to us, and we are grateful for your loyal support.

Throughout 195- and the years that follow, we shall do our utmost to provide the best service and the finest merchandise ever offered by The Keating Company. This, we believe, is the most convincing way to express our thanks for your confidence and friendship.

Sincerely yours,

Dear Mr. Finch:

We wish to compliment you and to thank you for your splendid record in the sale of Wearever Pens.

The fact that your orders have increased in size during each of the past three years is solid proof of your excellent sales work.

We sincerely appreciate your fine record, and we wish to co-operate with you fully to assure its continuance.

Cordially yours,

Dear Mr. Davies:

Today marks the fifth anniversary of business dealings between our two companies.

During the past five years I have watched with great interest your success in the sale of Sherman Products. Throughout this period you have continued to develop an increasing market for them; your fine record speaks for itself.

On this occasion I wish to express to you my personal appreciation of your alertness, your progressive spirit, and your wholehearted co-operation. All are factors in your outstanding success as a Sherman dealer. We, too, are proud of your record, and we assure you of our continued co-operation toward maintaining it.

Sincerely yours,

Dear Mr. Marsh:

Your purchases of Nelson Appliances during the first six months of 195- have exceeded your total for all of last year.

A record like this would delight any sales manager. It shows that a dealer is on his toes, helping to expand the market for the product in his community. It also indicates that his efforts are being rewarded by increasing sales and greater profits.

We warmly appreciate your business, as well as the fine manner in which you are representing Nelson Appliances in St. Joseph. You can be sure of our continued efforts to make this relationship always pleasant and profitable to you.

Sincerely yours,

For promptness in meeting obligations:

Dear Mr. Carlton:

Many of the letters I write as credit manager are requests for the payment of past-due accounts. But this one has a different purpose.

I think it is just as important that we express our appreciation to customers who meet their obligations with consistent promptness. Your fine credit record deserves both our compliments and our gratitude.

So this is just a note to tell you that we appreciate and thank you for the promptness with which you meet our invoices.

Sincerely yours,

Dear Mr. Asher:

It is a genuine pleasure to write this letter of appreciation for the splendid paying record you have established with Folger.

The fact that you consistently discount your Folger invoices indicates the careful attention you are giving to the operation of your business.

We just want you to know how pleased we are over the way you are handling your Folger account. We also want to wish you increasing success, not only with Folger's, but in every phase of the good work you are doing.

Cordially yours,

———————

Dear Mr. Stone:

In the regular course of business I have little or no occasion to write to you, since your account does not require correspondence from the credit department. So I wish to step from behind my desk for a moment and speak to you personally.

I want to tell you just how much you have helped me in my work for the house during the past year, as in other years, by the promptness with which you have followed your maturities and the consistency with which you have earned your discounts through both good times and bad.

I hope we have merited your confidence as fully as you have earned our high regard and enduring respect, and that we may rely on your wholehearted support in the future, as in the past, for bigger and better things to come.

Sincerely yours,

———————

Dear Mr. Grayson:

A credit man spends so much time and effort in saying "Please remit" that it's a real pleasure when he has the chance to say "Thank you."

That's why I get a real kick out of thanking you for the fine way you have handled your account.

If all customers were half as thoughtful and considerate as you have been, even a lowly credit man could occasionally go home to his family with a smile on his face and a song in his heart.

Sincerely yours,

———————

Dear Mr. Peters:

Sometimes, in the stress of daily business, we find ourselves overlooking some of the little courtesies that we should extend to one another. So we want to tell you right now how much we appreciate the promptness with which you have always taken care of our invoices.

Your loyal support has been most encouraging to us, and we thank you for your splendid co-operation.

Sincerely yours,

Dear Mr. Ranney:

Most of the letters that carry my signature are concerned with the daily routine of the credit department. But this one is different.

I want to speak personally for just a moment . . . long enough to tell you how much I appreciate your promptness in meeting our invoices. Customers like you certainly brighten the life of a credit man.

Because your co-operation has helped to make my work more efficient and more enjoyable, I am sending you this note to express my sincere thanks.

Cordially yours,

Dear Mr. Arnold:

Your consistent promptness in meeting your obligations has earned you something valuable—an excellent credit record—one of which you may well be proud.

It is true that in many credit departments accounts like yours go unnoticed and seemingly unappreciated. Those who are slow in paying their bills get most of the attention. This should not be so.

Please consider this letter an expression of our sincere thanks for the splendid way you have handled your account with us. It's a real pleasure to do business with you.

Cordially yours,

Dear Mr. Howard:

Because of the fine way in which you attend to your obligations, this department seldom has occasion to write to you.

You certainly do have a letter coming, though . . . a letter of real appreciation for the promptness with which you meet our invoices.

That old saying of Josh Billings, "The wheel that squeaks the loudest is the one that gets the grease," is all too true in most credit departments. A lot of time is spent on "squeaky" wheels, and we sometimes forget it's the solid, smooth-running wheels . . . made up of accounts like yours . . . that are the backbone of any credit system.

So this letter has just one purpose . . . to say "Thank you" for your splendid co-operation. We surely appreciate it.

Sincerely yours,

For act of special service or courtesy:

Dear Mr. Meeker:

Our new representative in your territory, Mr. Thomas Redding, has told me of your many courtesies to him last week.

It was certainly fine of you to help him so much on his first visit to Tulsa, and I wish to add my thanks to his. I share with Mr. Redding the desire to return your kindness at the first opportunity.

Very sincerely yours,

Dear Mr. Tolliver:

Your thoughtful expression of holiday greetings is much appreciated.

I, too, have enjoyed our association during the past year. It is my hope that it may continue for a long time to come.

I reciprocate most heartily your good wishes for 195-. May it bring you fulfillment of those things which you most desire.

Sincerely yours,

Gentlemen:

During the recent flood emergency which paralyzed activity in our main plant and delayed production schedules for almost a month, you showed us every consideration and co-operation.

We wish to express our appreciation to you for bearing with us in circumstances which could be neither anticipated nor prevented.

We regret the inconvenience which this situation must have caused you, but we shall long remember your spirit of understanding and helpfulness.

Now that we are operating at full efficiency again, we shall try to show our appreciation by giving you the best service you have ever received.

Cordially yours,

Dear Mr. Gaskill:

That was certainly a fine letter you wrote me November 6 about Fred Emmett, who called on you a week or so ago.

We are very glad to know that you liked Fred and enjoyed talking with him. He has done an outstanding job for us on the Pacific Coast the past five years, and we feel that he will be equally successful in the Southwest.

Whenever Fred, or any of us here, can be of service to you, please give us the opportunity. And meanwhile, thank you sincerely for your fine letter.

Cordially yours,

Dear Mr. Wales:

Thank you for writing to me about the contest you conducted recently to increase your sale of Sharpoint Pencils.

Your sales-promotion plan produced such remarkable results that we plan to outline it in detail to our dealers in other cities, as you suggested.

I compliment you upon your ingenuity in working out this clever promotional idea, and I thank you most sincerely for your generosity in making it available to our other dealers.

Cordially yours,

Dear Mr. Lambert:

It was good of you to send Harold Perkins in to see us. Many of our best employees owe their jobs to people like you, who take a friendly interest in our organization. You can be sure that, with your stamp of approval, this lad will receive very special consideration.

In the event we are unable to find an opening just now that would challenge his ability, we shall surely keep his application in mind for a future possibility.

Thanks again for your co-operation, which we are happy to regard as evidence of your good will.

Sincerely yours,

Dear Mr. Wagner:

I appreciate very much your cordial note, and I heartily reciprocate its friendly sentiments.

All of us in this firm who have come in contact with your concern feel that the fine spirit of co-operation between our two organizations has done much to benefit both.

You may be sure that we shall welcome every opportunity to work with you during the coming year, and that we stand ready to assist you in every way within our power.

I hope 195- will be the best year your business has ever had.

Sincerely yours,

Dear Mr. Greever:

Bob Watson has told me how much you did to help him get off on the right foot in Kansas City, and I feel just as deeply indebted to you as Bob does.

I shall try to stop in Kansas City to thank you personally the next time I make a trip to the West Coast. Meanwhile, please tell us of any way in which we can reciprocate the courtesy and fine co-operation you have extended to us.

Sincerely yours,

Dear Mr. McGinnis:

In opening an account with us recently, Mr. Fred Coleman of Price & Willoughby, Toledo, mentioned that he had heard some fine things from you about our merchandise and service.

This note is just to tell you how much we appreciate your recommendation. We shall try to live up to the good words you have spoken for us, and Mr. Coleman will receive our full co-operation in all his dealings with us.

In giving us so much credit for your success with Porter Products in Dayton, you underestimate your own excellent work in featuring them so effectively in your store. But we thank you most sincerely for your endorsement of our merchandise and business policies.

You can be sure of our continued effort to deserve your confidence.

Cordially yours,

Letters to Consumers [5]

For opening charge account:

Dear Mr. Fischer:

Thank you for opening an account at Van Winkle's. It is a pleasure to send you this personal note of welcome as a new charge customer.

We regard the opening of your account as an expression of your confidence in this store . . . its merchandise and service. Every effort will be made to satisfy you completely, and to make all your visits here enjoyable.

Cordially yours,

Dear Mrs. Hepperly:

This is just a note to thank you for opening a charge account at Pomeroy's.

We shall do our best to make your account a source of added satisfaction to you in shopping here. And when you find it more convenient to order by telephone, please make use of our Personal Shopper Service.

As a charge customer you will receive announcements of our sales and other special events. We hope you will enjoy these occasions.

[5] Letters of welcome to consumers (pages 142-145) contain an expression of appreciation for first patronage. Letters of seasonal good wishes to consumers (pages 128-130) include an expression of appreciation for business friendship.

In terms of courteous, efficient service, we shall try to show our appreciation of your confidence and patronage.

Sincerely yours,

———

Dear Mrs. Chapman:

I learned this morning that you have opened a charge account with this store, and I want you to know how much we appreciate your good will and the confidence you place in us.

We shall do our best to see that every contact you have with Kline's will be pleasant—every transaction completely satisfactory. Should you feel that we might serve you with a greater degree of efficiency at any time, I shall consider it a personal favor if you will let me know.

Cordially yours,

———

Dear Mrs. Parnell:

The personal charge account which you have just opened with this store is an indication of your confidence in us, which we will faithfully strive to deserve.

It is our aim to make the House of Russek a most pleasant, helpful place in which to shop, and we shall always appreciate any suggestion that you may offer toward bettering that service.

The opportunity to serve you as a charge patron is much appreciated, and we pledge our earnest efforts to please you.

Sincerely yours,

———

Dear Mrs. Clinton:

It was a pleasure to receive a report from the credit department this morning that you have opened a charge account with us.

The policy of this organization has always been to sell quality merchandise at prices comparable with those of other high-grade stores. In addition, we strive to maintain efficient, courteous service that will make your shopping here easy and enjoyable.

Please accept our sincere thanks for this opportunity to serve you as a credit patron. We shall try to make your charge account a real convenience to you.

Cordially yours,

———

Dear Mrs. Barnes:

This is just a note to extend my personal welcome to you as a new charge-account patron of Peck & Peck.

We hope you will enjoy wearing our fashions as much as we enjoy creating them, and that your account with us will prove a lasting pleasure and convenience.

The advantages of your account are available at any time in all of our Peck & Peck shops.

Yours sincerely,

Dear Mrs. Bernard:

It was a pleasure to learn this morning that you have opened a charge account here.

Thank you for this expression of your confidence in Burger-Phillips. We shall do our best to deserve it.

I hope the opening of your account will be the beginning of a long and mutually satisfactory association.

Cordially yours,

Dear Mrs. Gettman:

The opportunity to open a Capwell charge account for you recently was very much appreciated.

Though we've been serving Northern California for many years, nothing pleases us more than extending Capwell's credit services to a new charge customer.

You will find us always friendly and glad to be helpful. And on your part, please feel free to make suggestions and comments regarding this store. We really appreciate and use them.

It is a genuine pleasure to welcome you. We shall try to make all your shopping visits to Capwell's pleasant and satisfying.

Sincerely yours,

Dear Mrs. Rodney:

The fact that you have opened an account with Mason & Sons pleases us very much. We appreciate this expression of your confidence, and promise our earnest efforts to be deserving of it.

The enclosed folder, "How to Enjoy Your Charge Account," suggests many ways in which your account will add to your shopping convenience. Please make full use of these advantages.

It is a pleasure to welcome you as a charge customer, and we look forward to serving you often through your account.

Sincerely yours,

Dear Miss Sedgwick:

Thank you for opening an account with us.

The opportunity to serve you as a charge customer is most welcome. We shall try in every way to make your shopping here a very pleasant experience.

Cordially,

For first use of charge account:

Dear Mrs. Lyons:

Thank you for the first use of your charge account yesterday. We appreciate the opportunity to serve you as a charge patron . . . and promise our earnest effort to justify the confidence you have placed in us.

As you continue to visit Kingsley's, please tell us of any way in which your shopping can be made more convenient.

Cordially yours,

Dear Mrs. Jennings:

Sending our first statement for purchases made on your new charge account gives us a welcome opportunity to express our thanks for your patronage.

Whenever we can be of personal service to you, doing so will be a pleasure.

It is our sincere wish that you may find satisfaction in all your dealings with us, and that we may have the privilege of serving you for many years.

Cordially yours,

Dear Mr. Billings:

Thank you very much for your purchase here the other day, marking the first use of your new charge account.

It is a pleasure to serve you as a credit patron. We shall try to make your account a real convenience and time saver.

Your satisfaction with our merchandise and service is very important to us. Please let us know of any way in which your visits here can be made more enjoyable.

Sincerely yours,

Dear Mrs. Livingston:

This is just a note of appreciation for the purchases you made of Miss Marshall yesterday in our Ladies' Department. She mentioned to me that you had been in, and I want to add my sincere thanks for your patronage.

It was a pleasure to serve you, and your frequent visits will be most welcome. We shall do our best to make them pleasant occasions for you.

Cordially yours,

Dear Mrs. Finney:

The use of your new charge account is very much appreciated. We hope it is adding to your convenience in shopping at Bamberger's.

It is a pleasure to serve you as a credit patron, and we shall try to make your account a real advantage to you.

Sincerely yours,

Dear Mrs. Patterson:

Thank you for the visit you paid us yesterday. We appreciate your coming in, and we are sure your purchase will prove a useful, attractive addition to your home.

Now that you have found the way to our door, we hope you will visit us often. Whether you come in on a definite errand or just drop in to look around, you will always find a cordial welcome here.

Yours sincerely,

Dear Mrs. Johnson:

Thank you for the charge purchase you made at Bromberg's the other day, marking the first use of your new account. We appreciated the opportunity to serve you.

You will find us sincerely interested in your continued satisfaction with all your purchases here. We hope to deserve your reliance upon Bromberg's for things of quality and distinction.

Since many interesting pieces are being received from day to day, you will enjoy an occasional visit. Even your most casual one will be welcomed.

Thank you again for the opportunity to serve you as a charge patron.

Cordially yours,

Dear Mr. Lucas:

Thank you for selecting Clayton's for your purchase yesterday. It was a pleasure to serve you through your new account.

Please visit us again soon. We shall try to prove by our service how much we appreciate your patronage.

Cordially yours,

Dear Mrs. Hildebrand:

In sending the enclosed statement for your first month's purchases, we want to express our sincere thanks for your patronage.

We hope you are finding your account at Baker Brothers a real convenience, and that you will continue to use it for many years. Please let us know if there is any way in which your visits here can be made more enjoyable.

By providing the best of service and merchandise, we shall try to deserve an increasing amount of your patronage.

Sincerely yours,

Dear Mrs. King:

This is just a note to say "Thank you!"

The first use of your Morrison-Hayes charge account the other day pleased us very much. We shall try to make it a real convenience to you, whether you visit the store personally or shop by telephone.

It's a pleasure to serve you as a credit patron, and we hope you will use your account often.

Sincerely yours,

———

Dear Mr. Wheaton:

Thank you for your purchase today . . . and for the first opportunity to serve you through your charge account.

Your continued satisfaction at Howse's is important to us. Please tell us of any way in which your shopping here can be made more convenient.

Since new merchandise is arriving every day, you and Mrs. Wheaton will enjoy dropping in from time to time. Your visits will be most welcome.

Cordially,

———

For regular patronage:

Dear Mr. Robbins:

Do you remember when you opened your charge account with Marshall Field & Company?

You have been one of our charge customers for a long time . . . since 1934, to be exact . . . and we are proud of the confidence you have shown in us these many years.

Your long friendship and patronage are deeply appreciated. We shall try to express our thanks by maintaining the standards of quality and service that won your confidence years ago.

In addition, we shall be glad to know of any way that your visits here can be made more enjoyable. We look forward to serving you for many more years.

Sincerely yours,

———

Dear Mrs. Peterson:

A credit department does not often have the pleasant opportunity of writing to its charge patrons with no other purpose than to say

"Thank you." At this season of the year, before the last few busy weeks of 195- begin, we express our appreciation for your account and the confidence in us which it manifests.

Gratitude most deeply felt is often the hardest to express. We hope, however, that this letter will convey to some extent our genuine appreciation of your patronage and co-operation in the past.

It has been a pleasure to serve you, and we look forward to a continuance of our pleasant business relations.

Very sincerely yours,

Dear Mr. Long:

Not so very long ago the owner of a store greeted his customers at the door, and he knew many of them by name. Such a practice, of course, is impossible now; and yet it is just as much our desire to make you feel at home at Taylor's today as it was sixty-nine years ago.

Perhaps this letter will express in a small way our appreciation of your loyal patronage and of the fine way you have handled your account. It is our hope that this friendly relationship will continue for many more years.

Sincerely yours,

Dear Mrs. Reams:

You are certainly a loyal customer of Parker's, and we appreciate the frequent use of your charge account during the past year.

That is why we are writing to say a sincere "Thank you" for your patronage. This evidence of satisfaction and good will on your part gives us an added incentive to maintain, during 195-, the highest possible quality of merchandise and service.

Sincerely yours,

Dear Mrs. Kilbourne:

This note has just one purpose—to express to you our sincere thanks.

Year after year, you make a large percentage of your purchases at Burdine's. Your loyal support provides the strongest possible incentive for our efforts to serve you more efficiently and more completely. We value your confidence as much as your patronage.

This message, we hope, will convey to you something of the deep sense of gratitude we feel for your friendship. We shall strive to be worthy of it for many years to come.

Sincerely yours,

Dear Mrs. South:

This is just a note . . . before the dawn of another New Year . . . to express our sincere thanks for your patronage during 195-.

We regard the frequent use of your account as an expression of your confidence and friendship . . . and we shall do our best to be worthy of both.

Please let us know if there is any way in which Klingman's can better serve you during the coming year. And speaking of the New Year, may it be one of good health and happiness for you and yours!

Sincerely,

Dear Mr. Hudson:

It was just a year ago that we had the pleasure of extending to you the convenience of a charge account.

The activity of your account since that time has been most gratifying, and we hope we may assume from this record that we have justified in every way your reason for opening an account with us.

Back in the days when Carson Pirie Scott & Company was a one-story organization, this word of appreciation would have been expressed by one of the founders with a hearty handshake. Being big has its drawbacks, and not being able to talk with you when you come in is one of them.

But we hope you will accept this letter, though a poor substitute perhaps for the handshake, as no less sincere in thanking you for the many purchases you have made here.

Sincerely yours,

Dear Mrs. Walker:

As we come to the end of 195-, it is a pleasure to thank you personally for your patronage of Brandeis' during the past year.

We hope you have enjoyed your visits here as much as we have enjoyed serving you. Your confidence in us is deeply appreciated, and you can be sure of our continued effort to be worthy of it.

May our pleasant relations of the past continue for many years to come! Best wishes for a happy, prosperous, and successful 195-.

Sincerely yours,

Dear Mrs. Ruggles:

I wish it were possible for me to know each one of our customers personally, so that I could tell you, from time to time, just how much I appreciate your loyalty to us.

But I do want to thank you, nevertheless, for the friendship and patronage you have given us. Your charge account was opened just one year ago today. It is my sincere hope that you have enjoyed using it in proportion to the pleasure we have had in serving you.

During your second year as a charge customer, we want to make your account still more of a convenience to you. So please tell us of any way in which it can be made more useful.

Sincerely yours,

Dear Mr. Henley:

Since the opening of your Calloway charge account several months ago, you have made frequent use of it.

This is just a note to thank you for your patronage and for your confidence in us. Serving you is a real pleasure, and we appreciate each opportunity to do so.

Sincerely yours,

Dear Mrs. Elwood:

The dawn of the New Year brings a welcome opportunity to ex-press our appreciation for your patronage throughout the year just closed.

We sincerely hope that the use of your charge account during the last year has been as pleasurable to you as your patronage has been to us. Your loyal support has been a big factor in making 195- such an enjoyable year for us.

We look forward to the continuance of pleasant relations during the coming year, and hope that it will provide many opportunities for us to serve you.

Sincerely yours,

Dear Mr. and Mrs. Daniels:

Your charge account with us had a birthday this month—it is one year old.

Perhaps this doesn't mean much to you, but to us your patronage is an evidence of your faith in The LaSalle & Koch Company. All of us are sometimes inclined to take our friends too much for granted, and so we are glad to have this opportunity to say "Thank you."

We shall do everything we can to deserve your continued confidence.

Sincerely yours,

Dear Mr. Neeley:

It doesn't seem like ten years since you opened your charge account here, does it? But that's exactly what it is—ten years today.

So this seems an appropriate time to tell you something we have been thinking for a long time. That decade of friendship with you is something we value very highly. Your patronage and loyalty as a customer we have tried hard to deserve; and we shall keep right on trying, so that the second decade of our association will be just as pleasant as the first.

Cordially yours,

Dear Mrs. Gordon:

Years ago, Mr. Marshall Field used to shake hands with each of his customer friends at the State and Washington door.

I wish I could do that today, but since there are many thousands more friends of Field's in 195- than any one man could greet personally, I am writing instead to thank you for your friendship and for the confidence you have shown in us.

As always, we face the coming year with determination to attend our duties more adequately, to better our service, and to widen our comprehension of your wishes. In addition, we shall endeavor to keep pace with the rapidly changing economic and marketing conditions and to interpret them to your advantage.

It is our sincere hope that the year 195- will be a happy and successful one for you.

Cordially yours,

Dear Mr. Ulmer:

Just one year ago today! That was an important occasion to us, for on that day you opened your account at Van Winkle's.

On this "first anniversary" we want to express our appreciation of your friendship during the past year. It has been a happy year of association, and your patronage here is a source of genuine pride to us.

As you continue to shop at Van Winkle's, please tell us of any extra service that will make your visits more enjoyable.

Sincerely yours,

For prompt payment of bills:

Dear Mr. McVaney:

Your Myerson account is always paid so promptly that you seldom receive a letter from the credit department.

Perhaps you have never thought of it, but your fine co-operation means a lot to us. It makes the work of this department more pleasant and efficient.

So this is just a note to compliment you on your excellent credit record . . . and to say a sincere "Thank you!"

Cordially yours,

Dear Mrs. Givens:

At this season of the year, with Christmas only a few days off and 195- just around the corner, I pause to send you a message of appreciation.

Month after month, year after year, your account with Lit Brothers has been paid with prompt regularity. Such an account is the pride of any business executive. I feel a deep sense of gratitude for such co-operation, and I compliment you upon your superior record as a credit patron.

Before the holiday season passes, I want to thank you for the pleasant relationship which this firm has enjoyed in serving you over a long period of years.

Sincerely yours,

Dear Mrs. Wilson:

You happen to be one of our patrons to whom those of us in the credit department seldom have the pleasure of writing. The splendid manner in which you handle your account never requires a collection reminder.

So it seems very much in order to let you know that we are grateful, not only for the business you have given us, but for the manner in which payments have always been made.

It is a genuine pleasure to have you as a customer, and we thank you for your fine co-operation.

Sincerely yours,

Dear Mr. Downing:

As I review the work of this department during the past year, I realize what a splendid job you have done in handling your account with us.

Your fine record of promptness in meeting your obligations is a high personal tribute to you. Moreover, it has meant a lot to me, as credit manager, in making my work for the house more pleasant and efficient.

So this note is just to tell you how much I appreciate your co-operation.

Sincerely yours,

Dear Mrs. Blakeman:

This letter is a little different from those usually mailed by the department of accounts.

Its only purpose is to thank you for the splendid way in which you take care of your charge account at Russeks.

We appreciate your fine co-operation in all your dealings with us. You may be sure of our continued efforts to deserve your friendship and confidence.

Sincerely yours,

Dear Mr. Brownell:

For many years the Credit Granters of America have been trying to impress upon the buying public the advantages and justice of paying their bills promptly.

During that time very little and certainly not enough recognition has been given to those who have consistently paid their obligations promptly without being requested to do so.

It is a privilege to express to you, personally, my appreciation of the prompt manner in which you have always met your obligations.

I congratulate you upon an enviable credit record throughout your business dealings with Hink's.

Cordially yours,

Dear Mr. Ives:

Throughout your long patronage of Marshall Field & Company, it has never been necessary to remind you of a past-due payment.

Your fine co-operation in the use of your account marks you as a customer we are proud to serve.

By exerting every effort to make your shopping here pleasant and profitable, we shall try to show you how much we appreciate your splendid credit record.

Sincerely yours,

Dear Mrs. Donahue:

Your check for $24.15 in payment of your June statement came in this morning. Ever since you opened an account with us several months ago, you have paid your bills right on the minute, and we want you to know how much we appreciate it.

If you think of any way in which we can enhance the value of your charge account to you, please tell us what it is.

Sincerely yours,

Dear Mr. Harvey:

This is just a personal note to thank you for the promptness with which your Gimbel account is paid each month.

We appreciate your fine record of co-operation and consider it a privilege to serve you as a credit patron.

Please feel free to call on us if ever you have a problem concerning your account, or if we can be of assistance to you in any other way.

Cordially yours,

Dear Mrs. Garrett:

A year ago we suggested that you might enjoy the convenience of a charge account with us. Much to our pleasure, you accepted.

Now that your first year as a charge customer is drawing to a close, we are more pleased than ever that you accepted our offer. Throughout the year you have maintained a splendid record of promptness and dependability in meeting your credit obligations.

Charge customers like you add a lot to the pleasure of doing business. Every store would like to have more of them.

As you continue to use your account, won't you please tell us of any way in which we can make our service to you more complete?

Sincerely yours,

Dear Mr. Garris:

You certainly deserve a special letter of thanks for the splendid way you take care of your account at Mayo's.

We want you to know that your fine record does not go unnoticed. On the contrary, it is very much appreciated.

Please feel free to mention our name if you should ever have use for a business reference. It will be a pleasure to comment on your excellent credit record with us.

Sincerely yours,

Dear Mr. Kincaid:

Your account with us is marked "Paid in Full" . . . and right on the dot as usual.

This is just a note to thank you for the fine manner in which you handle your account. A customer like you, who pays his bills so promptly each month, makes the life of a credit man a lot brighter.

Though we seldom write to you about it, we do appreciate your excellent credit record . . . and the co-operation on your part that has helped to build it.

Sincerely yours,

For co-operation in correcting error:

Dear Mrs. Whitworth:

Thank you for your friendly co-operation in correcting the amount of your May statement.

Despite our best efforts toward complete efficiency, an occasional slip is inevitable. You were most helpful the other day in calling to discuss your account, thus giving us an opportunity to correct it promptly. We sincerely appreciate your doing so.

Cordially yours,

Dear Mr. Benning:

When a customer tells us of some way in which we can serve him more efficiently, we try our best to do so.

This is just a note of appreciation for your recent visit to my office. Your assistance gave us a welcome opportunity to correct an oversight on the part of this department. Thank you for your co-operation.

Sincerely yours,

Dear Mr. Ackerman:

Try as we will to make our operating efficiency one hundred per cent, an exception occurs every now and then. "The human factor," someone has called it—that inevitable fraction between one's best efforts and the goal of perfection.

We slipped up the other day on an item concerning your account, and we sincerely appreciate your calling it to our attention. More than that, we thank you for your friendly spirit of understanding and co-operation.

You can rely on our constant effort to serve you in a way that deserves your patronage and your confidence.

Sincerely yours,

Dear Mr. Finch:

When a mix-up occurred the other day in our delivery department, your co-operation helped us to straighten it out with the minimum delay.

This is just a word to say "Thank you" for both your patience and your assistance. Your co-operation is very much appreciated.

Sincerely yours,

For recommending firm to others:

Dear Mrs. Saunders:

This is just a note to tell you how much I appreciate your bringing Mrs. Martin to my office this morning. This evidence of your good will and your confidence in our service is deeply gratifying, and we shall do our best to deserve it.

We are very glad to have Mrs. Martin as a new credit patron, and every effort will be made to serve her in a manner worthy of your complimentary remarks about us.

Cordially yours,

Dear Mrs. Snyder:

Your courtesy in recommending The Young-Quinlan Company to Mrs. John Ansley is sincerely appreciated.

Thank you for the spirit of friendliness on your part that led you to speak a good word for us. You may be sure of our continued effort to be deserving of your confidence.

Yours sincerely,

Dear Mr. Spellman:

When one of our clients recommends us to a friend, we consider it a high compliment.

So we were very much pleased to learn that Mr. Howard Gleason had called upon us because of your recommendation. We shall do our best to serve him well, and to live up to the good things you said about us.

Thank you sincerely for your friendship and good will.

Cordially yours,

Dear Mrs. Gillespie:

This morning Mrs. James Allen called to inspect our selection of tea tables. She mentioned the fact that her visit was made at your suggestion.

I wanted to send you this word of personal thanks for recommending us to Mrs. Allen. I appreciate this evidence of your friendship, and I feel complimented that you thought of us in your desire to help a friend solve her furniture problems.

Sincerely yours,

Dear Mrs. Goulding:

It was fine of you to recommend our service and facilities to Mrs. Warren, who paid us a visit the other day. We appreciate this expression of your good will.

Naturally, we take pride in the confidence you have shown in us, and we shall strive to maintain high standards of service to you and your friends.

Sincerely yours,

Dear Mr. McAllister:

Yesterday I had a very pleasant visit with Mr. Walter Smith, who called to open an account with us. He explained that you had suggested his coming to see me, and that your recommendation of our services had induced him to do his banking here.

I was very glad to welcome Mr. Smith to this bank and to assure him of our best efforts to live up to the good things you said about us. But most gratifying of all is this indication of your loyalty and good will, and I want to express my sincere appreciation of your friendship.

You may be sure we will do everything possible to be worthy of your confidence in us. If ever you think of any means by which we can make our service more efficient, please tell me about it personally.

Sincerely yours,

Dear Mrs. Larkin:

This morning, when Mrs. J. H. Thayer paid us a visit upon your recommendation, I was very much pleased—both because she had come in and because you like our store well enough to recommend it to your friends.

I want to thank you personally for your confidence in us and in our merchandise. We shall always do our best to give you the kind of goods and service that justify your faith in us.

Cordially yours,

Dear Mrs. Eaton:

In opening a charge account with us recently, Mrs. John Bagby mentioned that she had heard some fine things from you about our service.

This note is just to tell you how much we appreciate your recommendation. In serving Mrs. Bagby through her account, we shall do our best to live up to the good words you have spoken for us.

Sincerely yours,

Dear Mrs. Moore:

When Mrs. Paul McHenry opened a charge account with us the other day, she mentioned that your recommendation had led her to shop at Davis Brothers.

It was a pleasure to arrange an account for Mrs. McHenry, and we gladly accept the responsibility of serving her well.

At the same time, we deeply appreciate the spirit of friendship and confidence that led you to recommend this store. You can be sure of our best efforts to deserve it in the years to come.

Sincerely yours,

For renewed patronage:

Dear Mrs. Leffler:

Thank you for your recent patronage. It pleases us very much that you have begun to use your charge account again.

If there is any courtesy that we can extend to you, it is yours for the asking. The entire Scruggs-Vandervoort-Barney organization joins me in the hope that you will visit us often.

Yours sincerely,

———

Dear Mrs. Ahlman:

It's always a pleasure to welcome back a friend. We are glad that you are again using your charge account here.

It is our earnest purpose to satisfy you completely, and we hope you will give us frequent opportunities to prove it.

Sincerely yours,

———

Dear Mrs. Sanders:

The renewed use of your charge account pleases me so much that I wanted to write you this personal note of appreciation.

The opportunity to serve you again is most welcome. We hope you will enjoy the convenience of your account often. If you think of any way in which we can make it more useful to you, please let us know.

Sincerely yours,

———

Dear Miss Jeffers:

The return of a good friend is as pleasant an occasion in the business world as it is in one's private life.

Your recent purchase marked the first use of your account in some time. We welcome you again to Taylor's and thank you for your patronage.

Please pay us another visit soon. We shall do our utmost to make it a pleasant occasion for you.

Sincerely yours,

———

Dear Mrs. Boynton:

It is a real pleasure to find that you have again used your account after an absence of some time.

The success of Russeks is based on the quality of merchandise we offer, and on the friendly and efficient manner in which our organization functions.

It is our purpose to serve you so well that you will enjoy shopping here regularly. Any suggestions you may have will be most welcome.

Sincerely yours,

Dear Mr. Brinkman:

Thank you for the opportunity to serve you yesterday in our Men's Department. We have missed you lately, so your return was an occasion of special significance to us.

Please visit us again soon. Whether you have a definite purchase in mind, or merely drop in to look around, you are always welcome.

Cordially yours,

Dear Mrs. Grant:

This is just a note to tell you how much we appreciate the renewed use of your charge account.

It's a real pleasure to serve you again through your account, and we hope you will make frequent use of its convenience.

Please tell us of any way in which your visits here can be made more enjoyable.

Sincerely yours,

Dear Miss Dailey:

Enclosed is your personal Charga-Plate. It is fine to have your account active once more, for we've really missed you.

The cordial business relationship with you, we feel sure, will be as mutually pleasant as it has been in the past. It will be our purpose to serve you so well that you will want to come in often.

Sincerely yours,

Dear Mrs. Weldon:

Welcome back! We are happy to see that you are once again using your Mandel Brothers charge account.

It's a pleasure to serve you . . . and your patronage here is very much appreciated.

Every effort will be made to make your further visits to Mandel's most pleasant and profitable.

Sincerely yours,

———

THREE

Letters of Seasonal Good Wishes

This chapter includes letter specimens made available through the courtesy of the following persons and organizations: Beaumont, Heller & Sperling, Inc., Reading, Pennsylvania; Boston Store, Fort Dodge, Iowa; Burroughs, Inc., Los Angeles, California; Mr. Richard P. Ettinger, New York City; Fairy Silk Mills, Shillington, Pennsylvania; Mr. Norman M. Focht, Reading, Pennsylvania; Mr. J. C. Holman, Oklahoma City, Oklahoma; Mr. F. M. Jones, Halifax, Nova Scotia; Professor John C. McCloskey, Oregon State College, Corvallis, Oregon; The Motor Sales Company, Baltimore, Maryland; Mullen & Bluett, Los Angeles, California; Mr. John G. Powers, New York City; Prentice-Hall, Inc., New York City; *Printers' Ink*, New York City; W. & J. Sloane, Beverly Hills, California; South-Western Publishing Company, Cincinnati, Ohio; University of Oklahoma Press, Norman, Oklahoma.

MESSAGES of seasonal good wishes are very effective in keeping business friendships active and business contacts alive. Usually written about mid-December, letters of this type emphasize (1) appreciation of the reader's friendship, confidence, and co-operation, and (2) an expression of good wishes for the holiday season and the coming year.

Ordinarily the message of seasonal greeting should be confined to a maximum of 150 words, and often a note of half this length or less is sufficient to cover the subject thoroughly. Too much elaboration makes the letter both effusive and repetitious, thus seriously impairing its effectiveness.

The following pages show notes of seasonal good wishes appropriate for mailing to business and professional associates, employees, dealers, and consumers. Though the tone and content of the message are influenced somewhat by the relationship involved, letters of seasonal greeting to all four of these groups should have in common the essential qualities of informality, friendliness, and sincerity.

Letters to Business and Professional Associates

Dear Carl:

In sending you my best wishes for a happy holiday season, I wish also to thank you for the generous co-operation you have extended on many occasions during the past year.

I have enjoyed the pleasant association with you, and I look forward to its continuance for many years to come. May the New Year bring you an abundance of the good things of life!

Sincerely,

Dear Mr. Converse:

As I look back upon the year just closing, one of its most enjoyable occasions was the fine visit with you in Detroit several months ago.

During the coming year I hope we shall have more frequent opportunities for such visits, and that our two organizations may continue to work together to their mutual advantage.

Best wishes to you for a happy holiday season and for health, happiness, and prosperity in 195-.

Sincerely yours,

Gentlemen:

It is a pleasure, on behalf of the entire Fletcher organization, to send you hearty holiday greetings and best wishes for 195-.

We feel sure that the New Year will see the continuance of your outstanding business record, and we look forward to many more opportunities to work with you.

Very sincerely yours,

My dear Charles:

One of my very real regrets for the year now drawing to a close is the fact that I have seen so little of you during the past twelve months.

I do hope you have had a good year, and that 195- will hold for you the best of health, happiness, and prosperity. I hope, too, that our paths will cross more frequently during the year ahead.

Sincerely,

Dear Mr. Ross:

It was five years ago this holiday season that we first met in Minneapolis.

In sending you my sincere good wishes for Christmas and the New Year, I wish also to tell you how much I have enjoyed the pleasant association with you during these past five years.

Yours sincerely,

Dear George:

Since you are an eminent paper man, your interest in pens must be somewhat more than trifling. As the ham complements the egg, as Damon complements Pythias, so doth the pen complement the paper.

Thus I have chosen a pen to express to you my warmest wishes for a truly happy holiday season. The wishes you have now, most abundantly. The pen should be along in a day or two.

Sincerely,

Dear Mr. Bartlett:

This is just a note as Christmas approaches to remind you of the pleasure that your visit in August gave to us here in Alexandria.

My wife joins me in conveying to you and Mrs. Bartlett the best of greetings, and in expressing the wish that your enjoyment of the Christmas season will be complete.

Yours sincerely,

Dear Roy:

Day in and day out, year in and year out, I write copy for others to help sell their wares.

Today I pause to write this note for myself—to tell you that I appreciate your friendship and wish you an abundance of health, happiness, and prosperity throughout the New Year.

Sincerely,

Dear Mr. Ramsey:

The association with you during the past year has been so enjoyable that I want to send you this word of good wishes for a happy and successful 195-.

I hope the coming year will afford more opportunities for pleasant contacts between your firm and mine, and that I shall have the pleasure of further visits with you from time to time.

Sincerely yours,

Dear Mr. Rickard:

As we approach the end of 195-, I realize that the enjoyable association with you has contributed much toward making it a very pleasant year for me.

In sending you these words of thanks for your kindness on several occasions, I wish for you the happiest of holiday seasons. May the New Year bring you continued health, happiness, and success!

Sincerely yours,

Dear Mr. Blevins:

Having enjoyed the very pleasant association with you last fall, I should like to convey to you my best wishes for your happiness during the holiday season.

I hope that the New Year will afford further opportunities for us to work together, and I wish you continued success and prosperity throughout 195-.

Sincerely yours,

Dear Mr. Walton:

As we begin another year of pleasant business dealings, I want to express my thanks for the most enjoyable association with you during 195-.

I hope the New Year will hold for you a full measure of health, happiness, and prosperity.

Sincerely yours,

Letters to Employees

Dear Mr. King:

As another Christmas season approaches, I send you my sincere wish that it will bring joy to you and your family.

I should like also to express my appreciation to you for having given so fully of your strength and loyalty toward making 195- such a successful year for Walters & Son. You have every right to be proud of your achievements during the past year.

May the year ahead hold for you and yours the best of health and a great deal of happiness.

Sincerely,

———

Dear Leslie:

We have come a long way together during the year now closing. It has been one of the most successful years The Miller Company has ever enjoyed.

As our thoughts turn again to the holiday season and the spirit it symbolizes, we have much to be thankful for. And you, personally, have full cause to look back with satisfaction upon your work for the house during 195-. You have done a good job; you have played a large part in writing our record of progress.

I hope that Christmas will be a happy day for you and your family, and that the New Year will hold for you a full measure of happiness.

Sincerely yours,

———

Dear Raymond:

Wishing you again this year a joyous Christmas and prosperous New Year brings back memories of the many years I have had this pleasure.

What is particularly gratifying is to review the optimistic forecasts of previous years—and to see how accurately they have come to realization.

The year just closing has been the best in our business history, and you have played an important part in making it so. In sending you this expression of holiday greetings, I feel sure that the thought of your personal record in 195- will bring you real happiness, and that your expectations for 195- will bring you substantial rewards.

Once again, my sincere best wishes and congratulations upon your splendid work this past year. And may 195- be the most prosperous year you ever had!

Sincerely,

Dear Mr. Massengill:

As 195- draws to a close, all of us at Nixon's can take pride in the record we've made during the past year.

Personally, I am well aware that such a record was made possible only by the fine co-operation of each department and each individual member of our organization.

You have played well your part in this story of progress. In both loyalty and efficiency, you have lived up fully to the Nixon tradition.

I wish to thank you for your substantial share in advancing our mutual interests, and to wish for you and yours a Merry Christmas and every happiness throughout the New Year.

Sincerely yours,

Dear Bob:

Christmas . . . marking the last short lap of our journey through 195- . . . is just around the bend. For us the road has been one of smooth, steady progress.

Before we branch off to another year, I want to tell you how much I appreciate your part in making the course we've traveled together such a direct route to greater achievement.

When old Father Time flashes the green light that means "Go" through 195-, we shall all go on together to still bigger accomplishments. I sincerely hope that you, personally, will find the road filled with health and happiness . . . with every passing marker bringing you closer to your goal.

Sincerely yours,

Dear Fred:

I have just returned from Washington. The factories along the way were brilliantly lighted—a 240-mile Christmas tree shouting as no human voice can, "Merry Christmas to Men of Good Will!"

In Washington I visited eight concerns in the same line of industry. The moment I mentioned Prentice-Hall, faces lighted up—men seemed proud to be associated with that name. We are all working hard to make association with it the badge of modern aristocracy—the aristocracy not of wealth nor of birth, but of service.

You are doing your full share toward that end through your outstanding work in the College Book Department. Your efforts have been a big factor in the progress we have achieved this past year.

As we pause to enjoy the holidays before setting our sights for 195-, I send you my very best wishes for a Merry Christmas and a New Year filled with happiness.

Sincerely,

Dear Ralph:

As we round out one of the best years Ellery Brothers ever had, I want you to know that your hard work throughout 195- has not only been noticed, but sincerely appreciated. You have carried more than your share of the load, and your efforts have contributed largely to our success.

Your enjoyment of the holidays should be more complete because of the satisfaction of a job well done. I hope that Christmas will bring an abundance of happiness to you and your family, and that the New Year will prove the best one you've ever had.

Sincerely,

Letters to Dealers

Dear Mr. Saunders:

In a few hours clocks all over the world will strike out 195- and chime in the New Year.

As we of Mullen & Bluett look back on the year just closing, we are grateful indeed for your friendly confidence and for the privilege of numbering you among our good customers.

With warm personal regards I send to you, for our entire organization, a sincere wish for your happiness, health, and prosperity throughout the New Year.

Cordially yours,

Dear Mr. Maybank:

Straight from our "house" to you comes this note with hearty good wishes for a Merry Christmas.

If we had the magic power of good old St. Nick to be everywhere at the same time, we could say it in person. But our thoughts at least can span the miles and wish for you all the good things that go toward making each holiday season one of happy memories.

For the New Year we wish you health, happiness, and a full measure of prosperity.

Sincerely yours,

Dear Mr. Shipley:

I wish it were possible to drop in for a visit with you this morning. I'd like to thank you personally for your confidence and good will, and to wish you the best of everything at this holiday season.

I am well aware of the substantial part you have played in making 195- such a successful year for us, and I wish to express my deep gratitude for your friendship.

Since I have not had a chance to greet you personally and wish you a Merry Christmas, I take this occasion to do so by letter. I sincerely hope that Christmas at your house will prove a fitting climax for 195-, and that the coming year will bring you more of success and happiness than any which has gone before.

Cordially yours,

Dear Mr. Ballard:

With the holiday season just around the corner, I am taking time out for a few minutes to write you a personal letter.

All of us at Baker-Jennings appreciate the confidence you have placed in us this past year. It is a pleasure to do business with you, and we are proud to have our products featured in your store.

Our 195- goal will be to provide for you the finest merchandise that has ever carried the B-J trademark. In this way we shall try to express our thanks for your business friendship.

Best wishes to you for a Merry Christmas and a New Year filled with success.

Sincerely yours,

Dear Mr. Faulkner:

There are some letters that it's fun to write, and this is one of them.

At this time of year, when all of us take "time out" from business cares to enjoy Christmas and everything that it represents, one of the greatest pleasures comes in writing a few words of good wishes to our friends.

And that explains this note to you. Throughout the year your friendship has made our work more enjoyable, and we want you to know that we sincerely appreciate it.

Here's hoping that yours will be a very Merry Christmas, and that 195- will hold for you a bumper crop of health, happiness, and prosperity.

Sincerely yours,

Dear Mr. Bennett:

This Christmas your friends in our company wish they could thank you in person for your friendship and for the confidence you have shown in us. But that isn't possible, so we are writing to you instead.

It has been a pleasure to work with you during the past year, and we shall try to deserve your continued confidence for many years to come.

It is our hope that your Christmas will be a merry one, and that 195- will be a happy and successful year for you.

Sincerely yours,

Dear Mr. Griswold:

In looking back over the year now drawing to a close, we realize that the cordial business relationship with you has played a very real part in making 195- such an enjoyable year for us.

This is just a note to wish you a Merry Christmas, and to express the hope that the New Year will hold for you a full measure of health and happiness.

Sincerely yours,

Dear Mr. McClintock:

On behalf of the firm, I send you the enclosed gift with holiday greetings and best wishes.

Each year at this time there comes to my mind a motto which has appealed to me ever since I first heard it as a boy: "Respice: Prospice." These words come to mind again now because I want to associate myself with you in "looking back" upon our happy partnership of the past year, and in "looking forward" confidently to continued good fortune.

For Christmas, a very merry holiday; for the New Year, heartiest best wishes. In these good wishes I am joined by the entire Prentice-Hall family.

Sincerely yours,

Dear Mr. Borden:

As the holiday season approaches, it is a pleasure to pause in the rush and hurry of business to write you a special letter—not trying to sell you anything—not having to ask for something—but just for the purpose of wishing you a Merry Christmas.

Reviewing the past year, we realize that the progress we have made is directly due to the confidence and co-operation of our friends, and we want you to know that your part has been sincerely appreciated. It is a privilege to have your name on our books and a pleasure to do business with you.

May the coming holidays bring to you and yours good health, happiness, and a full share of those things which make this world a better place in which to live.

Sincerely yours,

Dear Mr. Weidman:

"A Merry Christmas" . . .

What a wealth of meaning there is in those words! They stand for joy, good feeling, good fellowship. To me, they will never grow old or trite.

I want to extend that greeting to you in this letter, since I cannot greet you face to face with a warm handshake. I want you to know that all of us here are very grateful for your friendship.

I hope that 195- was a good year for you, and that the one ahead will be still better. You can count upon our 100 per cent co-operation to help make it so.

Sincerely yours,

Letters to Consumers [1]

Dear Mrs. Beemis:

This is just a note—as the holiday season approaches—to wish you all the joy and happiness that should go with Christmas time.

We want you to know, too, that you have our sincere gratitude for your business friendship during the past year. As another New Year dawns, we pledge our continued effort to be deserving of the confidence you have placed in us.

Best wishes for a Merry Christmas and a New Year filled with happiness.

Cordially yours,

Dear Mr. McInnis:

Thirty years ago, when this business was founded, I used to enjoy a friendly chat with each of our patrons at this season of the year.

But the rapid growth which has made this a larger, better organization has necessarily deprived me of the opportunity to shake hands with all our friends, and to wish them the best of everything at this holiday season.

You have played a substantial part in making 195- such a successful year for us, and I am sincerely grateful for your confidence and good will.

I hope that you will have a Merry Christmas, and that the New Year will bring you a full measure of success and happiness.

Cordially yours,

Dear Mr. Seavers:

As the holiday season draws near, we pause to express to you our sincere wish that yours will be a Merry Christmas and a Happy and Prosperous New Year.

----

[1] The letter specimens that appear on pages 104-105 and 106-107, thanking consumers for regular patronage, include also an expression of seasonal good wishes.

We hope that your association with Peterson's during the past year has been as pleasant to you as it has been to us. Your confidence in this store is much appreciated . . . and we shall try to be worthy of it during 195- and for many years to come.

Sincerely yours,

Dear Mr. Alcorn:

We welcome this opportunity to lay aside the cares of business— the buying and selling of merchandise—long enough to send you our sincere wish that yours will be a happy holiday season of long and pleasant memories.

You have our deep gratitude for the cordial business relationship we are privileged to enjoy with you. We hope the New Year will bring you 365 days of happiness, good health, and continued success.

Sincerely,

Dear Mrs. Lance:

At this season our thoughts turn naturally to customers whose friendship we have enjoyed throughout the year.

You are one of these loyal customers . . . one whose confidence we value and appreciate.

This note brings you a sincere "Thank you" on behalf of the entire Boston Store personnel. At the same time we wish you a Merry Christmas and much happiness in the New Year!

Cordially yours,

Dear Mrs. Cantrell:

In looking back over the year 195-, we are moved to a deeper, more sincere appreciation of our friends.

Each year we realize more fully that friendships are what make life worth living, and we feel that there is a spirit of friendship underlying our business relations with our patrons. Daily experiences confirm this feeling.

Appreciation of friends is manifest by a cordial word of greeting. And so, at this holiday time, we want to extend to you our sincere best wishes for a Merry Christmas and a happy, prosperous New Year.

Cordially yours,

Dear Mr. Kelleher:

The coming of the Christmas season brings me a welcome opportunity to write you this note of good wishes.

The pleasant business relationship with you has helped to make the past year an enjoyable one for us, and we thank you most sincerely for your friendship.

Best wishes for a Merry Christmas and a New Year of happiness and prosperity far beyond your expectations.

Cordially yours,

———————

Dear Mr. Truesdale:

At this season of the year the happy custom of thinking about the other fellow's well-being manifests itself. It's a fine custom—one in which we join most heartily.

A large measure of our success during the past year has been due to your loyalty and co-operation. We hope that you, too, have achieved success in your field of endeavor.

This note brings you cordial holiday greetings . . . and our sincere good wishes for your prosperity and happiness in 195-.

Cordially yours,

———————

Dear Mrs. Emory:

In pausing to review the activities of the year now closing and to prepare for those of the year ahead, we feel that we owe you a very real debt of gratitude.

Your business friendship has played a large part in the success and satisfaction that 195- has brought to us. We thank you sincerely for your co-operation and for the confidence you have placed in us.

As another year approaches, we look forward to the continuance of this pleasant association with you. Best wishes for a Merry Christmas and a New Year of genuine happiness.

Yours sincerely,

———————

FOUR

Letters of Welcome

This chapter includes letter specimens made available through the courtesy of the following persons and organizations: Battelstein's, Houston, Texas; Beaumont, Heller & Sperling, Inc., Reading, Pennsylvania; The William Boardman & Sons Company, Hartford, Connecticut; Bowers Battery and Spark Plug Company, Reading, Pennsylvania; The Dartnell Corporation, Chicago, Illinois; Mr. Norman M. Focht, Reading, Pennsylvania; B. Forman Company, Rochester, New York; Mr. L. E. Frailey, Columbus, Ohio; Franklin Co-operative Creamery Association, Minneapolis, Minnesota; D. H. Holmes Company, Ltd., New Orleans, Louisiana; Home Laundry, Washington, D. C.; Illinois Central Railroad, Chicago, Illinois; Lion Oil Refining Company, El Dorado, Arkansas; Lipman Wolfe & Company, Portland, Oregon; Charles Mayer & Company, Indianapolis, Indiana; Professor John C. McCloskey, Oregon State College, Corvallis, Oregon; National Retail Credit Association, St. Louis, Missouri; M. L. Parker Company, Davenport, Iowa; Prentice-Hall, Inc., New York City; J. J. Stangel Hardware Company, Manitowoc, Wisconsin.

THE MESSAGE of welcome to a newcomer is a courteous and friendly gesture. Often it lays the foundation of a warm and permanent business friendship. Such a letter may be mailed with propriety to any of the following groups of persons: (1) business associates, including new concerns beginning business as well as professional associates moving to the community; (2) employees who have just assumed their duties; (3) retail merchants who have just become dealers or distributors of a product by virtue of placing their first orders with the manufacturer or wholesaler; (4) consumers who have just given a retail concern their first patronage; and (5) prospective consumers who have recently moved to the community.

The content of the message naturally depends in some measure upon the type of business relationship involved. The letter of welcome to a new business house or to an associate establishing himself in the community ordinarily stresses an expression of best wishes for success, a friendly offer of co-operation, and an assurance that the newcomer will find the locality a desirable one. The message of welcome to a new employee usually emphasizes the outstanding qualifications that won him his job, the excellent opportunity for his advancement, and the confident belief that the new relationship will be mutually congenial. The note of welcome to a new retail dealer is highlighted by an assurance of complete co-operation in making the new business association pleasant and profitable to him. Finally, the letter welcoming the new consumer or the potential consumer emphasizes a promise to provide the best of merchandise and service, and a desire to make his visits to the store always pleasant and convenient.

In any message of welcome to one who has just become a customer—either as a dealer or as a consumer—particular stress should be given to the statement of appreciation for initial patronage. Otherwise the letter may seem to its reader more of a promotional effort than a gesture of courtesy.

The following pages present a variety of letters suitable for welcoming members of each group mentioned in the foregoing paragraphs. Despite the differences in their content, these specimens share the fundamental qualities of cordiality, genuineness, and brevity.

Letters to Business and Professional Associates

Gentlemen:

The Middleboro Electric Service Company is happy to welcome you to this community.

We feel sure you will find Middleboro a pleasant and progressive city. We know, too, that the opening of the Coombs & Allerton store will contribute materially to business activity here.

If there is any way in which we can co-operate with you, now or any time in the future, we shall be very glad to do so. Best wishes for the immediate and permanent success of your new store.

Yours sincerely,

Dear Mr. Wade:

I have just learned that you will join the firm of Simpson & Gillis on November 1.

This is very good news, and I am happy to welcome you—both personally and on behalf of our organization. You will find Mansfield a pleasant place in which to live, as well as a community of brisk business activity.

If there is anything I can do to assist you, by all means let me know and I shall do it gladly.

Sincerely yours,

Dear Mr. Stevenson:

It is a pleasure to welcome you as a new business associate, and to wish you every success in this community.

You are bringing to Milford an industry that will benefit its people, and we look forward to frequent opportunities to co-operate with you.

Cordially yours,

Gentlemen:

Welcome to Cedar Rapids! We are glad that your organization will soon become a part of this community, and we extend sincere best wishes for your lasting success in business.

Cedar Rapids is a city of rapidly expanding business enterprise; we are confident that the opening of your offices will be another forward step in its progress. We look forward to a cordial and mutually helpful association with you.

Sincerely yours,

Dear David:

I was happy to learn this morning that you will soon be coming to Hammond to join the accounting staff of Fischer & Company.

You will find Hammond a very pleasant place of residence, and I am sure your new business connection will likewise be conducive to your happiness here.

It will be a pleasure to welcome you, and I hope you will let me know if there is any assistance I can render before your arrival.

Yours cordially,

Gentlemen:

The John G. Lambert Company extends to you a cordial welcome as you open for business in Rockford. We hope that your success will be immediate and permanent.

It will be a pleasure to work with you toward the betterment of business standards in this community, and we look forward to a pleasant association with you for many years to come.

Yours sincerely,

Dear Mr. Bolton:

When your new shop opens for business in a few days, you will become a part of this community. We send you our sincere welcome and our best wishes for many years of success.

You will help to make Carthage a better city and we are glad you are joining us. If the Vincent organization can be of assistance to you in any way, please feel free to call on us.

Cordially yours,

Dear Mr. Fennimore:

On the eve of the Grand Opening of your attractive new store, we are happy to send you these words of welcome and best wishes.

Your organization will be a worthy addition to the business activity of Westport, and we look ahead with pleasure to a long and cordial association with you.

Sincerely yours,

Letters to Employees

Dear Mr. Peters:

This is a letter I am most happy to write, for its purpose is to welcome you as a new member of the Jones & Collingwood organization.

The fact that you have been chosen to fill a position of such importance is both a tribute to your ability and a fully warranted recognition of your past accomplishments.

That your record of achievement will continue and even grow with this firm I have no doubt. You have both a fine opportunity and the personal qualifications to make the most of it.

Hearty good wishes to you for complete success and happiness in your new work.

Sincerely yours,

My dear Fleetwood:

This is just a note to welcome you into our organization.

I am glad for several reasons that you have joined us. You have the qualities, both of mind and of training, to make a signal success of your new work. You have energy and enthusiasm. You have ambition based upon a sound sense of values.

I predict that you will go far in the Compton organization, and I wish you many years of success and satisfaction in your association with us.

Yours sincerely,

My dear Harrison:

It gives me genuine pleasure to welcome you personally into the Metcalf Brothers organization. The future of this firm will be in the hands of the young men who are learning the business today.

Believing as I do that you have the qualifications to achieve real success in your new job, I feel that the addition of your name to the Company roster is a step forward for both you and the firm.

As you begin your new work, I extend my sincere wish for your progress and happiness here.

Cordially,

Dear Edmondson:

It is always good to welcome to our ranks a young man who shows real promise of becoming a topnotcher in the retail merchandising field.

I feel sure that your work with us will bring you success and the high satisfaction that accompanies it. You have a bright future with Ames & Endicott, and I am confident that you will fulfill our expectations for you.

Sincerely yours,

Dear Miss Kimball:

As President of the Company of which you are now an important part, I extend a hearty welcome. I hope you will like all of us as much as I am sure we are going to like you.

Today will be the hardest you will ever spend in our organization. I know this is true because I still remember my first day on my first job. Things will seem strange, and some of the work you are asked to do will seem much more difficult than it really is.

But every worker in our office wants to be your friend, and wants to help you get adjusted on the job.

You are going to enjoy your work here—more, I think, than you can realize as a beginner. Our Company is the biggest and best of its kind in the world, and that's something for you to be proud of. We work as a team, and everybody in your department wants you to make good.

What may be even more important to you, and to your parents, is that you'll find things around our office pretty much as in your own home. It's a fine place for a young lady to be—with all the consideration and courtesies you have the right to expect.

So congratulations, and my best wishes! There are lots of others who wanted your job. I know you feel challenged—and will give your best.

Sincerely,

Dear Mr. Simmons:

It is a pleasure to welcome you into the Prentice-Hall family. We have every confidence that you will be both happy and successful in your work with this firm.

You have come to us after making an impressive record in publishing, and we feel that your association with our organization will be one of mutual profit and benefit. All of us extend to you a warm welcome and look forward to working with you.

Cordially,

Dear Mr. Wilkins:

Back in 1896, my first job on the Illinois Central was that of rodman. I was a graduate of Purdue University, having completed the general academic work and also the course in civil engineering.

While I was a rodman the thought never occurred to me that I might someday be President of the Railroad. My immediate concern was to be a good rodman, and after I had mastered that job I began thinking of what I might do next. The usual line of promotion in that department is from rodman to instrumentman, so I began to prepare myself to be an instrumentman. After a while my chance came, and I was promoted.

With each advancement in the organization, I went through the same experience—first endeavoring to do my immediate work thoroughly, and later undertaking to prepare myself for the next step.

There are several thousand employees in our organization, and only one of them can hold my present position at any one time. But every position in the organization is worth any man's best efforts.

Initiative and perseverance will accelerate your success. I hope your progress will be rapid and sustained.

Cordially yours,

Dear Clyde:

I am very glad that you have decided to join our sales division, and I am happy to welcome you into the A. J. Warfield Company.

The expansion and increasing scope of the sales division offers you an exceptional opportunity to grow and advance in your new position. I feel sure you will find inspiration in your work, and I send you best wishes for your outstanding success.

Sincerely yours,

Dear Mr. Fenton:

Welcoming you as a new member of the Wharton organization is a real pleasure.

We take a lot of pride in the past record of this profit-sharing institution, and all of us are working together to make it better each year. Building for the future is to the mutual advantage of us all.

Your joining us will add new strength to the firm, and we welcome you most cordially. We hope you will find satisfaction in your work and genuine pleasure in your new friendships here.

Sincerely yours,

Dear Mr. Herndon:

I should like to extend to you my warm personal welcome as you begin your work with The Charlton Corporation.

You are now a member of our organization for two reasons: first, because you have confidence that this firm holds for you a promising future; and second, because we feel that you are just the type of young man capable of making your future what you want it to be.

Mutual confidence and respect form the soundest possible basis for our new relationship. I wish you every success and a full measure of personal happiness in your work with us.

Sincerely yours,

Letters to Dealers

Dear Mr. Munson:

I am happy to welcome you personally as a new Glosstop dealer.

It will be our purpose to help you make an outstanding success of your Glosstop sales. We want your dealings with us to bring you new customers and increased profits.

You will find us eager to justify the confidence you have placed in us. To that end we shall do our best to see that our merchandise and service fulfill your highest expectations.

Cordially yours,

Dear Mr. Davenport:

I learned this morning that you recently sent us your first order. It is a pleasure for me to welcome you as a new customer friend of ours!

When I started out in the battery business, I made only four batteries the first month. I made them alone, and by hand, and then discussed their construction features with the first four men who ever used Bowers Batteries in their cars.

I was determined to satisfy them in every way. I made up my mind from the very start that every new customer of mine would always receive not only the best battery it is humanly possible to build, but also personal attention and 100% co-operation. So today, even though the busy company bearing my name has become one of the largest manufacturers of batteries and spark plugs in America, I still like to take the time to welcome personally each new customer.

Please let me know if ever I can help you, and feel free to write me of any suggestions, criticisms, or comments about our batteries, spark plugs, or our service. I am eager to work with you in a close, friendly manner.

Sincerely,

Gentlemen:

It is a pleasure to welcome you to the ever-growing family of Falco dealers. We appreciate the opportunity to do business with you, and we assure you of our unstinted efforts to make your association with us pleasant and profitable to you.

You will find us eager to co-operate in developing your Falco market, so that you may begin at once to benefit from its popularity. We look forward to a cordial relationship with you.

Sincerely yours,

Dear Mr. Meyers:

We are proud of our new friendship with you, and we want to say "Thank you" for your contract to sell Lion products. We really appreciate it. Our ambition will be to deserve fully your confidence and friendship.

We are sure that you, as one of our dealers, will be proud to sell Lion products. You will also find that Lion customers are loyal ones.

Just as soon as possible, we shall have one of our merchandising men call on you. He will be glad to assist you in every way toward increasing the profits of your business.

We take pride in the fact that every dealer who has signed a contract with Lion has been successful in increasing his gallonage. This, we think, is due to the superiority of our products, the help we give our dealers, and the natural preference of southern people for products made in the South.

Because this is your first association with us, we want to thank you for the confidence you have placed in Mr. Hinds, Mr. Clark, and our Company. We sincerely hope this is the beginning of a long and mutually pleasant association between you and our organization.

Cordially yours,

Dear Mr. Clayburn:

Welcoming you as a new Stapletite customer is the very pleasant purpose of this letter.

We feel sure that our products will find in your community the same ready market that has made them profitable to dealers all over the country. Moreover, we intend to give you active and energetic support in boosting your Stapletite sales.

The opportunity to supply you with our merchandise pleases us very much, and we shall try to express our appreciation in terms of good service and complete co-operation.

Sincerely yours,

Gentlemen:

Thank you for your initial order for Coleman Cravats. It is a pleasure to welcome you as a customer, and to extend to you our full co-operation in making the sale of our product profitable to you.

I am sure you will share the experience of our many other dealers in finding that the quality and inexpensiveness of Coleman Cravats makes them a profitable item among your customers.

For our part, we shall leave nothing undone to prove worthy of your confidence and your continued patronage. We hope your initial order will be the beginning of a pleasant and mutually profitable association between our two organizations.

Very sincerely yours,

Dear Mr. Sanford:

I want to send you, as a new customer, a friendly welcome from all the folks at Boardman's. For more than a century we have been making new friends, and we want to serve you in such a manner that we can count you among them.

Your business has a greater meaning to us than merely the sale of coffee or tea. We feel that you have placed in us the responsibility of helping you increase your reputation for fine coffee. We accept that responsibility.

Since 1841 we have been specializing in coffee and tea. Our trained coffee experts direct that accumulation of experience toward one objective—winning an ever-increasing reputation for the coffee our customers serve. We are waiting to help you, in a friendly way, with all your brewing and serving problems.

A special record will be kept of your individual requirements, including any special wishes you may have. We shall do everything possible to give you the satisfaction that will mean many years of pleasant business relations together.

Sincerely yours,

Dear Mr. Chapman:

It is with particular pleasure that we thank you for your initial purchase from us. With most cordial greetings we welcome you as a new friend.

Every effort will be made to give you the most efficient, satisfactory service possible. If you have any suggestions, we assure you they will be given our careful attention.

Your business is sincerely appreciated, and it will be a pleasure to serve you again soon.

Cordially,

Dear Mr. Dunn:

We are happy to welcome you as a new Burgess customer, and to accept the responsibility of serving you efficiently.

In thanking you for your initial order and for the confidence in us which it implies, we pledge our earnest efforts to make all your dealings with us both pleasant and profitable to you.

Cordially yours,

Dear Mr. Powell:

I wish it were possible for me to shake hands with every one of our new customers, and to welcome each one of you personally into the Sanotex family.

We feel that your first order for our products obligates us to provide you with the best of merchandise, service, and prices. We gladly accept this obligation, and we pledge to you our earnest effort to fulfill it.

Your patronage pleases us very much, and we thank you for it. You can depend upon us for full co-operation in making Sanotex products profitable to you.

Sincerely yours,

Letters to Consumers

Dear Mrs. Lacey:

There is no function I enjoy more than welcoming a new Brown-Amos customer. So I was very glad to learn of your recent patronage here.

Your visit was sincerely appreciated, and I hope you will give us the opportunity to serve you often. We shall try to express our thanks by making your shopping trips to the store pleasant and profitable to you.

Cordially yours,

Dear Mrs. Estes:

Your recent patronage of Lipman Wolfe & Company is very much appreciated. It was a pleasure to welcome you, and we hope you are finding Portland the enjoyable place of residence that we think it is.

We also hope that you will be a frequent visitor to this store, making it your stopping point when you are downtown. Meet your family or your friends here on your way to your shopping or to the theater, making use of our comforts with the same feeling that you would those in the homes of your other friends.

If there is any way in which we can be of service in making your life in Portland more pleasant, please tell us what it is.

Cordially yours,

Dear Mr. Merritt:

Welcoming you as a new customer of Payton's is a distinct pleasure.

We were glad to serve you in our Men's Department yesterday, and we shall do our best to deserve your frequent visits. Please come in again soon.

Cordially yours,

Dear Mrs. Farris:

We extend to you a cordial welcome as a patron of Bingham & Sons. It was a pleasure to serve you the other day, and we hope you will visit the store often.

It is our earnest desire to make your shopping here just as pleasant and convenient as possible. Your suggestions toward that end will be most welcome.

Sincerely yours,

Dear Mrs. Montague:

We are glad to welcome you as a user of Franklin Better Dairy Products, and we appreciate your joining our large family of customers.

The Franklin Creamery is a co-operative—a broad, human business that has won leadership because of quality products and efficient, cordial service. We are proud of the reputation we have built over an eleven-year period, and it will be our aim to uphold this reputation and merit your regular patronage by supplying you with dependable, quality merchandise at a fair price.

We thank you for your business and extend to you a cordial invitation to visit our plants whenever you find it convenient.

Yours sincerely,

Dear Mr. Drummond:

The purpose of this note is to extend to you a cordial welcome as a new patron of this store.

We feel that your purchase the other day was an expression of confidence which we shall make every effort to deserve. Please visit us often, and be sure to tell us of any way in which we can make your shopping at Harvey's more pleasant.

Sincerely yours,

Dear Mrs. Coburn:

It is a pleasure to welcome you as a customer of the Home Laundry and to express our thanks for the opportunity to serve you.

As I take a very real and personal interest in your satisfaction, I should appreciate your letting me know—by mail or telephone— how you liked our handling of your first laundry.

More than that, I want you to know that my interest does not stop with your first bundle. If ever our workmanship or service should not merit your enthusiastic approval, I should consider it a favor if you would call me at once.

We are ready and eager to serve you in every way possible.

Cordially yours,

Dear Mr. Randolph:

Thank you for your purchase in our Men's Department yesterday. I know you are going to enjoy wearing your new topcoat, and you'll be delighted with the excellent service it gives you.

It is a pleasure to welcome you as a Shapleigh customer. Your patronage is very much appreciated, and we are hoping for another opportunity to serve you soon.

Sincerely yours,

Dear Mrs. Beemer:

I am happy to welcome you personally as a new customer of Blake & Company.

Your confidence in us is much appreciated, and we shall try to serve you so well that you will visit us often.

Our sincere thanks for your recent patronage.

Cordially yours,

Dear Miss Glover:

It's a pleasure to welcome you as a Milburn customer, and to thank you for your purchase yesterday in our Dress Department.

Your further visits are cordially invited. You can be sure of our earnest efforts to deserve your friendship and confidence.

Sincerely yours,

Letters to Prospective Consumers

Dear Mrs. Sterling:

Welcome to Rochester! We feel sure you will enjoy living here.

It is our hope that this message will convey to you something of the friendliness that is traditional at Forman's.

You are cordially invited to pay us a visit whenever you find it convenient . . . to become familiar with our numerous departments and with the many Forman services that await you here.

We want this letter to be the initial link in a chain of friendship that will continue for many years.

Sincerely yours,

Dear Mrs. McClurg:

We learned today that you have recently become a resident of Indianapolis. It is with real pleasure that we welcome you to our city and to our store.

You will enjoy our many interesting departments. We hope to be of service many times . . . in supplying necessary accessories for your new home . . . and in providing distinctive gifts for the occasions you will be celebrating.

If you would like to open a charge account, your request will receive our prompt attention. In any event, it will be a pleasure to show you through the store at the time most convenient for you.

Cordially yours,

Dear Mrs. Ross:

Welcome to Lincoln! We sincerely believe you will enjoy living here.

As you become better acquainted in your neighborhood, you will find that many of your new friends are Bentley customers. It will be a pleasure to serve you, too . . . and we cordially invite you to visit us soon.

Here you will find complete selections of apparel . . . in all the latest colors and styles. You will like our efficient store personnel . . . and the friendly service for which Bentley's is noted.

To make your shopping more convenient and enjoyable, we have opened a monthly charge account for you.

Do pay us a visit soon. We'll try to make it so pleasant that you will want to come in often.

Sincerely yours,

Dear Mr. and Mrs. Landers:

We wish to welcome you upon the establishment of your residence in Houston. As one of South Texas' pioneer organizations, we feel that you have made a wise choice of a city in which to make your home.

It is also our desire to have you visit our new store. In addition to the enlargement of our famous men's departments, we now include complete departments of women's apparel and accessories.

Friendly service is traditional at Battelstein's and is extended to everyone, regardless of the amount of the purchase. We want you to make yourself at home when you visit us, and to take full advantage of the many services offered.

Please accept our invitation and allow us the opportunity of knowing you personally.

Cordially yours,

Dear Mrs. Beckwith:

It's a pleasure to have you as a member of this community. I am sure you will like Glenwood—everybody does.

As a token of my sincere welcome to you, I want you to accept the little bouquet that will be delivered to your home today. It may brighten things up a bit during the next few days, while you are getting your new home in order.

After a week or two, when you are completely settled and turn your attention to the stores and shops of downtown Glenwood, I'll be delighted if you will drop in sometime and say hello. Frankly, the building of this modern floral shop has taken me ten years, and it will be a lot of pleasure to show you through it.

Cordially yours,

Dear Mr. Hedges:

Welcome to New Orleans, "America's Most Interesting City." You have our sincere good wishes for success and happiness in your new work here.

The enclosed Charga-Plate is offered for your convenience. When presented anywhere in our store, it entitles you to the full courtesies and privileges of a charge account, which has already been opened. Additional Holmes Charga-Plates will be sent gladly for the members of your family upon request.

If there is any other service or information you desire in getting established in your new home, please feel free to call on me personally. It will be a pleasure to assist you in any way possible.

Cordially,

Dear Mr. and Mrs. Salisbury:

The Western Natural Gas Company extends to you a most cordial welcome to this community. We hope that you will enjoy living in Monroe, and that we shall be able to contribute to your comfort and well being.

If there is any way in which we can assist you in establishing your home here, it will be a pleasure. Please feel free to telephone or come in at any time and ask for me personally.

Cordially yours,

Dear Mr. and Mrs. Logan:

Welcome to our city! We are glad you have decided to make Manitowoc your home, and we want to extend to you every courtesy within our power.

If you have not yet paid us a visit, we shall appreciate your coming in to get acquainted. You will want to inspect our complete stocks of housewares, sporting goods, paints, and general hardware.

Whether you come in to buy or just to browse around, you will find a cordial welcome at our store.

Sincerely,

———

Dear Mrs. Sibley:

Establishing your home in Davenport means new things to do, new places to go, new friendships to be made; of course, the last is of greatest interest. We want to be one of your first new friends and to become well acquainted with you.

Parker's has a thirty-six-year-old reputation of the highest degree for serving and satisfying the people of this community. This is the store that every woman thinks of first when she starts on a shopping tour.

Will you let us have the pleasure of assisting you in your "discovery" of our store and its many features? We have opened an account for you, and our credit personnel will enjoy showing you about. Your most convenient time will be our appointment with you.

Sincerely yours,

———

Dear Mrs. Price:

Having just learned of your recent arrival in Richmond, we want to say "Welcome to our city." You will like it here, we know.

If you have not yet paid us a visit, please accept our cordial invitation to come and see us. We shall be very glad to meet you and to have you know us, too—for we feel sure that mutual benefit can be derived.

Our merchandise is smart and dependable; our service is courteous and friendly, as experience in shopping here will prove.

Please come in when you can, and see our attractive displays of "what is being worn" this season. A cordial welcome awaits you.

Sincerely yours,

———

Dear Mrs. Carmichael:

It is with genuine sincerity that we say "Welcome to Springfield" . . . and express the belief that you will enjoy living here.

We want this note to convey to you the friendliness that is traditional at Kennard's. Please consider this a cordial invitation to visit us and become acquainted with the many services of "Springfield's Leading Shop for Women."

A convenient charge account has been opened for you, and the personnel of this department will enjoy showing you about the store.

You will like Kennard's as much as your favorite shop back home. Please pay us a visit soon.

Cordially yours,

FIVE

Letters of Condolence and Sympathy

This chapter includes letter specimens made available through the courtesy of the following persons and organizations: Mr. Myron L. Boardman, New York City; The William Boardman & Sons Company, Hartford, Connecticut; Deltox Rug Company, Oshkosh, Wisconsin; Mr. Richard P. Ettinger, New York City; Mr. L. E. Frailey, Columbus, Ohio; John Geyer Company, New York City; Mandel Brothers, Chicago, Illinois; Prentice-Hall, Inc., New York City; Quaker Rubber Corporation, Philadelphia, Pennsylvania; Miss Bernice C. Turner, New York City; Mr. Howard Warrington, New York City.

BECAUSE many businessmen find the letter of condolence or sympathy difficult to write, this type of message is often the victim of procrastination. But postponement from day to day only adds complexity to the problem, with the usual result that the letter is not written at all.

By far the easiest time to formulate such a message is immediately after the occasion for it has developed. At this point the expression of condolence or sympathy should be a comparatively simple task, though many persons complicate it needlessly by their failure to realize when they have said enough.

A long, involved letter is a violation of good taste, especially when its purpose is an expression of sympathy upon the death of a relative or friend. Decision as to the length of any note of sympathy, whatever the occasion, should be based upon the following considerations: (1) the degree of friendship between writer and reader; (2) the situation that inspires the letter; and (3) the writer's knowledge of the tastes and temperament of his reader.

In any letter written to express sympathy, the two most vital qualities are sincerity and tact. If the writer uses simple and straightforward language to express what is in his heart, his message will carry warmth and conviction. If he carefully avoids any words or sentiments that could distress the reader, his message will satisfy the exacting requirements of tact. Under ordinary circumstances the practice of philosophizing upon the meaning of death, or quoting scripture or poetry, is altogether inappropriate. The bereaved person is almost certain to consider it poor taste; he may even resent it as an intrusion.[1] But when the occasion for the letter is an illness, accident, or material loss suffered by the reader, a well-expressed consoling thought may add conviction to the message and give encouragement to its recipient.

The following examples of condolence and sympathy letters illustrate good practice, and present a wide range of situations handled with varying degrees of formality.

Letters to Business and Professional Associates [2]

Upon a death in family:

Dear Mr. Hilton:

I know how little the words and acts of friends can do to ease the sadness that has come to you. Still, I want you to know how often I have thought of you today and how deeply I sympathize with you in your bereavement.

Sincerely,

Dear Ralph:

I was shocked this morning to learn that you had lost your brother. Though I did not have the pleasure of knowing him personally, I know he was respected and admired by all who did.

Words mean little at such a time as this, but still I want to send you this expression of my deepest sympathy. If there is anything at all that I can do to help, please call on me.

Sincerely,

---

[1] This practice is not to be confused with the perfectly appropriate one of paying a suitable tribute to a person whose death has occurred.

[2] Letters marked with an asterisk (*) are especially appropriate for mailing by manufacturing concerns or wholesale houses to their retail dealers.

Dear Paul:

Though there is little consolation in a note from a friend in one's hour of sorrow, I want to tell you how deeply I sympathize with you in the great loss you have suffered.

I have thought of you many times since I heard the sad news of your mother's death, and I wish so much there were some way in which I could help you. But I do want you to know that you are much in my thoughts and that you have my deepest sympathy.

Sincerely,

———

Dear Mr. Collins:

Upon my return to Richmond this morning, I was grieved to learn of the sudden passing of Mrs. Collins.

You have my deepest sympathy. I only wish there were some small way in which I could lighten your burden of sorrow.

Sincerely,

———

* Dear Mr. Jones:

It is with profound sorrow that we have just learned of the death of your wife.

We know there is little one can say or do to lessen the grief that must be yours, but we want you to know that the heartfelt sympathy of all your friends at Boardman's is with you. We hope that time will bring a cherished memory in place of present sorrow.

Sincerely yours,

———

Dear John:

There is little that even a good friend can do to help at such a time as this. I was deeply sorry to learn of the death of your father, and I know what an irreparable loss you have suffered.

If there is anything I can do, during your absence, to attend to things for you here, please call on me. I only wish there were some way in which I could soften the blow that has come to you.

Sincerely,

———

Dear Mr. Bates:

I learned with profound regret of the death of Mrs. Bates.

Though the words of friends bring little solace, I wish to express to you my heartfelt condolences in your affliction.

Sincerely,

---

* Dear Mr. Stephens:

It was a shock to us to learn of the passing of your brother, Mr. Otis K. Stephens, who had been our good friend for many years.

While the loss to us is very real, we know that the greatest loss is to Centralia itself.

We shall never forget how you and your brother carried on courageously during the years of depression. We well remember how you two helped to restore confidence among merchants in your community by building a beautiful new store while others were still holding back through fear of the future.

These are but two of the many things you and your brother have done to make Centralia a better city, but their importance to the general welfare in most trying times makes them especially memorable.

We sympathize with you in your sorrow, and feel that we share with many others the loss of a fine man and loyal friend.

Yours sincerely,

Dear George:

The sad news of your father's death reached me this morning. I know you have suffered a great loss, for I have never known a father and son who were more congenial or more devoted to one another.

No expression of sympathy, however sincere, can lighten the grief that has come to you. But you must find a measure of consolation in the realization that your father has lived a fine, full life—a life enriched by the friendship and respect of all who knew him.

I know you will carry on in the way your father would wish.

Sincerely,

Dear Bob:

I am more sorry than I can tell you to learn that you have lost your wife.

Words seem so futile at such a time; yet the sympathy of good friends may help just a little to give you strength and courage.

Since my thoughts have turned to you very often today, I wanted to tell you how deeply I sympathize with you in the great loss you have suffered.

Sincerely,

Dear Mr. Fairley:

This is just a word to let you know of my heartfelt sympathy.

Sincerely,

Dear Paul:

I was so sorry to read about the death of your mother and my heart goes out to you. I remember talking to your mother when you and I were working together in Troop 60, and I was much impressed by the sweetness of her personality and the pride that she seemed to have in you.

Life and death are beyond our control and we must accept things as they are—bravely. While no one has ever bridged the gap between this world and the next, I do believe that your mother is still with you, and that she will keep right on being proud of the good things you do.

Sincerely,

Dear Mr. Maybank:

It was with profound regret that I read this morning of the death of your son.

I know what a shock and irreparable loss you have suffered, and I realize that no words of mine can soften your sorrow. But I do want to express to you my deepest sympathy and the hope that the kind wishes of your many friends will make your grief just a little easier to bear.

Sincerely,

Dear Charles:

I was deeply shocked this morning to learn of the death of your wife.

Although I did not have the pleasure of knowing her as well as I should have liked, nevertheless I do know how you complemented each other and what an irreparable loss you will feel. You have my deepest sympathy in your sorrow.

When time has softened the severity of the blow, your many pleasant memories of your long and happy life together will be a source of great comfort to you.

If there is any way in which I can be of assistance, won't you please call on me?

Sincerely yours,

Upon personal injury or illness:

Dear Neil:

I was ever so sorry to learn from last night's *Transcript* that you are in the hospital, and I hope you'll be feeling a great deal better by the time this note reaches you.

You are much in the thoughts of your many friends these days, and all of us are hoping you will soon be well again.

Sincerely,

Dear Mr. Leland:

Your unfortunate accident was unknown to me until last night. I deeply regret that you have been injured, and I hope that your recovery will be rapid and complete.

If I should be in your city on business within the next week or ten days, which appears quite probable, I shall certainly come out to the hospital to see you. Meanwhile, sincere best wishes to you.

Cordially yours,

Dear Ralph:

This is just a word to tell you how very sorry I was to learn of your illness.

At least you have the consolation of knowing that an operation for appendicitis, like opportunity and the German measles, comes but once in a lifetime.

I hope that your convalescence will be rapid and that you will be enjoying the best of health again in record time.

Sincerely,

Dear Mr. Gordon:

I have just learned of your painful injury, and I send you my best wishes for a speedy recovery.

Since you will be confined to your home for a few days, I believe you will enjoy reading a new book which has given me a number of pleasant hours. I am sending it along with this note.

Cordially yours,

Dear Fred:

I was much relieved to learn this afternoon that you are reported "out of danger and making good progress."

You have been in my thoughts a great deal since I learned of your illness last week, and I am indeed sorry that you have had such a tough time of it. But the splendid news today has cheered the many friends who have been pulling for you.

I hope your progress from now on will be swift, and that you will soon be strong enough to return to your home. The well-wishes of this community have been with you throughout your illness, and all of us will be delighted at your homecoming.

Sincerely,

Dear Mr. Grantham:

When Mr. Mark Gilstrap called at the office this morning, he told me that ill health had forced you to give up field work for a somewhat less strenuous assignment in the home office.

I was extremely sorry to learn of your tough luck, and I shall miss those visits with you every couple of months. Your calls always brightened the day, and I found myself looking forward to them.

I hope that the change in your business duties will bring a rapid improvement in your health, and that you will come to enjoy your new work as much as you liked traveling. I hope, too, that we shall continue to meet from time to time, either here or in New York.

Meanwhile, you have my best wishes for your return to health.

Sincerely,

---

* Dear Mr. Blaine:

Jim Donovan told me this morning that you have been ill, and that you will be confined to your home for probably another week.

I was ever so sorry to hear it, and I do hope you will be well on the road to recovery by the time this note reaches you.

Jim joins me in this expression of regards and best wishes.

Sincerely,

Dear Mr. Carpenter:

I was sorry indeed to learn of your accident, and I hope that your recovery is progressing rapidly.

Tomorrow morning's delivery will bring you a little package that I hope will give you enjoyment. Please accept it with my sincere good wishes for your swift recovery.

Cordially yours,

---

* Dear Mr. Lewis:

I hope the ruffian who smashed into your car buys from your competitor and loses his shirt. In the meantime, you have my sincere sympathy. I realize that kind words won't heal a broken leg, so if there is anything we can do to help in your store, just let me know.

That's not an idle gesture. We very much appreciate your loyalty in the past—tell me how we can now give you a lift. It will be a pleasure.

Sincerely yours,

Dear Frank:

Word of your illness has just reached me, and I want to send you my best wishes for your quick return to health.

All your many friends will be sorry to learn that you must spend the next few weeks in the hospital, and it must help some to know that you have a host of well-wishers.

When you return home and are well enough to have visitors, I'll be over to see you. In the meantime, please have Mrs. Porter let me know if I can attend to anything for you here. I'll be delighted to help in any way I can.

Here's hoping the next few weeks will pass quickly for you, and that you'll be back home again in record time.

Sincerely,

Dear Jim:

Mr. Ledbetter told me a day or two ago that you have been in the hospital. I am ever so sorry to hear of this misfortune, and am not going to be content until I know that you are yourself again.

Without meaning to flatter you in any way, I can't help saying that I do like you a lot, and since I do, it grieves me to think that you have been ill.

Sincerely,

Dear Clyde:

I have been watching closely the reports in the paper each evening about your progress, and I am delighted at the news of your continued improvement. Tonight's item says that you and the doctors have won the fight, for which your many friends here are very thankful.

I hope you will be feeling more and more like your old self from now on, and that you will soon be returning home.

Sincerely,

---

* Dear Mr. Michaels:

Salesman Brown tells me that you went to the hospital a week ago for major repairs; that everything turned out fine, but you will be in bed another two or three weeks.

Knowing how strong you have been physically, I think you may fool these doctors, but just in case time passes slowly, I am mailing you today some books that I have read and liked.

The best of wishes for a quick recovery!

Cordially yours,

Dear Ted:

A couple of summers ago, when I spent several weeks in the hospital with my back in a cast and the temperature hovering around the one-hundred-degree mark, I developed a distinct antagonism toward those good people who tell you how lucky you are because "it might have been worse."

So I'll not try that strategy on you. I know it's a keen disappointment to be spending on your back the month you planned to be splashing about in Colorado trout streams. I was mighty sorry to learn that an accident had upset all your vacation plans.

But Jim Allison, who told me about your mishap, also said that you are coming along very nicely and will carry no permanent souvenir of it. This is very welcome news!

A little later on I'll drive over some evening to see you. In the meantime, do make the most of your first chance in many months to get caught up on your rest, and try to enjoy the luxury of breakfast in bed. You may never rate so much attention again.

Cordially,

Upon injury or illness of a member of family:

Dear Mr. Willison:

I was extremely sorry to read in the paper of Mrs. Willison's accident. I do hope it is not serious, and that her recovery will be rapid.

Please convey to her my best wishes.

Sincerely,

Dear Mr. Mallory:

I was very glad to learn today that your son is gaining strength rapidly and has now passed the crisis successfully.

Only another father who has gone through a similar experience can know the tremendous strain you have been under these past several weeks, and I am happy to know that your boy is now reported out of danger.

Though I have never met George, I have heard my own boy mention him with a lot of enthusiasm as one of the real student leaders on the University campus. It is good to know that his recovery is now assured, and that he will soon be able to continue his college work.

Cordially yours,

Dear Floyd:

I was very sorry to learn of the illness of your wife. Please pass on to her my sincere best wishes for her speedy recovery.

Cordially,

Dear Ted:

I learned with regret this morning that your son has suffered a broken leg. I hope he is already on the mend, and that the speed of his recovery will exceed all expectations.

Sincerely,

Dear Mr. Craig:

I was sorry indeed to learn this morning of Mrs. Craig's fall a few days ago.

Please convey to her my sympathy and best wishes. I hope she is resting comfortably, and that she will soon be fully recovered.

Sincerely,

---

* Dear Mr. Morris:

I was ever so sorry to learn that your little boy was stricken with polio recently, and that he has suffered partial paralysis of one leg.

Since our twelve-year-old youngster had the same experience two years ago, I know the moments of despair and helplessness that parents go through.

But time and corrective treatment work wonders. Our John has outgrown almost all trace of the illness, and I hope your boy will be equally fortunate.

Sincerely yours,

Dear Mr. Carson:

Our mutual friend, Claude Harrison, told me this morning of Mrs. Carson's painful accident.

I was very sorry to hear of it, and I hope she is recovering quickly. Please extend to her my sympathy and best wishes.

Cordially,

Dear Wallace:

During her visit at home between university semesters, Dorothy told us of the unfortunate illness that has compelled your daughter to withdraw from school for the remainder of this year.

Though I have not yet had the good fortune to meet your Helen, I was ever so sorry to hear this news, and I hope she is rapidly regaining her health. From what Dorothy has told us of her brilliant mind, I am sure she will have no difficulty in making up for lost time once her strength returns.

Mrs. Ellsworth and Dorothy both join me in this expression of sincere best wishes for your daughter's rapid and complete recovery.

Sincerely yours,

Dear Mr. Higby:

Please convey to Mrs. Higby my deep regret because of her illness, word of which reached me today.

I hope that she is already on the road to recovery, and that she will soon be completely well again.

Sincerely yours,

Upon death of a company officer:

* Dear Mr. Lewis:

I was shocked and saddened to learn of the sudden death of Mr. John Fraser. I wish to convey to you and to the other members of your firm my deep sympathy upon the loss of this remarkable man.

It was my privilege to know Mr. Fraser through most of the years he served as Secretary-Treasurer of your organization. He combined with his personal charm and unlimited energy the highest type of business ethics. All of us in the dry goods industry have suffered a heavy loss in his death.

Yours sincerely,

Gentlemen:

On behalf of the entire Bell-Whitney organization, I convey to you our deep regret at the untimely death of your President, Mr. James Ellis.

All of us here felt toward Mr. Ellis the same respect and admiration in which he was held throughout the profession.

We know that you have suffered a great loss, both personal and professional, and we extend to you our wholehearted sympathy.

Sincerely yours,

Gentlemen:

I am sure the death of Henry Whitman is almost as great a shock to the entire legal profession as it is to the members of your organization.

Few men have ever held the position of high esteem which has been his these many years. No man ever deserved it more than he.

Please count me among the many members of our profession, the country over, who share your great loss.

Sincerely yours,

---

* Gentlemen:

Every member of our organization joins me in this expression of sympathy upon the tragic death of your President, Mr. Howard Weston.

The genial personality and generous instincts of this fine man will be missed not only by his associate officers and directors, but by the executives of many other firms throughout the nation.

Mr. Weston's death is a severe blow to the hardware industry, and we feel a keen sense of loss in his passing.

Sincerely yours,

------

* Dear Mr. James:

It was with deep regret that I learned this morning of the sudden passing of Walter Conroy. I thought of you immediately, for I realize that the death of your good friend and business partner of some twenty years is an irreparable loss to you.

All of us in the furniture business will miss Walter. All of us admired the combination of kindness and honesty that his life represented. But since the loss to you is most direct and personal, I wanted to send you these words of sincere sympathy upon the death of a loyal friend and trusted associate.

Sincerely,

Gentlemen:

I know that the many friends of John Morton all over the country will share my deep regret in learning of his death.

To all of us in the field of retail credit he was, and always will be, an ideal. The example he set will long continue to influence and inspire us.

The loss of this fine man, who has been your President for so many years, is of course a tremendous shock to you. The other officers of this organization join me in expressing to you the deepest sympathy.

Yours sincerely,

Upon material loss or damage:

* Dear Mr. Harris:

Word has just reached me that your warehouse was severely damaged by fire this morning. I am indeed sorry to learn of this setback to your business, for I don't know of a merchant in Indiana whose record for fair dealing gives him a better right to the favorable breaks of the game.

I sincerely hope the damage to your warehouse and stock proves to be less than you expect. If you think of any way in which I can be of assistance to you, please call on me. It will be a pleasure to co-operate.

Sincerely yours,

----

* Dear Mr. Miller:

We learned with regret of the flood damage suffered by your firm last week.

Sometimes, when an emergency strikes without warning, there is something we can do to help a business friend. If we can assist you in any way, please tell us how.

Sincerely yours,

Dear Mr. DeWitt:

I have just read in this morning's paper that your home was damaged by fire last night. I know only too well how discouraging this experience is, for I have been through it myself.

If there is anything I can do to help you, such as providing packing boxes or storing household articles in our storeroom, please let me know. Any service I may be able to render will be a pleasure.

Sincerely yours,

----

* Dear Mr. Doss:

A letter is hardly an adequate instrument through which to convey our real feelings for you and your people. But we know that a letter will reach you, and we do want to tell you how deeply sorry we are about the misfortune that has come to you and the people of your city.

A pleasant business relationship serves to create a very real bond of human fellowship between buyer and seller; and it is this human tie that prompts me to tell you how sincerely we sympathize with you in this hour of distress.

It happened that I was caught in the great Arkansas flood of 1927. So I know, from personal experience, of the cold, hunger, and misery that go with these upsets in nature.

But soon the waters will recede. The sun will shine again. And with the great courage of the American people, you will rebuild to make a finer city.

Meanwhile, we shall welcome any opportunity to aid you, and we hope you will call on us for anything we can do to help.

Sincerely yours,

---

* Dear Mr. Warner:

All of us at Forster & Company were sorry to learn of the severe fire that damaged your store recently.

If there is any way in which we can co-operate with you in overcoming present difficulties, please feel free to call on us. We have been friends for a long time, and any department of this firm will be happy to extend a helping hand.

Sincerely yours,

Dear Mr. Bentley:

I have just heard through our mutual friend, Frank Smith, about the heavy loss sustained by your family during the recent floods.

At a time like this it is hard to put one's thoughts into words. But I do want you to know that I sympathize with you most wholeheartedly in this unhappy experience.

To lose your home is sad. The kindly thoughts associated with that home will linger long in your memory; you wouldn't want it otherwise. Yet, out of this catastrophe—from the masses of debris and ruins—bigger and better towns will arise. They always do, you know. so don't despair.

Hope pulls one through many a crisis, and it will pull you and yours through this one. As hard as it may seem, keep your courage and don't lose faith.

Sincerely,

Dear Mr. Rivers:

I am sure every businessman in Marion will share my regret in learning that your plant was damaged by last night's terrific storm. I hope the loss will prove much lighter than you now estimate.

Please count us as one of the many firms in this community that would welcome a chance to assist you in any possible way during this emergency. If there is anything we can do to help, please call on us.

Sincerely yours,

---

* Dear Mr. Kirby:

I have a friend in St. Louis whose business in the early days was twice destroyed by fire. But he never lost courage, and today he heads the largest company of its kind in the world.

Somehow, out of this adversity you have suffered, good will come, because you are the kind of merchant who will *make* it so.

In the meantime, if you need quick replacement of stock, longer terms—whatever it may be—please remember that we appreciate your loyalty, and are standing by to help you.

Yours sincerely,

Dear Jim:

I was ever so sorry to learn that your home was destroyed by fire recently. You and Alice have certainly had more than your share of tough luck during the past year. It seems only yesterday that your property was damaged by the flood.

But I've never known a couple better fortified, by perfect companionship and mutual understanding, to overcome the adversities that fate sends your way. I don't want to seem like a Pollyanna, for I realize it's a hard blow to lose your home, but I know you will take it in stride.

So this is just a word of good wishes to two fine people whose zest for life and capacity to enjoy it will survive any setbacks the elements can contrive.

Sincerely,

---

* Dear Mr. Lockett:

I have just heard of the heavy loss you suffered in the hurricane that brought so much destruction to your city.

At a time like this, words of encouragement bring very little cheer; but I do want you to know how sincerely sorry I am to learn of your plight.

While there isn't much we can do to help, we shall certainly be glad to ship you anything you may need in the rebuilding of your business. Of course, we'll gladly extend any kind of credit terms you desire.

May we have the privilege of doing that much, little as it is?

Sincerely,

Dear Mr. and Mrs. Densmore:

Announcement of the fire that destroyed your home just came to me in the form of a clipping from your local paper. What a sense of disappointment it must have brought to you who had so carefully planned that home!

Accept my sympathy in your loss. Your splendid hospitality had endeared the house to your friends, though even the most humble dwelling would be fascinating to us so long as it housed your family.

Sincerely yours,

---

* Dear Mr. Beckman:

We were extremely sorry to learn that your warehouse was damaged by fire last night.

Perhaps there is some special service that we can perform in this emergency. If there is, please feel entirely free to call on us.

You have been a friend and customer of Maybank Brothers for many years, and we shall welcome an opportunity to be helpful in any way possible.

Sincerely yours,

Letters to Employees [3]

Upon a death in family:

Dear Paul:

I want you to know how inexpressibly sorry I am to learn of the grief that has come to you.

[3] A number of the letters presented in the earlier sections of this chapter are also appropriate for mailing to employees.

Since I want very much to help, please tell me if there is anything I can do to lessen by some small fraction the strain of this sad hour.

Sincerely,

Dear Miss Manley:

I learned with the deepest regret of the sudden passing of your mother, and I extend to you my warm sympathy.

The news was the more shocking to me because your mother seemed somewhat improved when I last saw her a few days ago.

If I can do anything to lighten your burden in any way, won't you please call on me? I should like very much to give tangible expression to the keen sympathy I feel for you in your loss.

Sincerely,

Dear Roy:

I was ever so sorry to learn this morning of the sadness that has come to you.

Though words seem futile at such a time, I want you to know that you have my deepest sympathy. Please call on me if I can help in any way.

Sincerely,

Dear John:

It was with the deepest regret that I learned this morning of the death of your sister.

May the sincere sympathy of a host of friends, among whom everyone in this office wishes to be counted, bring some measure of consolation in this hour of your bereavement.

Sincerely,

Dear Howard:

I was deeply sorry to learn of the sadness that has come to you.

Though there is little that friends can do to help at such a time, I hope you will find some measure of consolation in the fact that your mother was with you for a considerable part of your life, during which you have done much to make her proud of you.

Moreover, I have never known anyone more thoughtful of his mother than you have been. You should find comfort in the knowledge that you did so much to make her life a happy one.

Sincerely,

Dear Bob:

I can only tell you in this note what I am sure you know already— that I am deeply sorry so much sadness has befallen you.

If there is anything I can do, either personally or in behalf of the Company, you have only to tell me what it is.

Sincerely,

Dear Mr. Wilson:

Mrs. Selby joins me in sending deepest sympathy. It was a shock to us both to hear of your bereavement.

Sincerely yours,

Dear Leonard: [4]

When I learned the sad news of your troubles, I was not as shocked as I might have been if I had not earlier heard of the illness of your wife.

But I do not write primarily to commiserate. I merely wish to say, as an older person who has had his crosses, that time is a great healer, and that my greatest regrets are for the moments when I permitted sorrow for what had passed to hold me up in moving forward toward solving the problems to come.

You have a bright, promising, and long life ahead, with much service you can render to others. Keep your eye in that direction.

Very sincerely yours,

Upon personal injury or illness:

Dear Dick:

I was ever so sorry to hear about your accident, and I hope you'll be feeling a lot better by the time this note reaches you.

[4] This letter was written to a young man whose wife had taken her own life.

Though I'm always telling the men that it's dangerous to lean back and rest on one's laurels, here is an exception. Your plan for reviving inactive accounts has just won the $100 first prize, and I hope this news will help to brighten your days in the hospital.

It will be fine to see you in the office again when you are completely recovered, but don't think of it a day earlier. Sincere best wishes to you.

Cordially,

———————

Dear Steve:

I was both surprised and sorry when your brother told me this morning of your emergency operation last night.

But it's fine that the operation was in time to prevent complications, and I am very glad to know that you'll be as good as new in a few weeks.

The manner in which you dealt with an obstreperous appendix is certainly consistent with your reputation for getting things done in a hurry. But please don't try to apply the same method to your convalescence.

Your work will be taken care of in your absence, and all of us want you to relax and rest until you are strong enough to think about returning to the office.

John, Dave, and the others join me in sending greetings and best wishes.

Sincerely,

———————

Dear Miss Owens:

I was very sorry to hear of the accident that has laid you up in the hospital. I am told that it was not serious, but I know it must be painful, and my sympathies are all with you.

My correspondence is being handled by the three other young women, but, without wishing to appear too critical, I feel as if I were working with my right hand tied behind my back.

We shall all be glad to see you when you are well enough to return.

Sincerely,

———————

Dear Bill:

There's just one good thing about a stay in the hospital. A fine fellow like you discovers how many friends he really has.

Jim Talbert told me this morning that the whole mail order department was planning to come out to see you Sunday—until he heard about it. Now Jim has set up a schedule, with just three callers to each day.

I hope you will be out of the hospital before Jim's date book reaches the second week. My warm good wishes to you.

Sincerely,

Dear Jim:

That flu germ must have packed a terrific wallop to floor a 200-pounder like you, but when bigger and better germs are bred, it will be in this kind of weather.

There's no need to tell you not to worry. In the first place, you have too much sense. And in the second, you won't have the energy for a while, anyway.

It will probably do you good to learn that your work on the Hanover people has resulted in an even better order than we hoped for. Judson sends his congratulations and regards.

Sincerely,

Dear Gene:

I was sorry to learn of your illness with ptomaine poisoning, and I hope you will be feeling a lot better by the time this letter reaches you.

The only wise course for you to follow is one of complete rest until you regain your strength. There are few forms of illness more enervating than ptomaine, and I hope you will realize the wisdom of placing your health first and your work second. Later on, I am sure we can work out plans that will take care of your territory.

Meanwhile, don't let business worry you. I send you my best wishes and those of the entire crew at the office.

Sincerely,

Dear Walt:

Letters and cheery sentiments don't help much, I realize, when one is flat on his back in a hospital bed. But I do want you to know that all of us here are thinking of you—and hoping you'll set a new record for a quick recovery.

We were relieved to learn this morning that your injuries are not critical, and that you are making excellent progress. Keep up the good work, and don't worry for a moment about things at the office.

Best wishes from all of us.

Sincerely,

———

Dear Mr. Saunders:

I am no doctor, but I know I can help you. Here is how:

Your regular salary check will be sent each week to Mrs. Saunders as long as you are incapacitated. This will relieve your mind of financial worries.

Your work at the office will not get behind, as your good friends here have offered to absorb your duties while you are away. You don't have to worry about your work.

Your job will be waiting for you when you are ready to go on with it—but no sooner.

That leaves you with practically nothing to do except get well.

The boys at the office send you their best.

Sincerely,

———

Dear Mildred:

The good news has just reached me that you are very much better, and that you will be able to leave the hospital in another week or ten days.

I am delighted to learn of your steady progress, but I hope you will continue to rest at home for as long a period as your doctor advises. There is no better investment of time than that spent in regaining one's health.

This point I emphasize especially because I know you are a most conscientious and enthusiastic worker. While we look forward to your return to the office, I want you to know that we can carry on without undue strain for as long a period as your complete recovery requires.

All of us are happy at the news of your progress. Keep it up!

Sincerely yours,

Letters to Relatives of Business Associates Taken by Death

My dear Mrs. Morgan:

I was saddened to learn of the passing of your husband, whose friendship it was my privilege to enjoy for many years.

John Morgan will be missed by all who knew him. To few was it granted to possess so large a capacity for friendship, and to enjoy the affection and esteem of such a large group of business associates.

I extend to you my deepest sympathy in your great loss. May you derive some measure of consolation from the knowledge that it is shared by every member of the textile industry who had the good fortune to know your husband.

Sincerely,

My dear Mrs. Winters:

It was with profound regret that I learned of the death of your illustrious husband.

His pioneering spirit and devotion to an ideal won the admiration of all with whom he came in contact; and his influence and guidance, so widely exercised, will long be felt.

May I personally, and in the name of Prentice-Hall, extend to you sincerest and deepest sympathy.

Sincerely,

My dear Mrs. Pittman:

I was shocked this morning to learn of the sudden passing of Mr. Pittman. I extend to you my deepest sympathy.

Although my association with your husband was not intimate, my business relationship with him during the past several years has given me a profound respect for his integrity and a sincere admiration for his loyalty to friends and his generosity in helping others.

While words are of little solace at such a time as this, still it is comforting to know that the entire community shares the loss of one who exemplified the highest ideals of his profession.

Very sincerely yours,

Dear Mr. Kellogg:

Some twenty years ago a tall, kindly man with a reassuring voice and a warm smile helped me to land my first job. From that day on he has been my friend—one of the best friends I've ever had.

I know that James Kellogg has played a similar part in the lives, accomplishments, and affections of many men. There are many, I know, who have been saddened today at the news of his death.

Though it has not been my privilege to know you as well as I have known your father, I feel impelled to tell you of my deep sympathy for you in this hour of sorrow. Your loss is great, but so is the heritage which is yours in the memory of this fine man.

Sincerely yours,

Dear Mrs. Griffith:

I learned with deep regret of the recent passing of Mr. Griffith and wish to extend my sincere sympathy in your bereavement.

Very sincerely yours,

My dear Mrs. Kent:

Upon my return this morning from San Francisco, I was saddened and shocked to learn of the sudden passing of your husband.

As one who felt toward him the greatest respect and admiration, I convey to you my profound sympathy in your great loss. To all who knew him, the name of Walter Kent stood for the highest type of manhood, integrity, and loyalty to worthy ideals.

While words can do little to mitigate your grief, I am sure you will gain a measure of strength and comfort from the knowledge that your husband's name will live in honor in the memory of all who share your loss.

Sincerely yours,

My dear Mrs. Truett:

Just yet I am too shocked to realize that we are to be denied Mr. Truett's guiding influence in this organization. He was a rock upon which we all built confidently, knowing that his unbounded sympathy and good judgment would help us steer our course aright.

The sympathy of this entire office force goes out to you and your family in this time of bereavement. You have assured us that there is nothing more we can do for you just now, but I invite you to consult me if you ever need the assistance of one whose close business association with Mr. Truett may enable him to help you.

Very sincerely yours,

My dear Mrs. Ackerman:

Every member of the Board of Directors of Morton & Hillary joins me in this expression of sympathy upon the death of your husband.

All of us in this organization who were privileged to know him felt a keen admiration for his great character and ability. In the truest sense, his life represented the best thought, most far-reaching vision and practical accomplishment of his generation in the public utility field. Beyond that, his personal contacts with men inspired and uplifted them. His memory will be one of our most treasured possessions.

Yours sincerely,

My dear Mrs. Clayton:

I was ever so sorry to learn of the passing of Doctor Clayton.

I want you to know that his many friends at Prentice-Hall have been deeply affected by the news, and our sympathies go out to you. We shall always remember Doctor Clayton as the completely lovable and energetic author who came into our lives with the manuscript of *Heaven Below*. He has left us with a feeling of warm admiration and respect.

Yours sincerely,

My dear Mrs. Sheldon:

I was deeply grieved to learn this morning of the death of your husband, whose friendship I have been privileged to enjoy for some eighteen years.

To me, and to all who knew him, John Sheldon exemplified the highest integrity and moral courage. I feel a deep sense of personal sorrow that the pleasant association of so many years with a man of his intelligence, rare judgment, and warm personality is ended.

I extend to you and yours my warmest sympathy in your great loss.

Sincerely,

Dear Miss Blakeman:

I did not know of your father's sudden passing until a few hours ago. I am deeply sorry to learn of it, and I extend to you my sincerest sympathy.

Each time I saw your father I was impressed with his keen intellect, his honesty, and his kindness. On several occasions, when I was a struggling young lawyer, he went out of his way to extend a helping hand to me. This I shall always remember, for he had already attained the heights of success and reputation; yet he always had time to help and encourage those who were working to establish themselves in the profession. I mention this because, to me, it symbolizes his entire life.

Though you have suffered a great loss, I know you will find consolation in the fact that your father was revered by all who knew him, and that his life was filled with the happiness that comes from giving generously to others.

Sincerely,

My dear Mrs. Watson:

Of the many business friends and associates who mourn the death of Mr. Watson, I am sure that none feels a keener sense of grief than I. The association with him will live on in my memory as an enduring inspiration. Time will not dim my deep appreciation of his qualities of mind and heart that made it a privilege to know him.

I hope you will not regard as an undue liberty the expression of my deepest sympathy to you and your family in your bereavement.

Sincerely,

Letters to Relatives of Employees Taken by Death

Dear Mrs. Grayson:

I am sure you know, better than any words of mine can tell you, how deeply I sympathize with you in your great sorrow.

John's death leaves me with the keenest sense of personal loss, for I have long thought of him first as a friend and second as a member of the Holmes organization.

Never have I known a man with a stronger sense of honor and loyalty. He will be missed by every person in this firm, for all were his good friends.

I know you will find strength and comfort in the memory of one whose every instinct was kind and generous. Your two fine boys will also find in his memory the inspiration of manhood at its best.

Sincerely,

My dear Mrs. Stanton:

I wish to express to you my deepest sympathy.

Everyone in this organization feels keenly the loss of one whose qualities of friendship, helpfulness, and loyalty will long be remembered by all who knew him.

To me, Paul Stanton personified all the high ideals that I would hope to instill in a son of my own. I could pay no greater tribute to any young man.

Sincerely,

My dear Mrs. Williams:

Every member of the Henley organization was shocked and saddened at the sudden death of your husband.

While sympathy is small consolation, even when it springs from the hearts of those who share your sorrow, I want you to know how keenly John's loss is felt by everyone here. I do not need to tell you of the respect and admiration in which he was held by all who worked with him.

Other members of the firm join me in this expression of our deep sympathy. We only wish it were within our power to alleviate the sadness that has come to you and your family.

Very sincerely yours,

———

Dear Mr. and Mrs. Dillard:

The loss of your fine son is a stunning blow, and I realize that no words of mine can lighten your sorrow.

But I am moved, nevertheless, to write you this note. Because of my close association with Jim and my very real affection for him, I am deeply grieved at his passing. There are many others in this organization who share my feeling of personal loss.

You have the deep sympathy of every one of us who knew Jim and worked with him. All of us were his friends.

Sincerely,

———

Dear Mrs. Webb:

The warm personal regard that I had for your husband makes me feel the keener sympathy for you in his passing. I realize my inadequacy in expressing it, but I want you to know that I feel it deeply.

Sincerely yours,

———

My dear Mrs. Kincaid:

This note comes to you belatedly because I was taken ill on the very day that the tragic news of Henry's accident reached our office. His death has shocked all of us, for every man in this firm counted him as a friend.

Henry's record was consistent and outstanding. Hilton-Wells representatives come in contact with all departments of its business; none was ever more respected and admired than Henry. "He was a prince of a fellow" came naturally to the mouths of our editors, accountants, correspondents, and sales administrators when they heard of his death.

I write this letter with the hope that the deep sympathy of Henry's many friends in this office will give you some little comfort in your affliction.

Sincerely,

———

Dear Mr. and Mrs. Wentworth:

The entire Dobbs organization was shocked and saddened at the news of Dan's accident.

Though your son had been with us less than a year, he had won the confidence and respect of all who worked with him. All of us admired his honesty, ability, and fine spirit of co-operation.

Personally, I had become very fond of Dan, and I shall miss him greatly. Words cannot convey the deep sympathy I feel for you in your loss.

Sincerely,

SIX

Letters of Recommendation

This chapter includes letter specimens made available through the courtesy of the following persons and organizations: Mr. Edward C. Ames, Toledo, Ohio; Mr. S. R. Bushnell, New York City; Credit Utility Company, Inc., New York City; Professor Roy Davis, Boston University, Boston, Massachusetts; Professor C. C. Parkhurst, Boston University, Boston, Massachusetts; Prentice-Hall, Inc., New York City; Mr. John Reed Spicer, Alfred, New York; Professor Brenton W. Stevenson, University of Toledo, Toledo, Ohio; Mr. Kenneth F. Van Sant, Chicago, Illinois.

THE LETTER OF RECOMMENDATION is a business courtesy performed occasionally in the interests of a personal friend, business or professional associate, or former employee.[1] The nature of its content depends largely upon the relationship involved and upon the kind of information sought by the prospective employer.

In seeking a report upon the record of a former employee, the inquirer usually expects specific details as to the period of employment, the extent of the employee's competence or efficiency, and such relevant personal characteristics as the former employer was in a position to observe. In seeking information from a personal friend or business associate of the individual under consideration, the inquirer frequently requests an evaluation of his character and personal integrity. Information of this kind, of course, results in an appraisal more general than specific.

Whatever may be the basis of the association between the writer and the person recommended, an enthusiastic tone adds to the favorable effect of the letter. Even a favorable report, written without warmth or enthusiasm, suggests that the writer himself is otherwise disposed toward the person about whom he writes.

[1] Now and then a businessman writes a letter recommending a person currently in his employ. Three letters of this type are shown on pages 190-192.

The letter of recommendation should always be made as complete and definite as possible. The mere assertion that an applicant is "a person of good character and attractive personality" is too vague, in itself, to carry much weight. Such a statement should be reinforced by the proof of supporting details. Moreover, the letter should be mailed directly to the intended recipient whenever possible, since it is obvious that the "To Whom It May Concern" message precludes any possibility of adapting its content to a specific situation.

The following pages show representative specimens of recommendation letters written in behalf of personal friends, business and professional associates, and employees and former employees.

Letters Recommending a Personal Friend

Dear Mr. Rogers:

I am happy to answer your inquiry of May 4, and to recommend Mr. Donald McGuire to you without qualification.

I have known Mr. McGuire well for more than ten years. In addition to being a gentleman of great personal charm, he is also an individual of exceptional ability and energy.

As Secretary-Manager of the Crescent City Chamber of Commerce, he has won the friendship and respect of this entire community. His is a record of high accomplishment, made possible only by his ability to work with others, his capacity for organization, and his stimulating enthusiasm.

In addition to his ability and personality, Mr. McGuire possesses the highest moral qualifications. He is a man of clean habits and fine ideals. He applies to both his business dealings and his personal life the highest of ethical standards and moral values.

There is no man in this community whom I could recommend to you more unreservedly or more enthusiastically.

Yours sincerely,

Dear Mr. Zachary:

This is a letter I am happy to write, for I can recommend John Winterson wholeheartedly for the position of traveling representative with your concern.

Having known this young man as a friend and neighbor for more than twelve years, I can vouch for both his character and his ability. He is honest and dependable. He is also extremely intelligent and energetic—a statement borne out by his brilliant record in college. His achievements at the University of Iowa, from which he was graduated a year ago, include both Phi Beta Kappa and the presidency of the senior class. This record is the more remarkable in view of the fact that he worked his way through the University.

John Winterson has also a splendid personality. He makes a fine appearance and wins friends easily. These attributes, I should think, would be particularly important in the kind of work for which you are considering him. I hope that he will be selected for the position with your organization, since I feel sure he has the qualifications to make a success of it.

Sincerely yours,

Dear Mr. Darnell:

Mr. Albert Findlay, about whom you inquire in your letter of March 16, has been a friend and associate of mine for ten years.

Mr. Findlay is an extremely intelligent, capable man. As you doubtless know, he has advanced very rapidly in his work with Pritchard, Jones & Company. In addition to his outstanding ability, he is also scrupulously honest. He combines tact with complete candor. Though he is always considerate of the feelings of others, one who asks for his frank opinion receives exactly that.

Because he possesses both the courage of his convictions and a broad-minded attitude toward those whose opinions differ from his, Albert Findlay is well liked and highly respected in Morrisville. The fact that he is now serving as President of our Rotary Club affords evidence of his standing among local businessmen.

I am sure that any responsibility you may entrust to Mr. Findlay will be diligently fulfilled. He is the type of man one can recommend with complete confidence, and without reservation.

Very sincerely yours,

Dear Mr. Askew: [2]

At the request of Harold Weston, I am writing you concerning his qualifications for a position in your College Book Department.

[2] The following recommendation was made upon the request of the applicant, and not in reply to an inquiry from a prospective employer.

I have known the Weston family for many years, and I have watched Harold's progress through grammar school, high school, and college. Since his personal data record is in your file, I shall not duplicate information that you have already. But I am happy to comment on some of the sterling qualities that I have observed in this young man.

Harold Weston has a quick intelligence and a fine personality. He is honest, conscientious, and energetic. He has a high moral standard and a sound sense of values. He is a young man of excellent family background—a gentleman in every sense of the word.

If young Weston enters your employ, you will find that he thrives on hard work and knows how to assume responsibility. I hope he will have an opportunity to demonstrate his ability as a member of your staff.

Yours sincerely,

Dear Mr. Shilling:

I welcome the opportunity to answer your inquiry as to the character of Mr. Howard Iverson, whom I have known well for fifteen years.

The position of respect and confidence which Mr. Iverson holds in this community has been well earned. He is a man of the highest integrity and moral rectitude. In the course of my close association with him, I have come to admire in him the qualities of frankness, absolute honesty, even temper, and sound judgment.

I recommend Mr. Iverson to you without reservation as a man in whom you can place complete confidence. If he becomes a member of your organization, I am sure he will measure up fully to your highest traditions.

Very sincerely yours,

Dear Mr. Rawlings:

Your association will be fortunate in securing the services of Milton Edwards, about whom you inquired November 5. Undoubtedly you are familiar with his academic record and the position he has attained as an author. Both are excellent.

Edwards is a "six-footer" of neat appearance. He is a delightful conversationalist, has an abundance of personality and enthusiasm, and makes friends readily. In the fifteen years I've known Milt Edwards, he has repeatedly demonstrated his fine emotional balance and his ability to evaluate properly the elements of everyday living. His habits are naturally temperate.

Your applicant is an excellent platform speaker. He has an analytical mind and thinks clearly on the problems confronting him. I am certain that Edwards is splendidly qualified to direct the educational program of your association.

To the organization that employs Edwards go my compliments. He's a fine fellow, and I wish we had a dozen like him on our pay roll.

Sincerely yours,

Dear Mr. Spencer: [3]

I hope you will excuse the liberty I take in writing you, but the circumstances are such that this unusual procedure seems justified.

Your organization has always been associated in my mind with the finest traditions in the commercial field, particularly as regards quality of service, reputation, and personnel.

I assume you are always interested in talking with persons who have the necessary background, breeding, and character to carry on this tradition.

With that idea in mind I am referring to you Miss Martha Ann Parker, who is very eager to obtain a connection with your company in any suitable capacity. She is particularly well qualified to fill any position where tact, appearance, intelligence, and the ability to handle detail and responsibility are necessary. She has had actual experience in stenographic and secretarial capacities.

I can recommend Miss Parker without reservation as to character and ability. Her appearance will speak for itself. I hope you can find a place for her; she would reflect credit on any company employing her.

Cordially yours,

------

[3] The following recommendation was made upon the writer's own initiative, and not in reply to a request from a prospective employer.

Dear Mr. Thorndike:

It is a pleasure to answer your letter of October 11 concerning John L. Kinsey, whom I have known well for more than twelve years.

John Kinsey is a man of the highest personal integrity and trustworthiness. He is also endowed with a keen intellect, a splendid personality, and the ability to win the confidence and co-operation of those who work with him.

On several occasions I have seen Kinsey demonstrate his unusual capacity to organize a promotional campaign and carry it through with remarkable success. His outstanding work as Director-Secretary of the Western Hospital Association, as well as his fine record in his present position, resulted in no small measure from his organizing ability and his capacity to work well with others. Both of these qualities, it seems to me, are essential in the type of position you describe.

In addition, Kinsey has other important assets. He is a very effective speaker. His appearance is neat and clean-cut. He makes a fine impression in meeting people, and lives up to it fully as they become better acquainted with him.

If John Kinsey becomes a member of your organization, I have every confidence that he will do an excellent job for you.

Sincerely yours,

Letters Recommending a Business or Professional Associate

Dear Mr. Harcourt:

It is with pleasure that I reply to your letter of October 16.

My acquaintance with Mr. Donald Harris dates back to 1937, when he came to Winfield to open a law office. Since that time I have been associated with him frequently in business transactions and civic enterprises, and I have the utmost respect for his ability and integrity. That feeling, by the way, is shared by business and professional men throughout this community.

Mr. Harris has been active in civic affairs, having served as a director of the Chamber of Commerce, as a member of the Board of Education, and as President of the Winfield Kiwanis Club. He has done much for this city.

I believe it is also significant that he has twice served as President of the County Bar Association, and that he was recently honored for his service to this organization.

My recommendation of Mr. Harris, therefore, is made without reservation. Everything I know about him is to his credit.

Very sincerely yours,

Dear Mr. Daniels:

Efficiency, honesty, enthusiasm, friendliness—these are the qualities that first occur to me in describing Fred Hubbard, about whom you inquire in your letter of May 19.

Throughout my dealings with Mr. Hubbard, which have covered a period of six years, I have found him absolutely trustworthy and highly co-operative. He is an energetic, enthusiastic worker; he stimulates those who work with him. In my personal association with him on several community projects, I have found him to be an extremely capable organizer, and to be unusually successful in working with others.

I think your organization would be most fortunate in securing Mr. Hubbard's services in your Sales Department. Though I have had little experience in selling, I feel sure that the qualities I have described would be essential to success in that type of work. I assure you that he has all of them in abundant measure.

Yours very sincerely,

Dear Mr. Crable:

I am happy to recommend Mr. Henry Bailey most enthusiastically for the position now open in your editorial department.

In publishing three of his books, we have found him to be accurate, neat, and painstaking in the preparation of manuscripts. He writes clearly and interestingly; his manuscripts have required practically no editorial work.

Mr. Bailey has also demonstrated, in his dealings with us, that he has the capacity to turn out work quickly without sacrificing its quality. Without exception his manuscripts have reached us before the date specified in the contract.

If Mr. Bailey is selected to fill the position in your editorial department, I feel sure you will find his work outstanding in every respect.

Very sincerely yours,

Dear Mr. Brinkman:

I have known Mr. Sherman Rollins for almost ten years, and I am happy to recommend him for the position in your bank.

As Assistant Cashier of the First National Bank of this city, Mr. Rollins has won widespread respect and confidence. One of his chief assets is a splendid personality, which enables him to win friends readily.

Mr. Rollins has been prominent in community affairs, having served for several years as Chairman of the annual Red Cross Drive, and for the past two years as a member of the Library Board. He is currently serving as Vice President of the Lions Club, and was recently elected a member of the City Council. His selection for these various offices of public trust indicates the high respect in which he is held by members of this community.

In my own association with Mr. Rollins, I have been impressed with his integrity, his keen intelligence, and his grasp of the problems of small business. I feel that his services would be a definite asset to any bank.

Yours sincerely,

Dear Mr. Myles:

Your letter of September 12 arrived during my absence on a business trip, from which I returned only this morning.

I am glad to give you the information you request in regard to Mr. Sidney Weyland, with whom I have been associated in a business way for the last seven years. In all my dealings with him, I have found him efficient, co-operative, and absolutely honest. In consulting him occasionally about investment problems, I have come to rely upon him with complete confidence. His judgment is sound; his business ethics, above reproach.

Mr. Weyland is also a man of likable personality and excellent appearance. He has a gracious, friendly manner that makes one feel completely at ease in his presence. This point I mention because it may well be significant in view of the public-relations character of the position for which he is being considered.

I hope the delay of a few days in the writing of this letter has not inconvenienced you, and that it has not worked in any way to the disadvantage of Mr. Weyland.

Very sincerely yours,

Dear Mr. Axelrod:

For more than ten years I have known Mr. Lee Fraker, about whom you inquire in your letter of May 17.

On numerous occasions I have worked with Mr. Fraker in Y.M.C.A. and Community Fund campaigns, and in the activities of our local Rotary Club. I have found him a conscientious and enthusiastic worker. He is a natural leader because others like him and respect his ability.

It seems to me that Mr. Fraker has an ideal combination of the qualities necessary for the type of fund-promotion work you describe. He makes friends easily; he wins and holds the confidence of others; he is a hard worker and a good organizer.

Because of his honesty, intelligence, and demonstrated ability, Lee Fraker is highly respected in this community. If he becomes a member of your organization, I feel sure he will prove worthy of the confidence you place in him.

Sincerely yours,

Dear Mr. Martens:

Your inquiry concerning Mr. David Sturgis reached me this morning.

My association with Mr. Sturgis covers a period of about ten years, during which I have worked with him on numerous business transactions and community projects. In all my dealings with him, I have found Mr. Sturgis completely trustworthy, dependable, and co-operative. I would not hesitate to place full confidence in his judgment and integrity.

From your description of the position for which Mr. Sturgis is being considered, I should say that he is very well qualified for it. He is a capable speaker, with a splendid personality and a good command of language. He meets people well and makes friends easily. In various community enterprises here, he has shown an unusual capacity to work with others and to impart to them his own enthusiasm and energy.

Every contact I have had with David Sturgis has merited my high regard for his ability and his character. It is a pleasure to recommend him for the position with your firm.

Sincerely yours,

Letters Recommending an Employee or Former Employee [4]

Dear Mr. Kilgore:

I am happy to comply with your request for information concerning our experience with Mr. Hanford Givens.

Mr. Givens was employed as superintendent of our printing division from 1945 until 1948. While in our employ, he fulfilled his responsibilities and performed his duties to our complete satisfaction. He was conscientious, painstaking, and punctual in his work. He managed our printing division with efficiency, and he was very well liked by the men who worked under him.

I can also vouch for the honesty and clean habits of Mr. Givens. He held the respect of everyone in our organization. It is a pleasure, therefore, to recommend him without qualification for the position as foreman of your printing department.

Yours sincerely,

Dear Mr. Talley:

I am pleased to tell you of our experience with Mr. Frank Gresham, who was employed in our personnel department from March 1, 1947, until his resignation became effective last July 15.

Throughout his period of employment here, Mr. Gresham did excellent work for us. Because of the failing health of his parents, he felt it necessary that he return to his family home in Cleveland. We were extremely sorry to lose him.

Mr. Gresham is an exceptionally capable young man who puts a lot of enthusiasm and drive into anything he tackles. He is alert,

---

[4] With the exception of the last two specimens in the following group of examples, each letter conveys a message completely favorable to its subject. The final two specimens are also favorable in part, but place definite limitations upon the recommendations.

resourceful, and highly intelligent. He is honest, conscientious, and dependable. Added to these attributes, his pleasant personality and willingness to co-operate make him unusually successful in working with others.

I recommend this young man to you without reservation, for I am confident that he will make good if given employment in your personnel division.

Sincerely yours,

Gentlemen:

We are glad to co-operate by supplying information about the qualifications of Miss Eleanor Simms, who was employed as a book-keeper in our credit department from January 2, 1943 to June 1, 1948.

Miss Simms was quick and accurate in her work. Her record was also excellent from the standpoint of punctuality. Moreover, she worked well with other members of the department; she was friendly, co-operative, and energetic.

Since we would not hesitate to re-employ Miss Simms, we feel justified in recommending her for a position in your accounting department. We feel sure you would be pleased with her services.

Very truly yours,

Dear Mr. Collins:

I am glad to give you a commentary on the qualifications and character of Mr. Richard Barnard.

Mr. Barnard entered our employ in June, 1942, following his graduation from college. He was placed in our accounting department and served as one of our junior accountants for three years. During this time we found his work highly satisfactory.

In 1945, as a reward for the efficient manner in which he fulfilled his duties, we promoted him to the position of accountant. This position has imposed upon him added burdens and responsibilities which he has performed in a most commendable manner.

Mr. Barnard is a man of unusual ability and energy. He is a certified public accountant and possesses a thorough knowledge of accounting problems such as confront the average business house today. His command of the English language enables him to write with unusual clearness and force. He has a most pleasant manner and is well liked by his associates.

For the past year we have hoped that we might advance Mr. Barnard again, but conditions have been such that we found ourselves unable to do this. Because I believe he is deserving of a promotion, however, I gladly recommend him for the position of chief accountant in your company. Our only regret is that we cannot offer him a comparable position within our own firm at this time.

Cordially yours,

Dear Mr. Gleason:

This morning's mail brought me your inquiry of May 23 concerning Miss Dorothy Lyons.

Miss Lyons has been my office secretary since September, 1947. She is the most capable secretary I have ever had, and I should regret losing her. But I feel that a young woman with her qualifications deserves every opportunity for advancement.

Miss Lyons has an excellent background and personality for secretarial work. She is efficient, intelligent, and thoughtful. She takes dictation rapidly and accurately; she is an expert typist. In addition, Miss Lyons is a pleasant, tactful office receptionist.

Because she combines a high degree of efficiency with such personal attributes as a cheerful disposition and a neat, attractive appearance, Miss Lyons is well qualified to fill the type of position described in your letter. If she becomes a member of your office staff, I am sure her work will confirm my statements concerning her capabilities.

Sincerely yours,

Dear Mr. Bowman:

Your inquiry of November 12, concerning Paul H. Wheeler, gives me an opportunity to recommend a very fine young man.

Paul Wheeler joined our organization July 1, 1948, shortly after his graduation from the University of Illinois. From the outset he has been a member of our sales staff, and his record has been excellent. He has sold our advertising services to many retail firms in this area, and he has earned the confidence of customers whose accounts he has handled.

Some time ago Paul talked with me quite frankly about his future with our organization, explaining that he hopes to specialize in selling direct-mail advertising. Since a concern such as ours—located in a city of 30,000 persons—does not concentrate its efforts in this field, I suggested to Paul that he explore the possibilities of a connection with such a firm as yours.

Paul Wheeler is the type of young man I should like to see remain with us permanently. He is energetic, resourceful, and dependable. His friendly, co-operative attitude wins and holds the good will of customers. His likable personality and clean-cut appearance are valuable business assets.

Because of Paul Wheeler's natural ability as a salesman, his "drive" and enthusiasm for his work, and his keen interest in direct-mail advertising, I feel that he would make an outstanding record as a member of your sales staff.

Sincerely yours,

———

Gentlemen:

I am glad to answer your query of May 14 about Mr. Frank Neely, who was employed by this company as one of three assistants in our chemical research laboratory from June 8, 1947 to September 19, 1947.

His work from the first was highly commendable and rather unusual for a college sophomore. By the end of the summer he was giving more reliable and satisfactory results than either of the other two assistants, who had been with us two and three years, respectively.

We found him industrious, responsible, careful in following instructions, and eager both to please his superiors and to learn all he could from the research in which he was employed.

We are happy to be of assistance both to you and to Mr. Neely.

Very truly yours,

———

Gentlemen:

It is a pleasure to recommend Mr. Ira Fulton for a position in the accounting department of your organization.

During his three years of employment with us—from October, 1944 to September, 1947—he proved himself to be honest, capable, and dependable. He did his work methodically and efficiently.

When he left our employ, it was to return to college—a purpose that speaks well for his initiative and ambition.

If there were a vacancy in our accounting division at this time, we should be happy indeed to re-employ Mr. Fulton. We believe he will fully justify your confidence if you offer him a position with your organization.

Yours very truly,

Dear Mr. Avery:

I am very glad to answer your inquiry of June 18 about the qualifications of Miss Helen Lennert as a private secretary.

Miss Lennert was employed in my office in that capacity from September, 1946 until April of this year. She resigned because it became necessary to take her mother, whom she supports, to California for reasons of health.

Throughout her period of employment in my office, her work was more than satisfactory—it was excellent. She is an expert stenographer, very well grounded in English and correspondence practice. She is quick, accurate, and industrious in her work. Among other things, she reorganized my files in a manner more efficient than I had thought possible. She is also completely reliable in the handling of confidential matters.

In addition to her efficiency, Miss Lennert possesses qualities of personality and appearance that make her a distinct asset to a business office. She is pleasant in her contacts with visitors; she is accommodating when an emergency requires overtime hours. She is neat and attractive in appearance.

I feel that you would be fortunate in securing Miss Lennert's services as a private secretary, and I recommend her without qualification.

Sincerely yours,

Gentlemen:

I am glad to give you information about our experience with Miss Wilda Mossman, about whom you inquire in your letter of November 17.

Miss Mossman was employed in our Correspondence Department throughout 1947 and 1948. She left us to accept a position in Pittsburgh that would enable her to attend a night business college there.

We feel that Miss Mossman is quite capable of performing most types of clerical duties to the satisfaction of any employer. Although she is not brilliant, she is very conscientious and entirely dependable. During her service with us, she did not demonstrate any great aptitude for work requiring resourcefulness or creative ability. Moreover, while she is pleasant and even-tempered, her personality would not equip her especially well for a position that would require contact with the public.

One other point deserves mention. Miss Mossman maintained with us a very good record of punctuality. She was seldom absent because of illness, and she was almost never late to work. I feel that she would prove a very satisfactory employee in any position within the limitations already mentioned.

Yours very truly,

Dear Mr. Knight:

I have just received your inquiry about Mr. Raymond Foley, who was employed in our Sales Department from January of 1948 until August 1 of this year.

There is much about Mr. Foley that is praiseworthy. He is both intelligent and honest. During his association with us, he never made a promise that he did not keep.

At the same time, I feel it is only fair to you and to Mr. Foley to say that his work in our Sales Department was not as resultful as we had hoped it would be. He was quite frank in saying that he did not enjoy his work, and that he thought it best for him to be transferred to another department. Since we had no other position open, he decided to leave our employ and seek some type of work that had more in common with his interests and talents.

Because Mr. Foley was completely honest with us, and also because we felt that his intelligence was far above average, we should have been glad to try him in some other capacity if there had been an opening. Personally, I like this young man, and I hope your firm will be able to fit him into a position that will enable him to demonstrate his ability.

Sincerely yours,

SEVEN

Letters of Introduction

This chapter includes letter specimens made available through the courtesy of the following persons and organizations: D. H. Ahrend Company, Inc., New York City; The Dartnell Corporation, Chicago, Illinois; Professor Roy Davis, Boston University, Boston, Massachusetts; Northwestern Furniture Company, Milwaukee, Wisconsin; Professor C. C. Parkhurst, Boston University, Boston, Massachusetts; Prentice-Hall, Inc., New York City; *Printers' Ink,* New York City; Miss Bernice C. Turner, New York City; United Autographic Register Company, Chicago, Illinois.

THE LETTER OF INTRODUCTION is a gesture of courtesy properly extended to a personal friend or to a business or professional associate. It may be prepared for direct mailing to the addressee, or written for delivery in person by the one introduced. In the latter case the envelope should be left unsealed as a courtesy to the bearer.

When there is sufficient time for the letter to reach its recipient before the arrival of the visitor, the preferable practice is usually to send the note directly to the addressee. This method eliminates any possibility that the caller may be embarrassed by assuming the initiative and presenting the message himself. It also permits the writer, if he wishes, to suggest that the recipient take the first step toward getting in touch with the visitor. But when it seems likely that the caller will arrive before delivery of the letter by mail, or when his plans are conditional or indefinite, it is frequently advisable to give him the note for presentation in person.

In either case the letter should include (1) the name of the person being introduced, (2) the purpose or reason for the introduction, and (3) all relevant and appropriate details, business or personal.

The tone of the letter should be determined by the degree

195

of acquaintance between its writer and the other person's concerned, and also by the purpose for which the introduction is being made. When the writer is introducing one of his personal friends to another upon a basis both social and business, the tone of the message is appropriately quite informal. When he is introducing one of his business associates to another for purely business reasons, the situation calls for a letter of a more conservative nature.

Whatever may be the purpose of the introduction, the letter is ordinarily written in the spirit of asking a favor, and usually includes a statement to the effect that any courtesy shown its subject will be appreciated by the writer.

The message introducing a new sales representative, while properly classified as a letter of introduction, is distinctly promotional in its purpose. After identifying the new representative, it should include a summary of his qualifications and background for his work, as well as an assurance of his desire to co-operate with the reader and to serve him well.

Each type of introduction by letter discussed in the foregoing paragraphs is illustrated in the following pages by a variety of appropriate and effective specimens.

Letters Introducing a Personal Friend

Dear Paul:

This note will introduce to you my good friend Bob Watson, of whom you have heard me speak many times.

Bob will be in Atlanta soon to gather material for his next book, which will deal with consumer-credit policies and practices. If it proves possible for you to be of assistance to him, I shall appreciate it very much, and I know he will, too.

It pleases me to think that you and Bob are finally going to meet. Each of you has heard me mention the other so often that your acquaintanceship is already off to a flying start. I only wish that I could be there to enjoy the occasion when you get together.

Sincerely.

Dear Kenneth:

I am pleased to introduce to you a very good friend of mine, John McBride, chief engineer for the William Merritt Company.

John is making a careful investigation of the heating and power plants of some of our largest industries, preliminary to writing a report upon the subject. He tells me that your company has one of the most modern plants in the country, and that he would like very much to inspect it.

Because I feel that you both might profit from knowing one another, I am writing this letter. I shall appreciate whatever assistance you can give John.

Sincerely yours,

Dear Frank:

When George Neeland told me this morning that the Globe Publishing Company is transferring him to the Pittsburgh territory, I insisted on giving him this note to you.

George has been calling on me for the past six years, during which we have become very good friends. He is one of the finest fellows I have met since I entered the book business, and I know you will like him. He is also a very capable bookman, and anything he tells you can be accepted as fact.

If there is anything you can do to help George get the lay of the land when he calls on you in Pittsburgh soon, I'll appreciate it as much as I know he will.

I hope your business is thriving these days and that your prospects are bright for the coming year. I am looking forward to a chance to "talk shop" with you at the Book Fair in Philadelphia next month.

Sincerely,

Dear Jack:

I have just learned that my good friend Gene Torrance will be in Dallas all next week, headquartering at the Professional Men's Club.

I have suggested to Gene that he call on you at your office, and I am sure he plans to do so if his business appointments permit. A couple of old Yale men should hit it off very well. Though you and Gene were not there at the same time, you will doubtless have many mutual friends. Furthermore, two top-notch merchandising experts should have a lot of interests in common.

If you and Gene do make connections, I am sure both of you will enjoy the occasion.

Cordially,

———

Dear Clarence:

My good friend Paul Davison plans to be in Akron next week, and will present this letter to you.

Paul is very much interested in developing a house magazine for Robert Gould & Company of this city, where he is in charge of the Sales Promotion Department. I have told him that you publish one of the finest house organs I have ever seen, and suggested that he drop in for a chat with you.

I know that you and Paul will like each other, and I am sure you can give him some valuable suggestions. I shall much appreciate anything you do to assist him, and I know that Paul will be sincerely grateful for your help.

It must be about time for you to make another trip to Cleveland, and I hope you will plan to have lunch with me at the Club.

Cordially,

———

Dear Alan:

My friend Bob Conaway, of whom you have heard me speak, will be spending the weekend of November 18-19 in Chicago, making his headquarters at Hotel Sherman.

Bob is much interested in commercial art; and this interest which you and he have in common makes me think that you would find him most congenial. If you find it convenient to make his acquaintance while he is in Chicago, I believe both of you will enjoy the occasion.

Sincerely,

———

Dear Roy:

I am writing this letter because I have felt for a long time that you and Jim Garnett really ought to know each other. You have so many interests in common that I feel sure each of you will enjoy knowing the other.

Jim does the same type of work for Ransome & Sons that you are doing for your firm. He also shares your enthusiasm for sports. While you were playing varsity golf for Dartmouth, Jim was doing the same for the University of Wisconsin. And incidentally, the two of you are members of the same fraternity.

Jim expects to be in Kansas City next weekend, April 9 and 10. He will be stopping at the Muehlebach. If you should find it convenient to call him, he would recognize your name right off, for he has heard me mention it many times.

I realize that suggestions of this kind sometimes arrive most inopportunely, and I don't want you to regard it as an obligation of any kind. But if you have a little free time during Jim's visit, I am sure both of you would enjoy getting together.

Sincerely,

Dear Arthur:

My good friend and former neighbor, Fred Halloran, will present this note to you when he stops in Omaha on his way to the Pacific Coast.

Fred is head of the advertising staff of Southeastern Airlines, and I feel sure that you and he will have much to discuss. In fact, it's because I think you both will enjoy a visit that I am writing these words.

Needless to say, I shall appreciate any courtesy you may extend to Fred during his brief stop in Omaha.

Sincerely yours,

Letters Introducing a Business or Professional Associate

Dear Mr. Hoke:

Mr. Harold Beeson will be coming to New York for the week of October 10-16, during which he plans to visit the headquarters of the Direct Mail Advertising Association.

As Credit Promotion Manager of the Palmer Dry Goods Company here, Mr. Beeson is naturally interested in the art of selling by mail. When he told me of his plans to spend a week in New York, I urged him to call at your office and by all means to see the excellent exhibits on display at DMAA headquarters.

If it is convenient for you to guide him about the displays and point out those of special interest to one in his type of work, I shall appreciate it, and I know you will have his gratitude for any courtesy you may show him.

Sincerely yours,

Dear Mr. Overbeck:

This letter will be handed to you by my friend and associate, Horace Bowes, a well-known writer of articles on business.

Mr. Bowes is engaged in the preparation of a book in which he hopes to outline the development of the textile industry during the past half century. He believes that through a talk with you he could obtain both information and inspiration that would be valuable to him in this work.

Since you are *the* authority on your particular phase of the industry, he has asked for an introduction to you. I shall appreciate any courtesies you may show him, and I know he will.

Sincerely yours,

Dear Mr. Kinney:

This note will introduce to you Mr. Harold Simpson, with whom I have often had the pleasure of working on civic projects.

Mr. Simpson is now engaged in planning the events of "Better Westland Week," which will be designed to stimulate community pride and interest in civic improvement. Since you were in charge of a similar project in the interests of your city recently, I am sure you can give Mr. Simpson some valuable suggestions. I understand, by the way, that you did a superb job and that your program in the interests of Columbus was an outstanding success.

Anything you can do to help Mr. Simpson will be appreciated by all of us who are working on the program for Westland, and we shall hope for a chance to reciprocate in some substantial way.

Yours sincerely,

My dear McKenna:

John Henry Mainwaring, my good friend and the company's valued client, is on his way to the Pacific Coast. He is accompanied by Mrs. Mainwaring, which means that it is a pleasure trip.

I told him that if his route led through Toledo, he should be sure to look you up, and he said he would. So if he presents this letter, he has!

Don't let him get away without seeing the factory. And ask him if he'd like to have any checks cashed. Take it from me, they'll be good.

I shall appreciate any courtesies you may show him.

Sincerely,

———

Dear Fred:

This morning one of the fellows who works with me at the plant—Warren Bullard—told me that he plans to be in St. Louis next week on his vacation.

For some time Warren has felt that he would like eventually to work into the promotional end of the firm, and he has developed a keen interest in direct-mail advertising.

When I learned that he will be spending a few days in St. Louis, I took the liberty of urging him to call on you. He is much interested in seeing the "inside" of a modern direct-mail concern. If someone in your department can find time to show him behind the scenes in the production department, I know he will be most appreciative.

When you meet Warren, I know you will agree with me that he is the kind of fellow one likes to help. I shall appreciate any courtesy you are able to show him.

Cordially,

———

Dear Ed:

I take pleasure in introducing the bearer of this letter, Mr. Frank J. Edmonds.

For some time Mr. Edmonds has been connected with the Denison circuit of Midwestern hotels, serving as chief accountant in the Erie Hotel in Detroit. He wants to secure a position in the eastern part of the country, and I shall appreciate any assistance you may be able to give to help him get located there.

He has an enviable record in the accounting field, and you need not hesitate to recommend him. Even if you are unable to give Mr. Edmonds any "leads," I am sure you will enjoy making his acquaintance.

Cordially,

———

Dear Harry:

When we had lunch together recently I mentioned Jack Hunt, who was doing some big things for one of our lines. Since that time he has decided that he ought to be handling something that will give him a bigger opportunity.

I do not know whether you are interested in getting additional sales right now or not. Perhaps you are too far behind in production as it is.

But seriously, talk to this fellow, won't you? Jack Hunt is a very likable chap.

The next lunch is on me.

Sincerely,

———

Dear Dick:

One day at lunch I told our Chamber of Commerce Secretary, Mr. George Payson, about the fine work you are doing for the Seattle Association of Commerce. He was much interested—so much, in fact, that he would appreciate an opportunity to talk with you when he visits Seattle next Friday and Saturday, May 21 and 22.

I have suggested to Mr. Payson that he telephone you to learn whether you can see him for a little while on either of those days. If you can do so conveniently, I shall appreciate your talking with him. He is a likable and capable young fellow, and I know he will profit from a chat with you.

I hope everything is going well for you these days, and that all your plans for 195- are working out perfectly.

Cordially yours,

———

Letters Introducing a New Sales Representative

Dear Mr. Corliss:

Within the next week Mr. Donald French, our new southern field representative, will call at your office.

You will find Mr. French well qualified to serve you. He is a Cornell University graduate with nine years of experience in publishing—six years in our central office and three more as our field representative in New England. We feel sure you will enjoy your contacts with him, for he brings to his new assignment a rich background, a keen intelligence, and a likable personality.

Mr. French will be eager to maintain the very pleasant relationship between our two organizations, and he will welcome any opportunity to co-operate with you. May I add that those of us here will also do our best to serve you well during the coming year. May it be one of the most prosperous in your business history!

Cordially yours,

Dear Mr. Ogden:

Last year Jim Davidson joined the sales staff of Morgan & Company. He has been working in and out of the Little Rock office, covering most of the Arkansas territory.

Next week Jim will take over the Iowa-Nebraska area, and about April 5 he will be calling at your office. He's a thoroughly capable, likable chap, and he is very well qualified to serve you. Born in South Dakota and educated in Illinois, he is familiar with farm conditions and problems in the Middlewest, and he prefers that section to any other.

Jim brings to his new work the experience of having lived and worked on a farm throughout his boyhood, plus three years of varied experience in the selling branch of the farm machinery industry. After talking with him for five minutes, you will see that he knows his business and that he'll be delighted to serve you in every way possible.

Sincerely yours,

Dear Mr. Culbert:

We'd like to have you meet Mr. Scott R. Gibson, our new office furniture representative in your territory.

Mr. Gibson comes to us with a wealth of practical experience in the world of business, advertising, and sales promotion. Such a background, coupled with his thorough knowledge of our merchandise, enables him to serve your equipment needs intelligently and efficiently.

Within the next few days Mr. Gibson plans to call and introduce himself to you personally. He will be pleased to discuss any problem you may have . . . be it the systematic arrangement of office equipment, a more efficient method of filing, practical layout of office furniture, or any other need that our merchandise can supply.

Not only will you find Mr. Gibson competent to render such a service, but you'll appreciate his conscientious interests in your behalf, and his pleasant, friendly manner. We feel sure you will like him from the start.

If you have an immediate question that you would like to discuss with Mr. Gibson before his regular visit, just write or telephone Marquette 5800 for an early appointment.

It is our hope that through Mr. Gibson we may continue our mutually beneficial association with you . . . and we assure you that your patronage in the past has been deeply appreciated.

Sincerely yours,

Dear Mr. Ellington:

He's heading your way!

These footprints, reduced of course, are those of Henry Vandenbosch, your new Uarco representative.

Van is well versed in systems work and will be happy to discuss any business problems that you may have concerning systems. He is a likable chap, and the many years of experience he has had in the business world—both in office procedure and in selling—should be sufficient recommendation for his ability.

Until he arrives—if there is anything you need or any service, a word to him at Box 3069, Beaumont, Texas, would be all it would take to bring him on the run. Or, if you'd prefer, a note to us here at the Home Office would be passed on to him pronto.

Van is eager to meet you and say "howdy" in person, so please have the "welcome mat" out for him, won't you?

Cordially yours,

Dear Mr. Dickerson:

We feel sure you will like our new California representative, Grant Morrison, who will drop in for a visit with you soon.

Grant is a very capable and likable young fellow. He will be eager to serve you well, and he is splendidly equipped to do so. A native of California and a product of Stanford University, he came to our organization a year ago. Recently he completed our Business Training Program with one of the finest records in its 18-year history, and since that time he has been in the sales division of the home office.

Please tell Grant of any way in which our service to you can be made more complete. He will appreciate it, and he will co-operate with you one hundred per cent.

Cordially yours,

Dear Mr. Kline:

It has been our privilege to serve you in the past through one of our most competent representatives, Mr. Clint Marshall.

Unfortunately, upon the advice of his doctor, Mr. Marshall must give up his New York territory and confine his activities solely to Westchester and Connecticut, in the vicinity of his home.

An equally able representative, Mr. Allen Brady, will replace him in New York City. Mr. Brady has had fourteen years of business experience—more than half of it as a member of our organization. He is thoroughly familiar with your needs and will bring you the same quality of Ahrend service you have received from Mr. Marshall.

We shall appreciate your co-operation and understanding in this matter, which was entirely beyond our control.

Sincerely yours,

Dear Mr. Paxton:

Stan McCandless, the new Clifford-Hines representative in Colorado, will be calling on you in a few days.

Born and reared in Indiana, Stan attended Purdue University. Soon after his graduation in 1948 he joined the staff of our Chicago office, where he has made an unusually fine record.

Stan is a capable, honest young fellow. We feel sure you will like him. He is looking forward to meeting you, and he'll be happy to assist you in any way he can.

Cordially yours,

———

Dear Mr. Peterson:

We should like to introduce our new representative in your territory, Mr. Frank Jamison.

He comes to us with a background of experience in advertising and retail merchandising, in addition to the excellent training he received at the Wharton School of the University of Pennsylvania.

If you like industrious, ambitious young men of character, then you'll like Frank Jamison. We are depending on Frank to get to know you as we know him, and we are pledging our unqualified co-operation to him in serving you well.

So when he appears in your store early next week, a friendly word will develop a pleasant relationship and trust with which we feel you will always be pleased.

Cordially yours,

———

EIGHT

Letters of Invitation

This chapter includes letter specimens made available through the courtesy of the following persons and organizations: J. N. Adam & Company, Buffalo, New York; The Auerbach Company, Salt Lake City, Utah; Bonwit Teller, New York City; The Brown-Dunkin Dry Goods Company, Tulsa, Oklahoma; Burdine's, Inc., Miami, Florida; B. Forman Company, Rochester, New York; The Honorable Joseph V. Gallagher, Brooklyn, New York; Hale's, San Francisco, California; Kline's, St. Louis, Missouri; Lit Brothers, Philadelphia, Pennsylvania; National Retail Credit Association, St. Louis, Missouri; Prentice-Hall, Inc., New York City; Schuneman's, Inc., St. Paul, Minnesota; Miss Bernice C. Turner, New York City; University of Oklahoma Press, Norman, Oklahoma; The Young-Quinlan Company, Minneapolis, Minnesota.

WHETHER its purpose is primarily business or social, the letter of invitation should be cordial and gracious in tone. It should also be complete in detail, telling its recipient *when* and *where*, and, if necessary, *why*. The last of these details is required when the occasion is essentially of a business nature.

As in other types of courtesy letters, the appropriate degree of formality—or, more accurately, of informality—is determined by the relationship between writer and reader (that is, personal friendship or mere business association), and by the nature of the occasion with which the message is concerned. In general, however, any personal letter of invitation used in business should carry a tone of warmth and friendliness, and should be entirely free of stilted formality.

The specimen letters presented in the following pages range from personal luncheon invitations to messages inviting consumers to make use of store facilities. It is natural, therefore, that these examples represent varying degrees of informality. But all of them capture the spirit of cordiality and enthusiasm so vital in making the letter of invitation a builder of lasting good will.

Letters to Business and Professional Associates [1]

To attend banquet, club luncheon, lecture, or entertainment:

Dear Carl:

When I learned today that John Wainwright will be the speaker at our Rotary meeting next Tuesday, June 20, I thought of you immediately. He will discuss his recent sojourn in Panama, where his experiences probably had much in common with yours.

If you can arrange to meet me in the lobby of Hotel Van Buren at noon, I'll be delighted to have you as my luncheon guest. We should be able to have a good visit before Mr. Wainwright's talk begins.

Cordially,

---

* Dear Mr. Ewing:

I am asking a few friends to be my personal guests at an informal dinner to be given by the Company on Thursday evening, April 6, at which Mr. Emerson Barnwell will speak on "The Dry Goods Business Today and Tomorrow."

Believing that Mr. Barnwell's remarks will hold considerable interest for you, I hope you will find it possible to be with us. If you can arrange to come over on the late afternoon train, I shall be glad to meet you at the station and take you to the Oklahoma Club, where the dinner will be held at seven o'clock.

Cordially yours,

My dear Landers:

I am hoping you will be able to join me Friday evening, May 7, to hear the address by Robert Ames Lawrence on "The Next Decade in American Industry." I understand that Mr. Lawrence will speak at the Civic Auditorium at eight-thirty.

---

[1] Letters marked with an asterisk (*) are especially appropriate for mailing by manufacturing concerns or wholesale houses to their retail dealers.

If you will be free that evening, I shall be glad to pick you up at your home a few minutes after eight.

Cordially,

---

* Dear Mr. Hines:

The Whiting Corporation is having a table at the annual meeting of the American Acceptance Council at the Hotel Roosevelt at seven o'clock on the evening of March 23. We shall be pleased to have you join us as our guest at the dinner.

In order that our guests may enter the dining room as a unit, we are asking that they assemble in Room K, at six-thirty, for a short informal reception.

Our travel department will be happy to attend to hotel reservations or make other arrangements for you relative to your stay in New York.

Very sincerely yours,

Dear Burt:

When the Sales Managers' Club meets on Thursday evening, April 12, George McQuillen will give his popular talk on "How to Make Your Prospects Say 'Yes.'"

I cordially invite you to be my guest at the dinner, which will be held at Hotel Bristol at 6:30 P.M.

Sincerely,

Dear Herb:

If you are free next Thursday noon, April 19, I hope you will be my guest at Kiwanis.

Paul Trimble will be in town that day on his way to the Pacific Coast, and will be attending the luncheon with me. I thought it would give the three of us a chance for a little visit, and I'll be delighted if you can make it.

Let's try to meet at the south end of the Jefferson Hotel mezzanine a few minutes before twelve.

Cordially,

Dear Ted:

Those members of the Inner Circle who linger after the meeting to consider the relative values, actual and speculative, of small rectangular pieces of cardboard will hold their next meeting at the West Side Country Club on Saturday, August 4, about nine o'clock in the evening.

Preceding the meeting an informal stag dinner of the group will be held at the Club, to begin at seven-thirty. It will afford me much pleasure if you will be my guest at this dinner.

As to your course of conduct after the dinner, a word of admonition seems in order. You may either continue in the role of guest or, throwing discretion to the winds, join the "innermost circle" of the Inner Circle and run the risk of becoming a host.

Arrangements will be made to keep you over night if you decide to make a night of it. I am leaving for the Club today and expect to spend most of my vacation there.

Sincerely yours,

Dear Mr. Britton:

About an hour after we were discussing James Rowe's new book at lunch yesterday, I discovered that the same Mr. Rowe is to be guest speaker at next Monday's Civitan luncheon.

I hope you will join me at Hotel Maybank a few minutes after twelve, for I feel sure the program will be an interesting one.

Cordially,

Dear Paul:

I have just acquired two complimentary tickets to the playoff hockey match at Madison Square Garden next Wednesday evening between Toronto and the Rangers.

Knowing that you are fully my equal as an ice hockey enthusiast, I thought of you at once. I believe it will be a lively evening, and I hope you can join me. Suppose we meet in the lobby of Hotel Taft about eight?

Cordially,

To be luncheon or dinner guest:

* Dear Arthur:

I learned this morning that you will be in town September 12 and 13 for the meeting of the Midwest Hardware Association. Do you think you could "play hookey" from the convention long enough to have lunch with me on one of those days?

It would be good to have a visit with you, and I think you would enjoy seeing the new Beaumont Club, which opened last week. Perhaps we can run over there for lunch and still get you back to the hotel in time for the first afternoon session.

If the idea sounds workable, and you think it won't crowd your schedule too much, just let me know which day is the more convenient for you.

Cordially,

Dear Harvey:

Walter Davis will be in town next week, and I am inviting a few of his old friends for luncheon at The Mayfair on October 12. Can you join us in Dining Room C at twelve-thirty?

Your presence will add to everyone's enjoyment of the occasion, and I do hope you can arrange to be with us.

Cordially,

Dear Wayne:

I was very glad to learn from your note this morning that you will be in New York next week, and I'll be delighted to see you on the 18th.

I believe, however, that we could have a much more satisfactory visit at lunch, away from the interruptions of the office. So why not come up about eleven-thirty? We can talk for a bit here and then adjourn to a quiet little restaurant a few blocks away.

It will be good to see you, and I am looking forward to a lengthy chat with you.

Cordially,

---

* Dear Mr. Jennings:

I learned with pleasure this morning that you will pay us a visit December 4.

If your plans for the day permit, I should be happy to have you join me for lunch. Since you will be in the building throughout the morning, perhaps we could meet in my office a little after twelve.

It has been much too long since you were here last, and I am looking forward to your visit with us.

Sincerely yours,

---

* Dear Mr. Kent:

I am writing this note in the hope that you can dine with me at the Tri-City Club when you come to Moline next week.

Since your days will be crowded with appointments, I shall gladly leave the date for your selection. Except for Thursday, when I must be in Des Moines, the most convenient day for you will suit me splendidly.

I can come by your hotel about a quarter past twelve or meet you at any spot that may better serve your convenience.

Cordially yours,

Dear Mr. Lowe:

I shall be very glad to talk with you about the proposed series of magazine articles when you are in town next Monday.

Would it be convenient for you to meet me for lunch at the Biltmore? Unless I hear further from you, I'll plan to meet you in the lobby about twelve-thirty. We can then come back to my office after lunch for a further talk about the series of articles.

If you have already made other luncheon plans, I shall of course be glad to see you in the office in the afternoon.

Cordially yours,

Dear Mr. Holloway:

Our mutual friend, Mr. Walter Haynes, has written me that you will be in Little Rock this week. Will it be possible for you to have lunch with me at the Commerce Club Friday noon?

You can reach me at the office by calling 2-2334, or at home by calling Spring 3110.

Yours sincerely,

---

* Dear Mr. Simmons:

During your stay in Cincinnati next week, I should like very much for you to be my guest at luncheon on any day that best suits your program.

If there is a day when no noon meeting is planned by the Retail Merchants' Conference, perhaps we could meet at the Cosmopolitan Club shortly after twelve.

It has been almost a year since our visit in Dayton, and I hope we shall have an opportunity next week to renew our pleasant association.

Yours sincerely,

Dear Jim:

Can you join me for lunch at the Fifth Avenue Hotel next Monday noon about twelve-thirty?

Don Moreland will be with me for the day, and I'd like to have you meet him. Aside from the fact that he is a fine fellow whom you would enjoy knowing, the contact with him might prove helpful from a business standpoint. He is making plans to add several new departments to his Boston and Worcester stores.

I'd have written you this note earlier, but I did not learn until today that Don will be in town next week. I hope you can make it.

Cordially,

Dear Ralph:

If you are planning to take the evening train home from San Francisco next Friday night, I hope you will be able to have dinner with me at the University Club.

There's nothing I'd enjoy more than a good, leisurely visit with you, and I believe dinner at the Club would give us a chance to talk in quiet and pleasant surroundings.

If you have a convenient moment when you're in the city **Friday,** you can reach me by telephone at 8-5567.

Cordially yours,

---

* Dear Mr. Franklin:

I am glad to hear that you will be stopping in Chicago on your way back to Fort Worth.

Though I realize that your day here will be a busy one, I'd be delighted if you could spare an hour to have lunch with me. I could meet you either at your hotel or at my office, whichever would be more convenient for you.

Cordially yours,

To be overnight guest at home or club:

Dear Fred:

I didn't know until this morning that the Bankers' Association will meet here next week. Doubtless you will be in town for some of the sessions, and I am hoping this note will reach you before your plans for the trip are complete.

Won't you accept our cordial invitation to stay with us during your visit here? If some of the meetings will run far into the night— and I know how conventions are—we can fit you out with keys to both garage and house. You can occupy a downstairs bedroom and come and go as you like.

It will be a real pleasure to have you as our guest, and I do hope you will plan to stay with us if you have made no other commitments.

Cordially,

---

* Dear Mr. Grady:

I was glad to learn from your letter this morning that you will be in Chicago next month. It will be good to see you again.

If you have no other plans, I should be happy to have you as my guest at the Illinois Athletic Club during your stay here. The local hotels are crowded even beyond capacity these days, and I believe you might enjoy the "peace and quiet" of the Club. If the idea appeals to you, just write me a word and I'll gladly make arrangements.

Sincerely yours,

---

* Dear Mr. Rutledge:

Mrs. Davis and I are hoping very much that your western trip next month will include a stopover in South Bend, and that you will be our guest for as long as your schedule will permit.

We should be genuinely delighted at an opportunity to repay in part your great kindness to us last summer, and the thought of a good visit with you is a pleasant one indeed.

Cordially,

Dear Mr. Floyd:

It has just occurred to me that you may be planning to attend the regional meeting of the United Hotel Association in Minneapolis on May 17.

If so, I hope you will accept the hospitality of our home during your visit here. It would be like the proverbial "postman's holiday" for a hotel man to spend the night at a hotel; and besides, Mrs. Gibbs and I would be delighted at the opportunity to enjoy a visit with you.

Cordially yours,

Dear Dave:

I want you to be my guest during your visit here next month, though a business trip to Seattle will deprive me of the pleasure of seeing you.

A room at the Colony Club will be waiting for you Tuesday evening, May 16, when you reach Cleveland. The reservation stands in your name, and the room will be held for your arrival.

For several months I have been looking forward to your visit, and it is disappointing to find that the Seattle trip will come at exactly that time. I must be there for a meeting of our western branch managers on May 17.

I hope your trip to Cleveland will be a pleasant one, and that you will enjoy staying at the Club. Mr. Leo Hendricks, the manager, will do his best to make you comfortable.

Sincerely,

Dear Mac:

Is there a chance that you will be driving through Joplin on your way east next week?

If you come this way, I hope you will plan to spend the night with us. I promise to let you get to bed early, and to start you on your way bright and early the next morning.

It would be a treat to have an evening's visit with you, and we'll be delighted if your plans work out so that you can make an overnight stop at our home.

Sincerely,

---

* Dear Mr. Bullock:

When you come to Kansas City next month for conferences with members of our organization, perhaps you would enjoy staying at the Coronado Club as my guest.

I have lived there for the past several years because it is equipped with a swimming pool and handball courts, because the atmosphere is quiet and pleasant, and because the location is convenient—less than three blocks from our offices.

If you think you would enjoy such a place during your stay here, it will be a pleasure for me to arrange accommodations for you.

Very cordially yours,

Dear Roy:

I have just learned that you will be coming to Springfield to speak at the Illinois Merchants Conference on May 7-8.

Both the guest room and a warm welcome will be waiting for you at 1406 Lincoln Drive. Dorothy joins me in this cordial invitation for you to be our house guest during your stay in Springfield.

Sincerely,

LETTERS OF INVITATION

To give address or informal talk:

Dear Mr. Urban:

I read with much interest the account in last night's pap
your recent experiences in Alaska.

Recalling your ability to put thoughts into words, I know you
could make a most entertaining and informative talk on Alaska, and
I am writing to invite you to speak informally to the Optimists Club
on Thursday, July 24. We meet in the Private Dining Room of Hotel
Livingston at 12:15 P.M. Our talks usually last about thirty minutes.

I hope your plans will permit your acceptance, for I know that
members of the Club would be delighted at an opportunity to visit
with you and hear about your experiences firsthand.

Very sincerely yours,

Dear Mr. Lee:

The subject of "How to Write Good Business Letters" is an interesting one to every business and professional man. For a long time I
have intended, when it came my turn to arrange a program for the
Business Men's Club, to invite a real authority in the field to talk to
the Club on that subject.

My turn came today, when I was asked to arrange the program
for Tuesday noon, November 17. I know of no other person so well
qualified as you to speak on the technique of writing business letters, and I am hoping very much that you will find it possible to
accept my invitation.

Our luncheon meetings are held in the Banquet Room of Hotel
Cleveland. They begin at 12:15 and are usually over about 1:30.
The talks range from thirty to forty minutes.

If you can be our guest on the 17th, you will receive a most enthusiastic welcome.

Sincerely yours,

Dear Joe:

I've heard so many good things about the talk you made before
the Merchants' Association last week that I'd be delighted if you
could give it at our Kiwanis Club meeting either October 8 or 15.

The subject of "Consumer Relations" is one of much interest to such a group as ours, and I know you would make a real hit with it.

If you can be with us on either of these dates, I'll begin spreading the good news at next week's meeting, and we'll have a peak attendance on hand to hear you.

Cordially,

Dear Mr. Fuller:

I noticed in the *Herald* the other day that you have recently returned from the annual meeting of the National Safety Council.

Having heard your talk before the ABC Club a year ago, at which you discussed new safety devices demonstrated at the 195- meeting, all of us on the program committee are hoping that you will speak to our members again at Hotel Randall next Wednesday noon, September 17.

If you could give us about a thirty-minute talk on new safety devices, just as you did a year ago, I know that you would find your audience just as receptive as it was the other time.

In short, we liked your talk last year so much that we hope you will come back for a "return engagement."

Cordially yours,

Dear Mr. Leslie:

Already the program committee is hard at work on arrangements for the annual meeting of the Pacific Coast Retailers' Association next February 10 and 11. We are inviting the participation of men who are outstanding in several fields related to retailing.

It is for this reason that I am writing to you. Members of the committee have decided unanimously that you are the ideal man to address the meeting on the subject of effective credit correspondence. No use of the written word is more important to the successful management of retail credit; and yet, few retail houses are making the most efficient use of credit letters.

In view of your long experience and your accomplishments in this field, we know our members would count it a privilege to hear you discuss this important subject. We should be happy to schedule your talk for 2:00-2:45 P.M. February 10, or for 10:00-10:45 A.M. February 11. In the past these hours have been particularly favorable to maximum attendance. All sessions, by the way, will take place at Hotel Biltmore.

We can schedule your talk for either day, according to your preference. Perhaps it could be announced as "How to Write Better Credit Letters" or "What's Wrong with Our Credit Letters?" Or quite possibly there is some other title you would prefer.

We should be proud to have you participate in the program, and we sincerely hope you will be able to accept our invitation.

Very cordially yours,

Dear Mr. Jordan:

I read in last night's paper of the unusual experiences you had on your recent trip to Mexico, and of the study you made of economic conditions in that country.

Since members of the Burlington Lions Club would be much interested in your research, I hope you will find it possible to be my guest at the meeting September 22 and to speak to us for thirty or forty minutes. If this date is convenient for you, I shall gladly call for you at your office about 11:30 A.M. and drive you back to Newport after the luncheon.

I hope very much that you will be able to accept.

Sincerely yours,

Dear Jack:

I know it's a bit heartless to call on you for a talk so soon after your speaking trip across the state. Yesterday, however, Ralph Pinkert told me about the hit you made in Durant the other day with your talk entitled "History Repeats Itself."

Would your schedule—and your vocal cords—permit you to give that same talk before the Young Men's Dinner Club in the Pheasant Room of the Blackstone next Thursday evening, March 21? I know our full membership will be on hand for the occasion if you find it possible to accept. The dinner is informal, and is planned for six-thirty.

Sincerely,

Dear Mr. Hughes:

As program chairman of our local Business Men's Dinner Club, I asked our members recently to indicate the subjects they would like to hear discussed during the coming months. One of the topics of greatest interest was "The Future of Retail Credit."

I can think of no man in this state who is better qualified than you to speak on this subject. Both your training and your present work seem to make this topic a "natural" for you. So I am hoping very much that you can be our guest on either May 9 or May 16. Our meetings, for which we dress informally, are held in the Crystal Room of Hotel Fenmore at 7:15 P.M. The Club, by the way, pays a fee of fifty dollars to each speaker. The talks usually run from forty-five minutes to an hour in length.

We shall be delighted if you can be with us on either of the dates mentioned, and you can be sure of a warm welcome.

Sincerely yours,

Dear Mr. Gregg:

I was very glad to learn last night that you will be coming home from Washington for a vacation the first of August.

Though I know the purpose of your trip will be to get away from your work for a little while, I am hoping that you will attend the Chamber of Commerce banquet as my guest on the evening of August 6, and that you will talk to the group informally for twenty or thirty minutes about recent developments in industrial planning. No subject could be of greater interest to our members.

I am very glad you will be in Kingsbury for a week or two, and I am looking forward to seeing you.

Sincerely yours,

Letters to Employees [2]

To attend company social event:

* Dear Mr. Glenning:

This is a cordial invitation for you to be the guest of Jenkins & Company on Friday evening, February 26, at an informal banquet

---

[2] Letters marked with an asterisk (*) are also appropriate for mailing by manufacturing concerns or wholesale houses to their retail dealers.

in honor of Mr. Timothy White. On that day Mr. White will complete his fortieth year of service to the firm.

Dinner will be served at six-thirty in the Walnut Room of Hotel Bellevue. The occasion will be one of interest to all of us who know Mr. White, and I hope you will be able to join us in paying him this tribute.

Sincerely yours,

Dear Miss Tinsley:

Davenport's is going to usher in the holiday season Thursday evening, December 20, with a Christmas party for company personnel at Hotel Mayview.

Festivities will get under way at 8:30 in the private meeting room on the mezzanine. There will be candy, cookies, popcorn balls, coffee and mince pie. And Santa Claus will drop in with his pack loaded with presents for everyone.

You are cordially invited, and we hope you will be there to join in the fun.

Cordially,

Dear Al:

Next Tuesday, May 1, will be the tenth anniversary of Mr. Elliot's service as President of the Company.

Plans have just been completed to honor him with a dinner at the Athletic Club that evening, and we hope you will find it possible to attend. We have reserved Banquet Room A, where dinner will be served at seven o'clock. Dress will be informal.

You will be the guest of the firm, and we promise not even to call on you for a speech.

Cordially,

Dear Mr. Halsey:

You are cordially invited to attend the Nelson Brothers Open House next Sunday afternoon, April 12, to be held from two-thirty until five o'clock.

As you know, this event will mark the opening of our new building, and we should like for you to share the enjoyment and satisfaction of the occasion.

Sincerely yours,

Dear Bill:

A few of us in the Sales Department are planning a little celebration for Dan Gilmore in honor of his recent promotion.

We are inviting members of the sales staff to set aside next Saturday evening, January 6, if they can do so conveniently, and to be our guests at a smoker. It will get under way in Banquet Room 2C of the Carlton Hotel at eight-thirty.

Later in the evening there will be doughnuts and coffee, and we are planning a "home talent" show that will amaze you. We hope you'll be able to make it.

Cordially,

Ahoy there, Shipmate Parker!

We're shining up the brass and tightening up the rigging, and getting everything shipshape, because on September 18 we're going to haul up anchor and set sail for Bear Mountain. Our strategy for this expedition is all mapped out, and since you are a seaworthy old salty, we'll let you in on it.

At one o'clock sharp on September 18, Prentice-Hall, en masse, will board the good ship *Peter Stuyvesant* at the foot of West 42nd Street, and chug merrily up the Hudson to Bear Mountain. We expect to arrive about 3:45, and we'll soften up the old hill for the invasion with a barrage of laughs, hilarity, and fun. Since you are the laddie-buck with plenty of that kind of ammunition, we're counting on you to be on deck with everything you've got.

At seven o'clock, after supper in the Bear Mountain Inn, we'll board our good ship again and sail for home port, arriving at 42nd Street at ten. We'll have our own orchestra and show on the boat.

I'm not putting any R.S.V.P. on this, for shiver-me-timbers if I'll take any answer from you but "Aye, aye, sir!"

Sincerely,

---

* Dear Mr. Walker:

On Friday evening, September 24, J. L. Jones & Company will observe its Fiftieth Anniversary at an informal banquet to be held in the Biltmore Hotel junior ballroom at seven o'clock.

We hope very much that you will attend as a guest of the Company. Since you have played a substantial part in its progress, your presence on this happy occasion seems particularly appropriate.

The program following the dinner will be varied and entertaining, and we feel sure you will have a most enjoyable evening.

Cordially yours,

Dear Ralph:

Saturday afternoon, August 5, will find the Wellman Company crew off to a picnic at Medicine Park.

There will be golf, tennis, boating, softball, swimming, and horseback riding—according to one's taste in sports—followed by a picnic supper along the shore of Lake Winnetka.

I hope that you will join us in an afternoon of fun and relaxation. We shall meet at the Sixth Street entrance at one-thirty, and bus transportation will be provided to and from the Park. One bus will return about eight o'clock and the other will follow an hour or so later to bring the slow eaters and overeaters.

There is nothing for you to bring but yourself—and your swimming suit if a plunge in the Lake appeals to you.

Cordially,

---

* Dear Mr. Brown:

I should like to invite you to be the guest of the Company at an informal dinner in the Banquet Room of Hotel Palace at 6:30 Thursday evening, May 18.

Plans for the immediate expansion of our organization will be announced at the dinner, and I am sure they will be of interest to everyone associated with the Company. They will assure an even brighter future for all of us.

I hope very much that you will be able to attend the dinner, since I am sure the occasion will be a happy one for us all.

Sincerely yours,

Letters to Consumers [3]

To open charge account:

Dear Mrs. Nichols:

The Auerbach Company has selected your name from a limited and preferred credit list, and is happy to extend to you an invitation to open a charge account.

You need merely sign and return the enclosed card or call at the Department of Accounts whenever convenient and leave your signature so that we can make up a Charga-Plate, the most modern convenience in shopping. This affords you protection and quicker service. It also eliminates any possibility of error.

An itemized statement is mailed to you each month. By charging, you avoid the delay of waiting for change; you also eliminate the nuisance of sales tax tokens by having the tax included in the bill at the end of the month.

We sincerely hope you will accept our invitation to enjoy the convenience of a charge account here.

Cordially yours,

Dear Mr. Reddick:

Your visits to the store as a cash customer are very much appreciated, and we wish to make your shopping here just as pleasant and convenient as possible.

Though we already count you as a friend of J. N. Adam & Company, we feel that you will find added convenience in the use of a charge account.

An account will make shopping easier, whether in person or by telephone. Your purchases will be recorded. Your name will be placed on our mailing list to receive regular information about our special events.

[3] Letters of welcome to prospective consumers (pages 145-149) include an invitation to visit the store.

Just fill out and send us the enclosed card, and we shall complete the arrangements for your charge account at once. We shall appreciate this opportunity to make your visits here more enjoyable.

Sincerely yours,

Dear Mrs. Jackson:

You are cordially invited to open a Forman charge account.

Every day more and more of our friends are finding that an account really does help in shopping. It provides a convenient record of total purchases for budget-control purposes, and it makes available the many friendly services offered by this store.

So we should like you to enjoy a Forman account. The procedure is simple. Usually arrangements are made during a brief interview; but we are making it even easier than that in this special invitation to you. Just fill out and return the enclosed card, and within a day or so the account will be ready for your use.

Cordially yours,

Dear Mrs. Carpenter:

It was a real pleasure to serve you when you paid us a visit recently. We hope you will return often.

Our new fashions are ready now . . . selections are complete for you to see . . . and we're sure you will find shopping more convenient with the aid of a charge account.

So you are cordially invited to open an account with us. Just fill out the enclosed folder with the information requested for our records, and mail it to us in the postpaid envelope.

That's all you need to do to enjoy the credit convenience at Kline's. We'll let you know as soon as your account is ready for use.

Sincerely yours,

Dear Mr. Thornton:

Thank you for the promptness with which you have met every payment on your Club Plan Account, recently completed.

You may be interested in having a regular charge account at Lit Brothers. We are sure you will find it a real advantage and time saver because when you buy, all you need say is "Charge it." For your convenience, too, an itemized bill will reach you the early part of the month, payable in full during the month following that of purchase.

As you have already established such an excellent record, no further credit investigation will be necessary. Will you just sign the enclosed form and return it to us? Then your account will be ready for use.

It will be a pleasure to serve you through a charge account, and we hope you will make frequent use of its conveniences.

Cordially yours,

Dear Mrs. Fleming:

There are so many delightful things in our store, unusual gifts as well as distinctive apparel, that we believe you will find a Young-Quinlan charge account convenient.

We shall be glad to open an account for you if you will merely mention this letter to the saleswoman the next time you are in the store. Shopping on a charge account will save your time and eliminate the need of carrying money with you for cash purchases.

Each of your visits to the store we shall endeavor to make a pleasant occasion for you.

Cordially yours,

Dear Mrs. Kenyon:

"Charge it, please." That's what we'd like to hear you say the next time you shop at Morris Brothers.

There are many conveniences in a charge account here. It speeds up service, eliminates the bother of tax tokens, and brings you an itemized statement of each month's purchases.

A Morris Brothers account also provides complete Personal Shopper Service, placing our four floors of distinctive apparel and accessories as close to you as your telephone. And you'll be notified in advance of sales, style shows, and all other special events.

Will you take just a moment to sign the enclosed request card and return it to us in the prepaid envelope? This is all we need to open your account for immediate use.

Cordially yours,

Dear Mrs. Burdick:

Since you do not live so close to Burdine's as many of our customers, we should like to bring Burdine's to you by placing many of our services right at your door.

You will enjoy the convenience of a monthly charge account. Naturally, this service is limited to persons in whom we have absolute confidence. You are one of them.

With a Burdine charge account you may shop from your own home. Just write us a note or postcard, and our stocks of quality merchandise are open for your selection . . . to be sent wherever you wish.

When in Miami, you can shop here without the bother of bringing along "shopping money" or checkbook. You have until the tenth of each month to pay the previous month's bill.

If you will just sign the enclosed card and return it to us in the attached envelope, your account will be ready for use immediately.

We want you to feel that Burdine's is your store . . . where every shopping convenience is extended to you. It will be a pleasure to serve you in your home or in Miami.

Sincerely yours,

Dear Miss Werner:

It is so much more pleasant and businesslike to shop where you can charge your purchases. It saves you time and effort. You get an exact statement of your expenditures at the end of each month.

There are other reasons, too. Charga-Plate, for instance, speeds up service, eliminates errors, and provides instant identification.

We should like to have you enjoy the advantages of a Schuneman charge account. To do so, you need only sign and return the enclosed card.

This closer relationship will enable us to provide a more complete service for you . . . and will add to your convenience in shopping here.

Sincerely yours,

Dear Mrs. Kendall:

The charge customers of Rand & Company are leading citizens in this community, and we should like to include you among them.

A charge account here will simplify your shopping amazingly. It will save your time and assure you of many conveniences. There will be no waiting for change, no need of carrying large sums of money to pay for your purchases, no C.O.D. bother on telephone orders.

A Rand account will also simplify your budget keeping. Each month you will receive an itemized statement showing all purchases.

If you will just sign the enclosed card and return it to us in the business-reply envelope, your account will be opened immediately. It will be a pleasure to provide this convenience, and we hope you will use it often.

Sincerely yours,

Dear Mrs. McCall:

It is gratifying to know that we were able to accommodate you in a small way by cashing a check for you the other day.

We should like to suggest to you that a charge account with J. N. Adam & Company would afford real convenience in matters like this. With an account there is no waiting, no bother about checks . . . you need only say "Charge it."

In addition, a charge account gives you a monthly record of your purchases, and places your name on our mailing list to receive regular information about our special events.

Opening an account for you will be a pleasure. Just fill in and sign the enclosed form, mail it back to us in the prepaid envelope, and your account will be ready for use. We shall welcome such an opportunity to make your visits here more enjoyable.

Cordially yours,

To renew use of account:

Dear Mrs. Ellenwood:

A satisfactory charge account like yours is never closed.

At times it becomes inactive as yours is just now; but the account is always there, ready for your use without the formality of reopening.

Now that large shipments of winter merchandise are arriving each day, you will find a visit to the store both interesting and profitable. We cordially invite you to renew the use of your charge account, with our promise that everything possible will be done to make your shopping here enjoyable.

Your Charga-Plate is the token . . . bring it with you for speedier shopping at all Hale stores.

It will be a real pleasure to serve you . . . and to see your account active again.

Sincerely yours,

Dear Mr. Page:

We'd rather serve an old
customer than two new ones.

That short sentence sums up the whole business philosophy of Crandall's. So we're genuinely concerned because you haven't used your account here in recent months.

If any detail of our service . . . or any article purchased here . . . has fallen short of your expectations, won't you please let us know? We'll appreciate an opportunity to correct it, and we won't be satisfied until you are.

Please accept this cordial invitation to pay us a visit soon. Attractive new stocks of spring and summer merchandise are here for your inspection, and you'll find exceptional values in every department.

Sincerely yours,

Dear Mrs. Douglas:

Though Burdine's wins a host of new friends each year, we take still greater pride in our old customers, such as you, whom we have been privileged to serve for a number of years.

This letter comes to you because several months have passed since you last used your charge account. Perhaps you have been out of town. But we want to be sure of your complete satisfaction in all your dealings with Burdine's. If there has been any exception, please give us an opportunity to correct it promptly.

Now that our stocks are complete for the holiday season, you will find a visit to the store especially interesting. Anything in this wealth of useful and beautiful merchandise is yours by simply telling the salesperson to "Charge it." And even when you are at home, you can shop with convenience at Burdine's. A telephone call will bring you what you want . . . often on the very next delivery.

It will be a real pleasure to serve you again. Please give us an opportunity soon.

Sincerely yours,

Dear Mrs. Jarman:

It has been many months since you last used your Tillman charge account, and we really miss you.

If anything has occurred to interrupt your visits, won't you tell us frankly? Your complete satisfaction is our goal, and we shall welcome a chance to make amends if we have fallen short in any way.

Large shipments of fall merchandise are coming in almost every day, so it's an ideal time to pay us a visit. Our selections have never been more attractive and complete.

It will certainly be a pleasure to welcome you back to Tillman's, and to hear you say "Charge it" again.

Sincerely yours,

Dear Mrs. Jacobsen:

With spring just around the corner and Easter only two weeks off, we extend to you a special invitation to visit our five floors of distinctive, up-to-the-minute apparel for women.

Right now our stocks are more complete than they have been in several years. They include a wide assortment of the latest spring and summer fashions in many alluring colors. There is so much here to interest you that we are sure you'll enjoy visiting us.

And please remember . . . your charge account will make your shopping pleasant and convenient. We look forward to serving you . . . and hope you'll come in soon.

Cordially yours,

Dear Mr. Leland:

You may have thought that because this store is large your patronage would not be missed. On the contrary, we are genuinely concerned because you have not used your charge account for some time.

If there has been anything in our relationship to cause you to stop using our facilities, please give us an opportunity to correct it. We want you to be fully satisfied in all your dealings with Hale's.

Incidentally, this is an ideal time for the use of your account. The entire store is ready for our annual Mid-Winter Sale, with selections more complete and varied than we have had in years.

Do pay us a visit soon. You will find it both pleasant and profitable.

Sincerely yours,

Dear Mrs. Payton:

This is just a note to tell you that we've missed you. Several months have passed since you last used your Brown-Dunkin charge account, and we are wondering why.

There must be some reason, and we are anxious to know if it is through any shortcoming on our part. If any transaction in the past has not been entirely satisfactory to you, it is never too late to let us know and give us an opportunity to adjust it.

Right now the store is aglow with up-to-the-minute fall apparel, and all sorts of fascinating new items are arriving each day. You will find a visit here most interesting and worth while.

So won't you come in soon? Your charge account is waiting to be used, and we shall be glad to see you once more enjoying its advantages.

Cordially yours,

Dear Mr. McEver:

With the coming of September and its crisp fall days, probably you are planning to supplement your wardrobe with a new suit, topcoat, hat, or pair of serviceable all-weather shoes.

Our shipments of new fall merchandise have just arrived . . . and we cordially invite you to come in and look around while selections are still complete. This year we have the largest and most attractive stocks of men's apparel in all our thirty-seven years in Portland . . . and we are sure you will find a visit to the store enjoyable.

Since your account is already established and ready for use, you need only say "Charge it." A cordial welcome awaits you, and we hope you'll come in soon.

Sincerely yours,

Dear Mrs. Poole:

Your charge account has not been used for several months, and we've really missed you.

If any shortcoming on our part has resulted in your long absence from the store, we are anxious to correct it, for we want you to be entirely satisfied in all your dealings with us.

At this busy season your charge account will be a greater convenience than ever, with its Charga-Plate identification for faster and easier shopping. And there are sure to be many things you will want . . . for yourself, your family, and your home.

Please give us further opportunities to prove that your satisfaction is important to us.

Sincerely yours,

To attend special event:

Dear Mrs. Corwin:

Won't you be our guest?

On Wednesday evening, March 23, at eight o'clock, we invite you to attend an illustrated lecture by Miss Frances Murdock, well-known New York authority on interior decorating. Miss Murdock will discuss "Home Furnishing on the Budget Plan." After her lecture she will answer questions brought up by her listeners.

Elevators at either door will be ready to take you to the lounge on the seventh floor. We hope you will save next Wednesday evening for Miss Murdock's lecture. It will be both entertaining and practical.

Cordially yours,

———

Dear Mr. Ryerson:

If you can't get rid of that exasperating "slice," or if your putts refuse to "drop," we invite you to consult one of golf's leading specialists without any consultation fee.

At 7:30 next Tuesday evening, May 26, "Chuck" Farmer will be at the store to talk on "How to Lick Golf Nerves." Afterward he will demonstrate the cure for those irritating faults that drive golfers crazy.

We know you will want to hear what one of America's leading professionals has to say, and we promise you an enjoyable evening.

Cordially,

———

Dear Mrs. Clark:

We have good news for you! Beginning next Thursday afternoon, July 18, McIntire's will conduct a series of ten weekly book reviews of the latest outstanding fiction. You are cordially invited to attend, and an easy chair is being reserved for you.

The book to be reviewed next Thursday is *Barnaby House*, an exciting new novel by Doris Hampton. The reviewer will be a well-known Kansas Citian, Miss Elizabeth Larrimore, herself a novelist of established reputation.

This review, and all others in the series, will be given in our air-conditioned lounge on the third floor. All will begin at 2:30 P.M. On Thursday we shall announce the name of next week's reviewer and the title of the novel to be discussed.

We are sure you will enjoy this Thursday feature during the next ten weeks, for we have engaged only persons whose background and experience distinguish them as experts in the art of book reviewing.

Please plan to be with us next Thursday afternoon at 2:30.

Cordially yours,

———

Dear Mr. Boardman:

On Thursday, December 2, we are having our Annual Stag Party in honor of the opening of our 721 Club for men, where we have assembled all the gifts that men like to give women.

It will start about 5 P.M. and will include such attractions as a fashion showing modeled by famous beauties of stage, screen, and magazine.

I do hope you can be with us for the party at the 721 Club, Fourth Floor.

Sincerely,

————

Dear Mrs. Turner:

In an effort to make our service to you just as complete as possible, we'd like to make a suggestion.

All next week, March 12-17, our Kitchen Karnival will be in full swing. This is an annual feature of our Household Department in the Basement. There will be special displays and demonstrations of the newest time- and effort-saving devices in kitchenware. In addition, our entire stock of up-to-the-minute kitchen utensils will be on sale at a ten per cent price reduction.

We are sure you will find a visit to our Household Department next week both interesting and profitable, so we cordially invite you to come in.

Sincerely yours,

————

Dear Mr. Cox:

"Ladies and gentlemen: The batteries for today's game . . ."

It won't be long now until that familiar prelude to the World Series echoes through the Yankee Stadium.

We invite you to "take in" the series with us, from a comfortable easy chair behind radio's home plate. One side of the store will be converted into a men's lounge for the occasion, and cigars will be "on the house."

Our sports party begins next Wednesday afternoon at one-thirty. We hope you'll join us, and bring along your friends.

Cordially yours,

————

Dear Mrs. Osborne:

Short Cuts to Better Meals, by Elizabeth J. Karsten—probably there's a copy of this famous book in your kitchen at this moment.

Next Wednesday afternoon, March 7, at three o'clock, Miss Karsten will be here in person to discuss and demonstrate "Ten-Minute Meals." She will speak from the stage of our auditorium on the fifth floor.

You are cordially invited to hear Miss Karsten as our guest. Her talk will be the third in our 195- Timely Topic Series.

We hope you can arrange to be with us for this outstanding event, for we know you will find it entertaining, practical, and helpful.

Sincerely yours,

NINE

Miscellaneous Courtesy Letters

This chapter includes letter specimens made available through the courtesy of the following persons and organizations: D. H. Ahrend Company, Inc., New York City; Boyd's, St. Louis, Missouri; Mr. Perry W. Branch, Lincoln, Nebraska; Burdine's, Inc., Miami, Florida; Mr. L. S. Crowder, St. Louis, Missouri; The Dartnell Corporation, Chicago, Illinois; Duplex Envelope Company, Richmond, Virginia; *The Eagle Magazine,* South Bend, Indiana; Mr. Charles A. Emley, Philadelphia, Pennsylvania; B. Forman Co., Rochester, New York; Thomas W. Garland, Inc., St. Louis, Missouri; Mr. Stewart Harral, Norman, Oklahoma; Mr. F. Heywood, London, England; Kerr Dry Goods Company, Oklahoma City, Oklahoma; Professor Edward J. Kilduff, New York University, New York City; Livingston Bros., San Francisco, California; Mr. C. E. Lovejoy, Chicago, Illinois; Mr. Harley E. Miller, Greencastle, Indiana; C. F. Mueller Company, Jersey City, New Jersey; National Retail Credit Association, St. Louis, Missouri; *Nation's Business,* Washington, D. C.; Prentice-Hall, Inc., New York City; Mr. T. J. Ross, New York City; *Sales Management,* New York City; Miss Bernice C. Turner, New York City; University of Oklahoma Press, Norman, Oklahoma; Mr. S. L. Weisskerz, Columbus, Ohio.

THE SEVERAL TYPES of correspondence discussed and illustrated in the following pages are concerned with a variety of business and personal situations. Some of the subdivisions of this chapter deal with occasions that may develop only infrequently, but that present something of a human-relations problem when they do arise. The numerous specimen letters are designed to point the way to effective handling of these various problems in a manner that will maintain, and often strengthen, cordial relations with business friends and associates.

Letters of Acceptance [1]

A personal letter accepting an invitation should convey both appreciation and enthusiasm on the part of the writer. If the

[1] Two types of messages included in the following section—(1) the letter

invitation has left certain details to the convenience of its recipient—such as the time or place of meeting—the acceptance must, of course, deal specifically with these points. Otherwise, a brief note of thanks and acceptance is sufficient. The degree of informality most appropriate in a note of acceptance is determined by the nature of the association between writer and reader, and also by the occasion with which the invitation is concerned. A letter accepting an invitation to a symphony concert or grand-opera performance, or accepting membership in a professional association, would naturally tend to be more restrained in its tone and language than a note accepting an invitation to a smoker or a civic-club luncheon.

Whatever may be the occasion for a message of acceptance, the letter should manifest a spirit of gratitude and pleasant expectancy. Although the writer should avoid effusiveness, his reply should make the reader feel that the invitation was warmly received and accepted with genuine pleasure.

Specimen Letters of Acceptance

Of invitation to banquet, club luncheon, lecture, or entertainment:

Dear Loren:

I appreciate very much your inviting me to attend the Chamber of Commerce Banquet the evening of May 20, and I accept with pleasure.

It is very kind of you to include me at your table, and I am looking forward to what I know will be a most enjoyable evening.

Sincerely yours,

Dear Mr. Harter:

I shall be pleased to accept your invitation to attend the Anniversary Banquet as your guest. Under such able guidance as that

---

accepting a resignation from a position, board, or committee, and (2) the letter accepting a resignation from a club or association—are exceptions to the following summary of essential qualities. In accepting a resignation, the writer usually expresses his regret at losing the services of the person concerned (if such a statement can be made with sincerity), recognizes the accomplishments of this individual, and conveys personal good wishes.

of your company, I am looking forward to a perfect evening, starting with that informal reception in Room K.

Your kind offer leads me also to accept the services of your travel department and to ask that they reserve a single room with bath for me at the Commodore. I shall arrive in New York at eleven o'clock Sunday evening, October 17.

Thank you for your kind invitation, and for your thoughtfulness in offering to make hotel reservations for me.

Very sincerely yours,

Dear George:

I'll be delighted to be your guest at the Business Men's Club on Thursday, October 12. For several months I have wished that I might hear Carl Heaton's widely discussed talk on "Personality in Selling," and the opportunity to hear it in your company will make it doubly enjoyable.

As you suggest, I shall be in the Claremont lobby a few minutes after twelve. Thanks a lot for thinking of me.

Cordially,

Dear Mr. Trent:

I accept with pleasure your thoughtful invitation to attend the Kiwanis Club luncheon next Tuesday, April 16.

It was fine of you to think of me, and I am looking forward to the occasion with a lot of pleasure.

Sincerely yours,

Of luncheon or dinner invitation:

Dear Jim:

I'll be delighted to have lunch with you when I come to St. Paul next Friday. As you suggest, I'll meet you in the lobby of the Spartan Club at twelve-thirty.

Thanks a lot for asking me.

Sincerely,

Dear Mr. Kimball:

Everything about your invitation pleases me—even the hour. I shall be most happy to accept your hospitality.

It will be a pleasure to recall those early days in Chicago, and I thank you for your kindness in inviting me to your home.

Sincerely yours,

Dear Walter:

Many thanks for your note of May 9.

I shall look forward with pleasure to having lunch with you when I am in Rochester next Thursday.

If it is really convenient for you to stop for me at Hotel Columbus, as you suggest, I'll be waiting for you in the lobby at twelve.

Sincerely,

Dear Mr. Dollard:

I was very much pleased to receive your note this morning, inviting me to have lunch with you next Friday. I shall be delighted.

Your suggestion that we meet at Hotel Mayflower is a good one. I shall be in the lobby at twelve-thirty.

It will be good to see you and visit with you again, and I thank you for your kindness in inviting me.

Sincerely yours,

Of hospitality of home or club on overnight visit:

Dear Mr. Fellows:

Nothing could have been more welcome than your letter this morning inviting me to stay with you during my weekend in Portland. I am happy to accept.

It is fine of you and Mrs. Fellows to extend to me the hospitality of your home, and I look forward to seeing you next Saturday.

Sincerely yours,

Dear Mr. Ferris:

Thank you for your cordial note inviting me to be your guest at the University Club the night of September 26. I shall be delighted to do so.

Since our evening meeting will also be at the Club, your thoughtfulness will simplify my stay in Chicago. It is very kind of you to arrange accommodations for me, and I appreciate it.

Yours sincerely,

Dear John:

I was delighted to receive your letter this morning, inviting me to be your house guest during my stay in Wichita. I accept with pleasure.

It will be good to see you and Mrs. Harcourt again, and the prospect of a good visit with you adds a great deal to my enthusiasm in preparing for the trip.

Though it is generous of you to offer to meet my train, please let me take a cab to your home instead. I know that early afternoon is a busy time for you at the office, and cabs are always plentiful at the Wichita station.

Thank you again for your welcome letter. I'll look forward to seeing you Thursday.

Sincerely,

Dear Mr. Bullins:

I accept with pleasure your kind invitation for me to stay at the Athletic Club when I come to your city April 16.

Your thoughtfulness is much appreciated. I know it will add a great deal to the enjoyment of my trip.

Sincerely yours,

Dear Paul:

It was nice of you to write me about the class reunion, and to invite me to stay overnight at your home on June 8. I shall be very happy to do so.

Since I'll reach Champaign only a little while before the reunion dinner, I shall go directly to the Urbana-Lincoln and plan to meet you there.

It will be good to see you again, and I sincerely appreciate your invitation.

Cordially,

Of speaking invitation:

Dear Mr. Parkinson:

I appreciate your inviting me to speak before the Advertisers' Club at the meeting to be held Tuesday noon, October 11. I accept with pleasure.

If you think it would be suitable, I shall use as a subject "New Trends in Radio Advertising." This phase of the advertising field has occupied a lot of my time lately, and I believe some of the recent research of this office will prove interesting to retail advertising managers.

Should you prefer that I speak on some other aspect of advertising, however, please let me know and I shall do my best to oblige.

It will be a pleasure to visit with the members of your club, many of whom I know, and I thank you again for your invitation.

Cordially yours,

Dear Mr. Johnson:

Thank you for your letter of November 21, outlining the 195- program of the Central States Bankers Association.

It is nice of you to invite me to speak at your March 2 meeting in Chicago. I shall be happy to do so.

In a similar talk before a group of bankers in New York some time ago, I used the topic "Bank Public Relations by Letter." Perhaps this title would also prove appropriate for your meeting on March 2.

You deserve a lot of credit for the fine work you are doing in the field of bank public relations. I shall feel complimented to have a small part in the program you are developing for the coming year.

Cordially yours,

Dear Mr. Fitzgerald:

Thank you for inviting me to speak to members of the Business Forum on Thursday noon, May 27.

While I make no pretense of being an expert at public speaking, I shall be glad to outline current trends in retailing as I see them, and I'll try to bring along some charts to illustrate major points.

I shall meet you as suggested in the lounge of the Athletic Club at twelve-fifteen. It will be a pleasure to visit with you and the members of your organization.

Cordially yours,

My dear Paul:

I feel very much complimented at your invitation for me to speak before the Oklahoma City Advertising Club on Friday evening, January 26. I accept with pleasure.

If you think it appropriate, I shall try to bring into my talk some of the current findings of the Bureau of Advertising Research with regard to advertising psychology. These new developments, I feel, will play an important part in the progress of American selling technique during the next decade.

Thank you for inviting me to speak before your club next month. I shall look forward to the occasion with pleasure, and I shall try to bring to your members something of interest to them.

Sincerely yours,

Dear Mr. Morse:

I shall be happy to speak to the Rotary Club on Monday, June 26. Thank you for asking me.

The subject you suggest is quite satisfactory, and I shall do my best to give your members an interesting half hour. I know that prompt adjournment is an important requirement of most luncheon clubs, and I assure you that my remarks will be confined to the allotted time. I mention that point because long-winded speakers are among my pet aversions, and quite probably you share my sentiments.

I shall be glad to meet you in the Biltmore lobby at twelve o'clock, and I look forward with pleasure to the visit with your club.

Cordially yours,

Of invitation to attend meeting or convention:

Dear Mr. Wellman:

Thank you for your March 18 letter inviting me to attend the Sales Management Conference in Houston on May 5 and 6. Your invitation is much appreciated, and I accept with pleasure.

The 195- convention should be one of the best in years. You and your committee deserve a great deal of credit for arranging such an excellent program.

Cordially yours,

Dear Jack:

I'll be very glad to attend the meeting you have arranged for 2 P.M. on May 12 at the Chamber of Commerce office. Thanks for inviting me.

Your project deserves the wholehearted support of this community, and I believe you will find the business and professional men solidly behind you.

Sincerely,

Dear Mr. Farnam:

Thank you for your note of July 8, inviting me to attend a meeting of the Foundation Board of Directors at the University Club on Thursday, July 21.

I shall be happy to attend. It will be good to hear the annual report of activities which have made the past year one of outstanding success for the Foundation.

Sincerely yours,

Dear Charles:

Thanks for your interesting letter this morning.

I shall be glad to attend the meeting you have set up for 7:30 P.M. on Wednesday, November 16, at your office.

The idea of a young men's business club sounds most worth while, and you can count on me to help in any way I can.

Sincerely,

Dear Mr. Gilchrist:

Thank you for inviting me to attend a meeting of Sigma Delta Chi members at your home at eight o'clock Friday evening, April 11.

I accept your invitation with pleasure. It will be good to see you again, and to get acquainted with other SDX members who live in this community.

Cordially yours,

Of membership in professional or civic organization:

Dear Mr. McMann:

Your letter of June 4 is very much appreciated. I shall be delighted to become a member of the Sales Executives' Club.

I consider it a privilege to join such an outstanding group of sales managers and consultants, and I welcome the opportunity to participate in your activities.

Since I am scheduled to leave tomorrow noon for a divisional sales conference in Wilmington, it will not be possible for me to attend the meeting next Monday. But I shall be on hand the following Monday, and regularly thereafter.

Please express to the others on your membership committee my sincere thanks for the invitation to join your group.

Cordially yours,

Dear Mr. Foley:

Your cordial invitation for me to join the American Business Writing Association pleases me very much, and I accept with pleasure.

I realize that your membership includes many recognized authorities on the subject of business writing, both in academic ranks and in business circles. I am highly complimented at the opportunity to become associated with such a group.

Sincerely yours,

Dear Mr. Cordell:

I sincerely appreciate your cordial letter of April 10, conveying the invitation of the Business Men's Club for me to become one of its members.

It is with much pleasure that I accept this invitation. I feel that it is an honor to become a member of your group, and I shall make every effort to fulfill the responsibilities that membership implies.

I shall look forward to attending the meeting next Wednesday noon.

Sincerely yours,

Of invitation to serve on civic or professional committee or board:

Dear Mr. Armstrong:

Thank you for your letter of June 15.

I shall be glad to serve on the Membership Committee of the Newspaper Men's Association during 195-. Your suggestions as to committee procedure appeal to me as being sound and practical.

I know the association with you in this work will be most enjoyable, and I am looking forward to it.

Sincerely yours,

Dear Mr. Warrick:

I appreciate your inviting me to become a member of your Committee on Civic Improvement, and I am happy to accept.

It seems to me that this committee has an important job to do, as well as a splendid opportunity to contribute materially to the progress of Northfield. I feel complimented that you wish me to participate in such a worth-while work, and I shall do my best to justify my place on the committee.

Sincerely yours,

Dear Mr. Anderson:

Thank you for your May 17 letter inviting me to serve on the Editorial Board of the American Business Writing Association during the coming year.

Your invitation pleases me very much, and I accept with pleasure. You can be sure of my best efforts to help in maintaining the high standards established by the Editorial Board in past years.

Cordially yours,

Dear Mr. Camp:

I was both pleased and complimented to receive your letter yesterday.

It will be a pleasure to serve on the Planning Committee for the "Better Burlington" campaign, and I am looking forward to a pleasant association with you and Mr. Norton in this work.

Yours sincerely,

Of resignation from position, board, or committee:

Dear Leonard:

It is with genuine regret that I accept your resignation as Assistant Sales Manager.

I appreciate the outstanding work you have done in this position for the past three years, during which I have come to have the utmost faith in your judgment. Naturally, I am sorry to see you leave us.

At the same time I can understand your feeling that the position now open to you in New York will give you an exceptional opportunity to develop a technique for which you have special talent. I am sure you will make a success of your new work, and my very best wishes go with you.

Sincerely yours,

Dear Clifford:

I regret, indeed, to receive your letter of resignation from the Editorial Board of the R. E. A. *Bulletin*.

Of course I realize that your decision was reached because of your first obligation to your business, and I know that its demands upon your time have increased materially during recent months.

All of us who have worked with you on the *Bulletin* will miss your sound counsel and your genial presence at Board meetings. I know that the others share with me a deep sense of gratitude for all you have contributed to the progress of the *Bulletin*.

Sincerely yours,

MISCELLANEOUS COURTESY LETTERS

Dear Mr. Lamont:

At its meeting yesterday the Board accepted with reluctance your resignation as Director of Special Functions, to take effect October 1.

The fine work you have done in this capacity is appreciated by every member of the Board. You have developed the scope and effectiveness of the Special Functions office to a point far in excess of our expectations when it was created five years ago.

While we shall be sorry indeed to have you leave this organization, we wish you the best of success in your new endeavor.

Yours sincerely,

———

Dear Charles:

When the Board of Directors accepted your resignation today, effective next July 1, its members expressed their deep regret that you will soon be leaving us.

You have done a splendid job as Director of Correspondence, and it will be difficult to replace you. All of us know that you have done far more than your duties required. We appreciate your excellent work, as well as the co-operation you have given the members of other departments.

Though we shall be sorry to see you go, we realize that you have been offered a fine opportunity in your special field. You will take with you our best wishes for success and happiness in your new work.

Sincerely yours,

———

My dear Jim:

You have acted as I should have done in your place.

I accept your resignation with deep regret, which I know will be shared by all my colleagues.

The loyal support you have given the national government through five strenuous years will always be remembered by those who have worked with you.

Very sincerely yours,

Dear Mr. Rollins:

It is with a great deal of regret that we accept your resignation as Educational Director, to take effect January 1, 195-.

You have done an excellent job during your three years in this position, and it had been our hope that you would remain with us permanently. Your many friends among the R. M. A. membership will be sorry to learn that you are leaving the Association.

I realize that the position you will assume the first of the year offers you a great opportunity in the educational field. You have the background and the qualifications to make an outstanding success of it. Our very best wishes will go with you.

Sincerely yours,

Of resignation from club or association:

Dear Sidney:

Your resignation from the Business Men's Club has been accepted with genuine regret. We are indeed sorry to learn that you will soon be leaving Portland.

As one of the first members of the Club, you have been identified with it for almost twelve years. During this period you have contributed much to its progress and prestige. The entire membership will miss you.

When you leave Portland, our good wishes will go with you. May you enjoy many years of success and happiness in your new work!

Sincerely,

Dear Ben:

We received your resignation from Rotary with deep regret. It has been both an honor and a pleasure to have you as a member of the Greencastle Club.

Whatever your future plans may be, we wish you the success that you so well deserve. And please remember that you have a standing invitation to visit us whenever you return to this community.

Sincerely yours,

Dear Walter:

Your letter of resignation as a member of the Elmwood Merchants Association was read at today's luncheon.

We learned with deep regret that health considerations make it necessary for you to leave Elmwood for a warmer climate. You will take with you the best wishes of every one of us.

The Association owes you a big debt of gratitude for your loyal interest during the past ten years. You have contributed much to its growth and progress.

It is our hope that life in the South will bring a quick and lasting improvement in your health. Whenever you return to Elmwood for a visit, a warm welcome will await you at the Friday luncheon.

Sincerely,

Dear Dick:

Your letter of resignation from the Columbus Kiwanis Club was read at the Board meeting this noon.

All of us will miss you, and we are extremely sorry to learn that you will soon be leaving Columbus. Your membership in the Club these past four years has made it a better organization. In every Club activity you have carried your part of the load—and more!

You have made a host of friends, Dick, and all of us wish you well as you undertake your new assignment. The best of luck to you.

Sincerely,

Letters of Declination [2]

The message declining an invitation must combine cordiality with tact. It is essential that the writer express his regret with a sincerity that carries conviction. Often the letter is strengthened by an explanation of the circumstances that prevent acceptance.

The declination should also include an expression of appreciation for the invitation. Without it, the tone of the

[2] The following section is confined to letters declining invitations. Letters declining requests are discussed and illustrated on pages 288-295.

message would be almost certain to indicate an attitude of indifference.

To be entirely effective, the letter of declination must convince its recipient that the writer was pleased to receive the invitation, and that he is genuinely regretful because other commitments or obligations make his acceptance impossible.

Specimen Letters of Declination

Of invitation to banquet, club luncheon, lecture, or entertainment:

Dear Bob:

I regret very much that a business trip to Cincinnati, scheduled for the week of October 20-26, will make it impossible for me to attend the Better Business Forum with you on the evening of the 24th.

It was fine of you to invite me, and I'd be delighted to be your guest at the Forum if I were to be in town.

Sincerely,

———

My dear Mr. Emory:

Thank you very much indeed for sending me an invitation to the dinner to be held in honor of Mr. Richard Everett at the Virginia House on October 14.

Much as I should like to be with you on that occasion, I sincerely regret that another engagement to which I am definitely committed will deprive me of that pleasure. So I hope you will hold me excused and at the same time accept my best wishes for an auspicious gathering. No one more richly deserves this tribute than the man in whose honor you are meeting.

Very sincerely yours,

———

Dear Mr. Miller:

I appreciate very much your inviting me to attend the July 28 luncheon of the Junior Chamber of Commerce as your guest. Doing so would be a pleasure and a worth-while experience, I know, and I'd like nothing better than to accept.

Unfortunately, however, I am scheduled to leave tomorrow night for the East on a ten-day business trip. Since hotel reservations and business appointments have already been made, I am now committed to a definite itinerary. But I want you to know how sincerely I regret being unable to accept your kind invitation, and I do hope you will give me another opportunity later on.

Cordially yours,

Dear Mr. Stiles:

Only this morning I accepted another invitation to be a guest at the Acceptance Banquet. This makes it impossible for me to enjoy your hospitality.

It is a pleasure, however, to know that I am going to see you during that week. Thank you for your kindness in remembering me in arranging your table.

Very sincerely yours,

Dear John:

For several weeks I have expected that you would be holding the annual Foundation banquet sometime in June, and I've been keeping my fingers crossed in the hope that I could be present.

Unfortunately, however, June 15 is out of the question for me. I'll be in Boston at that time attending a company sales conference.

My sincere thanks, nevertheless, for your gracious invitation. I hope this year's banquet will be the best yet; and under your capable guidance, I am sure it will be.

Cordially,

Of luncheon or dinner invitation:

Dear Mr. Wolfe:

I should like nothing better than to dine with you Tuesday evening, March 8, if only my train schedule would permit. But since I must be in Philadelphia the following morning, it will be necessary for me to take a late afternoon train eastward.

Your invitation is none the less appreciated, however, and I thank you most sincerely for your thoughtfulness.

Very cordially yours,

Dear Mr. Seymour:

It was gracious of you to ask me to have lunch with you in Denver next Tuesday.

I regret that a company luncheon for Argo dealers will make it impossible for me to accept your invitation, much as I should like to do so. But I thank you sincerely for your kindness, and I hope you will let me have a "rain check" on the luncheon visit with you.

Cordially yours,

Dear Carl:

The thought of recalling the "old days" with you over one of Monty's juicy steaks is a pleasant one indeed. There is no way I'd rather spend my noon hour in Reading next Friday.

But a luncheon meeting of our Executive Board has been announced for that day, which means that line of duty must prevail over personal pleasure.

I do thank you, though, for an invitation that I'd accept with delight if circumstances gave me even a fighting chance. And I'll try to stop by your office during the day with the hope of visiting with you for a little while.

Sincerely,

Dear Harold:

Your note has just arrived, and I do appreciate your inviting me to have dinner with you and Walter Nesbit at the Missouri Athletic Club next Friday evening.

Unfortunately, I must leave late this afternoon for Boston and New York, and I'll not be back in time to join you for dinner Friday evening. This I regret very much, for I remember spending a delightful evening with you and Walter when he was here three years ago.

Again my warm thanks for your invitation. Please give Walter my regards, and tell him that I am very sorry to be away during his visit.

Sincerely,

Dear Mr. Bradley:

It is very kind of you to invite me to have lunch with you on the fourteenth, and I appreciate your gracious letter.

Only yesterday, however, I agreed to make a few remarks to members of our Altoona sales staff at a luncheon to be held that day. So I shall have to forego the pleasure of lunching with you, much as I should like to accept your hospitality.

I am looking forward to a chat with you during my day in Altoona, and I shall stop at your office for a few minutes in the afternoon. Thank you again for your thoughtfulness.

Cordially yours,

Of hospitality of home or club on overnight visit:

Dear Mr. Logan:

Your gracious invitation for me to spend next weekend in your home is keenly appreciated. I only wish that my traveling program were such that I could accept.

Immediately after my talk in your city, I must catch a night train to St. Louis. There I shall make connections for Topeka, Kansas, where I am scheduled for a talk Monday afternoon.

I am sure you can imagine how welcome would be the respite of a pleasant visit in your home. Though the situation does not permit me that privilege, I thank you most sincerely for your kindness.

Cordially,

My dear Will:

I appreciate very much your invitation for me to spend the night as your guest at the Mayfair Club when I come to Spokane on May 12.

In view of this tempting inducement, I would certainly postpone my departure from Spokane until the next morning if the closely planned itinerary of my trip permitted it. Unfortunately, however,

I must be in San Francisco for a business conference at nine o'clock the following morning. This will necessitate my taking the night train from Spokane.

It was most generous of you to offer me the luxury of a comfortable night's rest, and I wish that circumstances permitted my acceptance.

Very sincerely yours,

Dear Mr. Danvers:

My sincere thanks to you for your letter of June 19. It is generous of you to extend to me the hospitality of your home.

I should like to accept your kind invitation if only circumstances permitted. It happens, however, that my stop in Sioux City next Thursday will be only four or five hours between trains, since I must be back in the office the following morning. But I am looking forward to seeing you during my stopover, and I wish the situation would allow me the pleasure of visiting in your home.

Sincerely yours,

Dear Bob:

Thanks ever so much for your letter this morning. It was fine of you to invite me to stay over in Chicago after the Law Alumni Banquet next Tuesday evening. The hospitality of your home offers a great inducement.

But I succeeded only last week in making my "get away" from the hospital, and on the condition that I would spend only an hour or two at the office each day for the next couple of weeks. It's nothing serious—just my periodic bout with stomach ulcer.

This year I'll have to pass up the Chicago trip, much as I regret doing so. But your letter was a real tonic, and I sincerely appreciate your invitation.

Cordially,

Of speaking invitation:

Dear John:

Thank you for your gracious letter of June 6. I appreciate your inviting me to speak before the ABC Club of your city on the afternoon of Tuesday, June 18.

Under normal circumstances I should gladly accept your invitation. It happens, however, that Mr. Phillips of our Chicago office is scheduled to arrive at the plant the morning of June 18 for a one-day visit, leaving the same evening for Kansas City. I know you will understand why I must be here on that day, much as I should like to spend it visiting with you and the members of your club.

It was fine of you to invite me, and if your program schedule should work out so as to give me another chance in the months ahead, I'll do my best to come.

Sincerely yours,

Dear Mr. Bell:

Your letter of March 16 reached me this morning, and I surely appreciate your invitation to speak at the University of Illinois Foundation banquet the evening of April 8.

This reply would convey a most enthusiastic acceptance if only my schedule permitted. But sales meetings in St. Louis, Kansas City, and Omaha will keep me on the jump throughout the week of April 6-11.

Though I know you will understand the circumstances, I am extremely sorry they will prevent my coming over to Urbana. Thanks again for sending me such a cordial invitation.

Best personal regards to you.

Sincerely,

Dear Bill:

Your letter was a pleasant surprise because it has been quite a while since we have seen each other. But through our mutual friends I know of the fine work you are doing.

You know how everything seems to happen at once. On checking my schedule for January 14, I find that I am to make a special report to the Board of Directors that day. So it will be impossible for me to address the weekly luncheon of the Tulsa Merchants' Club.

Will you give me a "rain check" on the invitation so that I may speak to your organization and enjoy a visit with you sometime in the future? Many thanks for your welcome letter.

Sincerely yours,

Dear Mr. Roberts:

It was good to hear from you this morning, and to learn that the Toledo Merchants Association is completing another successful year.

I appreciate your inviting me to speak at the Business Forum to be sponsored by the Association on November 25. This is an invitation I should like very much to accept, for I share many interests with the members of your group. But I am scheduled to speak at a businessmen's luncheon in St. Louis on that date, and it would not be possible to reach Toledo in time for your afternoon meeting.

Again my thanks for your cordial invitation. Best wishes for many more years of success in your work with the Association.

Sincerely yours,

———

Dear Mr. Myles: [3]

This is a difficult letter for me to write, since I know that it can only result in inconvenience to you.

Two days ago Mrs. Dunn was suddenly taken ill. This morning the local doctors told me it would be necessary to take her to the Mayo Clinic as quickly as possible. My doing this, of course, will make it impossible for me to speak before your organization next Thursday noon as I had intended.

Much as I regret to put you to the inconvenience of arranging for another speaker, I feel there is no alternative under the circumstances, and I am sure you will understand. I am indeed sorry that I cannot be with you as planned, and I hope that other arrangements can still be made without difficulty.

Sincerely yours,

———

Dear Mr. Higdon:

It was good of you to invite me to give the commencement address at Middlebury High School. Visiting your school would be a pleasure, for I have heard a lot about its progressive methods and outstanding program.

But a quick glance at my calendar tells me that I am already booked for the evening of May 28 at the Chamber of Commerce rally in Little Rock.

[3] The following letter cancels a speaking engagement that had been previously accepted.

I appreciate your thinking of me, and I hope that you will keep me in mind for future occasions.

On your next visit to Norman be sure to stop at my office for a visit.

Sincerely yours,

Of invitation to attend meeting or convention:

Dear Harvey:

Thank you for your letter of February 18. Your outline of plans for the annual convention of the Iowa Retailers Association makes me want very much to attend.

But I left the hospital only a few days ago after major surgery, and it appears that the Cedar Rapids trip is out of the question. It will be a real disappointment to miss the convention, as well as the opportunity for a visit with you and other friends.

You have arranged a splendid program, and I am sure the 195-convention will be one of the best the Association has ever had.

Sincerely yours,

Dear Mr. Cunningham:

Thank you for your letter of April 10, inviting me to attend the spring meeting of the University of Illinois Citizens Committee on May 6.

I am sincerely sorry that business commitments in the East will make it impossible for me to be present. Otherwise this letter would be an enthusiastic acceptance.

Best wishes for a highly successful meeting. The program as outlined in your letter is unusually attractive, and I am sure you will have a large turnout.

Cordial personal regards to you.

Sincerely,

Dear Mr. Welch:

Thank you for inviting me to attend the meeting of the Southern Business Writing Association in Atlanta on April 17-18.

I regret very much that engagements here on those days will prevent my attending the Atlanta meeting. From reading the program you so thoughtfully sent me, I can see that you have an excellent group of speakers, and I hope you will have the best attendance in the history of the Association.

Again my thanks for your cordial letter.

Sincerely yours,

Dear Frank:

Thank you for your letter of October 3, inviting me to attend the next meeting of the Foundation Board of Directors.

I am extremely sorry that an all-day sales conference here on October 25 will prevent my coming to Champaign for the Board meeting that afternoon.

The order of business indicates an unusually interesting session, and I should like very much to be present for it. Please express my regrets to the others.

Cordially,

Of membership in professional or civic organization:

Dear Mr. Haskell:

I consider it a high compliment to be invited to join the Professional Men's Club. Thank you sincerely for your letter.

Just now, however, my work requires that I spend about two weeks of each month in the Omaha office. Any consistent participation in club activities on my part would therefore be impossible.

In view of this situation, I do not feel that it would be advisable, or entirely fair to the members of your organization, for me to undertake the responsibilities of membership. I know you will fully understand the basis of this conclusion.

Thank you again for your kind letter. Please convey my deep appreciation to members of the club.

Very sincerely yours,

Dear Mr. Malone:

It would be a pleasure to become associated with your splendid organization, and I sincerely appreciate your courtesy in inviting me.

Unfortunately, however, I am compelled for reasons of health to leave next week for Florida, where I expect to remain through most of the winter. I regret exceedingly that these plans will deprive me of the pleasure of joining the University Club at this time.

I want you and the other members to know, however, that I am deeply grateful for your kindness.

Very sincerely yours,

Dear Mr. Geary:

Please accept my sincere thanks for your note of August 27, inviting me to become a member of the Kiwanis Club. There is no group of men with whom I would rather be associated.

Because of the nature of my work, however, I must be out of town a large part of the time. It would therefore be impossible for me to attend meetings with any regularity. Since I realize that membership in the Kiwanis Club carries with it both privileges and responsibilities, I do not feel justified in enjoying the former without being in a position to fulfill the latter.

I want you and your fellow members to know, however, that I feel highly complimented at your invitation, and that I am most appreciative of it.

Sincerely yours,

Of invitation to serve on civic or professional committee or board:

Dear Mr. Dillingham:

I consider it a compliment that you have asked me to serve on the Editorial Board of the *Journal of Economics*. Thank you for including me in your plans for the coming year.

Recently, however, my work has been materially increased because of the absence of a member of our department, who is in Washington doing special work for the government. I feel, therefore, that it would be both unwise and unfair for me to accept a post to which I cannot devote my full share of attention.

But I want you to know that your invitation is deeply appreciated, and that I shall be happy to hear from you if there is any way in which I can co-operate with you and your Board.

Sincerely yours,

Dear Herbert:

I appreciate very much your letter inviting me to serve on the Christmas Fund Committee, although I am frank to say that it places me in a difficult position.

I realize the fine work that is done each year through the Christmas Fund, and the thought of having an active part in it appeals to me strongly. On the other hand, the Christmas season is the busiest of the entire year in my business, and I know from past experience that the next month will find me working nights and Sundays.

As a result, the time I could devote to the work of the committee would be far short of the amount necessary to carry my full part of the load. So I feel that my acceptance would actually work a hardship on the other members.

If you will be good enough to excuse me in view of these circumstances, and give me an opportunity to do an equivalent amount of work in some Chamber of Commerce activity that comes at another time, I shall appreciate both your understanding and your co-operation.

Sincerely,

My dear Mr. Cavanaugh:

Thank you for your kind letter of March 6, in which you invite me to become a member of your Committee on Professional Standards in Advertising.

I should like very much to be in a position to do as you wish. Unfortunately, however, my present business duties will not permit me to give such an undertaking the time and consideration it deserves; and I have always made it a policy to refrain from association with any project to which I cannot devote a worth-while measure of personal attention.

Nevertheless, I want you to know that your invitation is much appreciated, and that you and your associates have my very best wishes.

Yours sincerely,

Letters of Apology

A situation arises now and then that calls for a note of apology. When forgetfulness, procrastination, or some unavoidable factor results in a seeming discourtesy, a sincere, straightforward letter of apology will often restore the writer to the good graces of the recipient.

Regardless of the circumstances, any situation that occasions a letter of apology requires a tone of warmth and friendliness. When the letter deals with an incident for which there is an adequate and convincing explanation, a few words can well be devoted to this explanation. If no such justification exists, a frank admission of that fact usually has a disarming effect upon the reader.

Specimen Letters of Apology

For delay in returning borrowed property:

Dear Mr. Fowler:

In returning your bound volume of Dineen Business Reports, I want to express to you both my thanks and my apologies.

I am afraid the length of time I have kept this material is nothing short of disgraceful, but my study of the reports has been interrupted frequently, and I finished reading them only last night.

It was generous of you to make this information available to me, and I do hope you have not been inconvenienced by the delay in their return.

Sincerely yours,

Dear Peter:

Probably you will be just as surprised to get your book back as I was to discover I hadn't returned it.

Thank you again for sending it over to me when I was laid up. It gave me several hours of most enjoyable reading. And please forgive my tardiness in returning it.

Sincerely,

Dear Mr. Gould:

It was generous of you to let me borrow your folder of information on inactive-account solicitations, and I am ashamed to be so slow in returning it.

I have read this material with much interest, and I have profited largely from it. Please accept both my thanks for your generosity and my sincere apology for having kept your folder so long.

Cordially yours,

Dear Mr. Huntington:

In thanking you for sending me the enclosed summary of last month's Sales Management Convention, I wish also to apologize for having kept it so long. I hope that my tardiness in returning it has not inconvenienced you.

I enjoyed looking over the summary, which made me wish all the more that I could have attended the meeting. Thanks again for your thoughtfulness in sending it.

Sincerely yours,

For delay in acknowledging favor or courtesy:

Dear Mr. Goodman:

This is a letter I intended to write weeks ago, and I apologize to you for its tardy arrival.

I really did appreciate the generous assistance you gave me when I stopped in Little Rock, and I fully expected to write you upon my return to Indianapolis. Upon reaching the office, however, I discovered that I must leave immediately for Pittsburgh. Within a few hours I was on an east-bound train, and I returned from this second jaunt only last night.

I hope you will give me an opportunity to return your kindness whenever there is some way in which I can be of assistance to you.

The help you gave me in Little Rock saved me a great deal of time and effort, and I shall not forget it.

Sincerely yours,

Dear Will:

I am ashamed to think how long it has been since you sent me those samples of your promotional mailings. I had intended to examine them at once and then write you about them, but a ten-day tussle with the flu prevented my doing either until a few days ago.

It seems to me that you are doing a remarkably fine promotional job by mail. Each piece is splendidly adapted to its particular purpose, and I can readily see why the results of your efforts have been so gratifying.

I know you went to a lot of trouble in sending me both the samples and the sales data that accompanied them. Despite this long-delayed acknowledgment, I do appreciate your generosity in letting me have this material for my files. It will be the subject of further study as soon as time permits.

Sincerely,

Dear Mr. Norton:

Forgive me for not answering more promptly your gracious letter of November 4.

It happens that, since the afternoon I spent so pleasantly with you and your associates discussing the subject of "Employer-Employee Relations," I have been constantly engaged in that practical problem myself. Reply to your letter has been delayed because I have been in Detroit most of the time since it came.

I appreciate your thoughtfulness in writing to me, and I thank you most sincerely for your kind remarks.

Cordially yours,

Dear Mr. Dodge:

For weeks I have intended to thank you for your kindness in writing Mr. George Tinker about my stay in Sacramento. Meeting him was a most enjoyable experience, and he did a lot to make my visit there enjoyable.

I appreciate the thoughtful courtesy on your part far more than the date of this letter might indicate. Please accept my apology for what must have appeared as ingratitude. Since returning to the office two weeks ago, I have spent more than half of the time in bed with tonsilitis, and only now am I catching up with my personal correspondence.

Yours sincerely,

Dear Arthur:

I have long intended to thank you for writing me about Paul Millard's article on installment selling in *Business Trends* for November. I profited much from reading it; moreover, if you had not called my attention to it, the chances are that I would not have seen it at all.

Please accept my apology for this belated expression of thanks. It was thoughtful of you to tell me about the Millard article.

Cordially,

For delay in sending promised material:

Dear Mr. Richards:

When I wrote you on August 12 that you would receive sample copies of our credit-promotion mailings within a few days, I did so with the best of intentions.

Naturally, I was embarrassed to discover this morning that this material had not yet been mailed. Please accept my apology for the delay.

The credit-promotion samples are being sent you today in a separate wrapper. They should reach you very shortly, and I hope you will find them useful in your work.

Cordially yours,

Dear Mr. Johnson:

I am sorry it has taken me so long to get together the material on letterhead design, which I promised to send you several weeks ago.

An unexpected field trip through New England took me away from the office for almost two weeks, and I returned to find my desk stacked with correspondence to be answered as quickly as possible. As a result, last weekend was my first opportunity to get the letterhead items together, and I am sending them this morning in a separate package. I do hope you have not been seriously inconvenienced by the delay.

Please let me know if there is any other way in which I can cooperate with you, and I shall try to do so more promptly next time.

Sincerely yours,

Dear Mr. Emley:

I am ever so sorry we overlooked sending you the catalog you requested.

When I passed the carbon copy of my acknowledgment of your letter along to my stenographer with instructions to mail the catalog, she inadvertently filed the letter without sending the catalog. You don't know how sorry both of us are.

I am sending a catalog with this letter, and I hope you will find just what you want in it.

Sincerely yours,

Dear Mr. Wayland:

During our visit in your office a couple of weeks ago, I promised to send you our booklet entitled "Courtesy Wins Customers." Upon returning to Dayton I discovered that the supply was exhausted, and that a reprinting was under way.

When the new stock of booklets reached us this morning, several copies were mailed to you in a separate container. I regret this unavoidable delay, and I hope the material will measure up to your expectations.

Cordially yours,

Dear Arthur:

Here are copies of the collection letters that we talked about last week at the Detroit convention. They should have been on the way to you several days ago, but a heavy accumulation of work during my absence has kept me hopping all week.

I am sorry about the delay, and hope it has not inconvenienced you. If I can co-operate in any other way, please call on me.

Cordially,

For absence from meeting:

Dear Mr. Morton:

I hope you will accept a sincere apology for my absence from the Credit Association meeting yesterday afternoon.

When I told you earlier in the week that I planned to be there, I fully intended to be. But a meeting of our own credit department staff yesterday afternoon lasted much longer than expected, and it was quite impossible for me to get away.

When I see Jim Davis at lunch tomorrow, I shall ask him to bring me up to date on yesterday's developments.

Sincerely yours,

Dear Mac:

I was sorry to miss last night's meeting of the Finance Committee, and this note brings you my sincere apology.

As you know, I have been in the Southwest on business throughout the past week. I had expected to return to Chicago at noon yesterday. But my work in Dallas required an extra day, and I did not get back home until noon today.

You can depend on me to be present at the next meeting. I'll try hard to pull my weight in the boat from now on.

Sincerely,

Dear Mr. Robbins:

I certainly owe you an apology for my absence from the meeting of your committee yesterday afternoon.

To be quite honest about it, the meeting slipped my mind completely and I did not think of it until last night. I am sorry to make such a poor showing at the committee's first meeting, and I'll do my best to make up for it in the future.

Sincerely yours,

Dear Mr. Dixon:

I regretted missing last night's meeting of the Chamber of Commerce Directors, at which I had fully expected to be present.

Returning from Portland on the evening train, which was scheduled to arrive at 7:25 P.M., I had supposed the margin of time would be ample for me to reach the Board meeting. But the train was more than two hours late.

I wanted you to know that my absence was caused by a situation over which I had no control, and that I was very sorry to miss the meeting.

Sincerely yours,

For inability to keep appointment:

Dear Mr. Hampton:

I sincerely regret that my secretary had to telephone you about the postponement of our conference yesterday.

A transportation tie-up at our Akron plant made it necessary for me to drive over there on very short notice, and I hope you will be generous enough to understand the unavoidable nature of the situation.

If you can come to the office conveniently any time Wednesday or Thursday, I shall be glad to see you and to be of assistance in any way possible.

Yours sincerely,

Dear Mr. Long:

During the past year I have been absent from the office only two days because of illness. I regret that one of them had to be the day for which our conference was planned, and I hope the change in your program for the day did not incommode you too much.

Would it be convenient for you to come over either next Thursday or Friday morning at ten? I should be happy to see you on either day, and this time I shall try to elude the flu germ that played havoc with our plans last week.

Sincerely yours,

Dear Mr. McFadden:

Please accept my sincere apology for the inconvenience I caused you yesterday.

When I suggested over the telephone that you come out at four o'clock, I fully expected to be back in the office by that time. But a Board of Directors meeting at the plant lasted until almost four, and I was delayed by heavy traffic on my way back to the office. Upon my arrival Miss Preston said you had just left to catch a train back to Joliet.

Please let me know the next time you plan to be in Chicago, and do give me a chance to make amends. I shall be glad to meet you either at my office or in the Loop.

Sincerely yours,

Dear Mr. Harris:

I regret that I was out of the office when you called yesterday. Having told you the other day that I would be in all week, I feel that an apology is due you.

Quite unexpectedly I was called over to the plant to help straighten out a shipping mix-up, and I was away for some two hours. I am sorry that you were inconvenienced as a result, and I do hope you will drop in during the next day or two.

Cordially yours,

Letters of Regret

The note of regret deals with a situation that has developed through no fault of either the writer or his reader. It expresses disappointment and regret that adverse circumstances have prevented some occasion that would have brought pleasure to both. Often, too, it expresses hope that the occasion will still materialize at some later time.

The spirit of the letter should be that of cordiality and friendliness. Through sincerity of tone, the letter should make its recipient feel that any chagrin or disappointment on his part is shared equally by the writer. Such a letter is a manifestation of courtesy that often serves to strengthen a personal relationship even in the face of unfortunate circumstances.

Specimen Letters of Regret

For absence during call of out-of-town visitor:

Dear Jim:

I was disappointed to learn, upon returning to the office this week, that you had been in Baltimore while I was away. It would have been good to see you, and I am sorry to have missed the chance for a visit with you.

I hope your work will bring you back this way soon, and that next time I'll be in town. In fact, why not send me a word when you are planning another trip southward, and we'll try to get together for lunch or dinner at the Oriole Club.

Sincerely,

My dear Whitcomb:

When I returned to the office this morning, I was much disappointed to learn that my three-day illness with the flu had made me lose out on a visit with you. Our attempts to make connections have certainly been ill-fated these past several months.

Do you plan to come through Detroit again during the summer? If so, please try to include a stopover here. If the Detroit Tigers are playing at home, we'll go out to see them unless you would prefer to play golf.

Most cordial personal regards to you.

Sincerely yours,

Dear Mr. Ashton:

I am sorry, indeed, that I missed seeing you when you were in Lincoln recently. As my secretary probably told you, I was in Colorado on my vacation.

It was nice of you to stop at the office to see me, and I hope you will do so again the next time you are here. It has been a long time since we have had an opportunity to visit together, and I shall hope to see you the next time you come west.

Sincerely yours,

Dear Mark:

I really felt cheated this morning when my secretary told me of your call yesterday. It would have been good to see you, and I am sorry we missed connections.

Here's hoping your new work is going very well, and that it will bring you to Chicago again within a few months. I shall hope for a good visit with you the next time you come this way.

Cordially,

Dear Willis:

Upon returning to the office this morning from a ten-day vacation in Michigan, I learned that you had called to see me last week. I am extremely sorry to have missed a visit with you.

Please let me know when you plan to be in St. Louis again, so we can arrange to have lunch together. Many months have passed since our last visit, and we have a lot to talk about.

Thanks for stopping when you were in town last week. I hope you will be coming this way again soon.

Sincerely,

For inability to call upon associate during visit to his city:

Dear Mr. Engles:

It was a real disappointment not to see you during my all-too-brief visit to Los Angeles last week.

I had fully expected to call at your office, and would certainly have done so if my stay had not been cut short after I had been in Los Angeles only two days. I had intended to spend a week there, but an unavoidable change in my business appointments in San Francisco required a sudden and complete revision of plans.

It now looks as if I would be on the West Coast again within a few months. In this case several days will be spent in Los Angeles, and I shall call at your office with the hope of having that long-expected visit with you.

Cordially yours,

Dear Mr. Updike:

The one disappointment of a very strenuous trip to your city was that I did not have an opportunity to see you. I had fully intended to give myself the pleasure of calling on you, and several times I included it in my daily program.

Unfortunately, unexpected developments prevented my making even a single call. I hope you will forgive me for this seeming discourtesy, and I assure you my disappointment was great.

I trust, however, that the pleasure is only deferred, and that I shall see you shortly either here or in New York.

Yours sincerely,

Dear Mr. Dumond:

I regretted not seeing you on my way through Chicago last week, for I had counted on dropping in for a chat with you at your office.

My train from Kansas City was very late into Chicago, and an expected stopover of several hours was cut to fifty minutes. As it turned out, I had barely time to get from one station to another and to make final arrangements about my sleeper space to New York.

Next time I hope to be more fortunate. You may be sure I shall call at your office for a visit the first time circumstances permit.

Sincerely yours,

For inability of associate to call at office as planned:

Dear Mr. Markham:

I was sorry to learn from your letter this morning that you have had to postpone your trip to Nashville. The prospect of a visit with you was a very pleasant one, and I was looking forward to it.

It is my sincere hope, however, that your trip will materialize before the end of the year, and that I may then have the pleasure of seeing you.

Cordially yours,

My dear Mr. Henderson:

Thank you for your letter of March 24, which reached me this morning.

I was sorry not to see you during your recent business trip to Boston. But I can well understand how your good resolutions were nullified by insistent demands in connection with your business.

Next time I hope we shall have an opportunity to lunch or dine together. It has been a long time since our last meeting in St. Louis, and I should be happy to renew the very pleasant association with you.

Cordially yours,

Dear Mr. Rogers:

It was a disappointment not to see you on your recent trip to New York, and I was particularly sorry to learn that your visit here was cut short by the sudden illness of Mrs. Rogers.

I know how relieved you are now that she has safely passed the crisis, and I am very glad she is on the road to recovery. As for our visit, I hope that it has only been postponed for a few weeks, and that you will plan to have luncheon or dinner with me the next time you come east.

Cordially yours,

For absence of associate from meeting or convention:

Dear Mr. Mossman:

I had hoped to see you at the Southwestern Bankers' Association meeting in Dallas last weekend, and I was genuinely disappointed that you were unable to be present.

The meeting was quite successful, I believe, and unusually well attended, but we missed your genial presence and your sound counsel on matters of Association policy.

I hope that you will allow time to lunch with me at the Alamo Club when you next come through Houston.

Cordially,

Dear John:

It was a real disappointment not to see you at the Boston convention of the N.R.C.A. at the Statler last week. I asked Harold Evans if you were registered at another hotel, and he told me that illness had prevented your making the trip.

I hope you are fully recovered by now, and that you are planning to attend the district meeting in Louisville next month. Perhaps we can have lunch or dinner together during the convention.

Sincerely,

Dear Charles:

I was very sorry to learn from your letter of November 6 that you will not be with us at the M.A.R. convention in Detroit next week.

Since you and I drew exactly the same committee assignments, I shall be glad to send you a brief report, upon my return, of what decisions were reached in the committee sessions.

An M.A.R. convention will not seem quite the same without you, and I know we shall all miss you.

Cordially,

Dear Fred:

I was indeed sorry that last-minute developments prevented your attending the meeting of the Southern Credit Men's Association in Birmingham last week.

One of the things to which I had looked forward was a session with you, and I was disappointed in not seeing you. I shall hope to make connections with you on my next trip to Atlanta. Meanwhile, please let me know if your plans include a stop in Chattanooga.

Sincerely,

Letters Explaining Delayed Action

There are times when definite action upon an inquiry or request cannot be taken immediately. Perhaps the granting of a request for information or material will require the expenditure of considerable time on the part of the addressee, thus making immediate compliance impossible. Sometimes, too, an inquiry arrives while the addressee is ill or out of town.

In such cases an immediate note of acknowledgment is a business courtesy. It lets the reader know that his request will receive careful attention, and that he may expect a detailed reply as soon as circumstances permit. If the request is personally acknowledged by its recipient, the reply usually explains the reason for the delay and indicates approximately how long it will be. If the acknowledgment is written by a secretary in the absence of the addressee, it is usually noncommittal, merely stating the date upon which the intended recipient will return, and assuring the reader of prompt attention to his message at that time.

Specimen Letters Explaining Delayed Action

Requesting additional time in which to make final reply:

Dear Frank:

Your letter of March 20 has just arrived, and I was glad to hear that your work is going well.

I shall be happy to prepare the figures you want, and to get them off to you as quickly as possible. Doing so will take me some little time, however, and it may be four or five days before I can complete the tabulations. At any event, you may expect to hear further from me within a week.

If there is any other way in which I can co-operate, please feel free to call on me.

Cordially,

Dear Mr. Hanley:

Your letter of February 18 has been read with much interest.

I shall be glad to send you whatever information I have on mailing-list testing that is relevant to your problem. You are quite right that I have been interested in this aspect of promotional work for some time, and I have accumulated a considerable amount of material.

It happens that I must leave this evening on a business trip to Boston and Providence, and I shall be away from the office for the next three or four days. As soon as I return, I shall check over the mailing-list material and send you anything that I think may prove helpful.

Very cordially yours,

Dear Bill:

Just a short note to tell you that I have received your letter of April 24. May I have a few days to think this over?

You will hear from me further within the week, and I hope it will be possible for me to be helpful to you.

Sincerely yours,

Dear Mr. Jordan:

I was glad to receive your letter of October 2.

It will be a pleasure to co-operate with you, and I shall look through my files within a few days and pick out any examples of special-event announcements that I think might be of interest to you.

At the moment I am working almost feverishly on a sales report that must be ready for a Board meeting day after tomorrow. I know, therefore, that you will let me have a few days to collect the material in which you are interested.

Your project sounds like a thoroughly worth-while one, and I wish you every success with it.

Cordially yours,

Dear Mr. Shelley:

Your letter of December 2 has reached me just as I am preparing to leave for the East on a ten-day business trip.

I shall be very glad to compile the information you wish, and to send it to you within a very few days after my return to the office.

The opportunity to be helpful to you is most welcome, and I hope the unavoidable delay will not cause you any inconvenience.

Cordially,

Dear Mr. Donnelly:

It was a pleasure to hear from you this morning. I shall be glad to send you the summaries requested in your letter of October 7.

It will take a few days to make up this material, but the summaries will be on the way to you by the end of the week. You can expect to receive them not later than October 15.

If your eastern trip next January brings you through Cleveland, I shall look forward to a visit with you.

Sincerely yours,

Acknowledgment by secretary in absence of addressee:

Dear Mr. Wales:

Your letter of March 17 finds Mr. Gleason out of town on a short business trip. He will return to the office on or about March 24, and I am sure you will hear from him shortly thereafter.

Very sincerely yours,

Dear Mr. Greenwood:

Mr. Conley left last week for the East, and he will be away until April 20. When he returns on that date, I shall see that your letter of April 12 comes to his attention immediately.

Very truly yours,

Dear Mr. Cantrell:

Your June 23 letter to Mr. Farber reached his office this morning.

For the past several days Mr. Farber has been confined to his home because of illness, and he is not expected back at his desk until the first of next week. Your letter will be handed to him immediately upon his return.

Very truly yours,

Dear Mr. Stanleigh:

In the absence of Mr. Smith I am acknowledging the arrival of your letter of July 10. It is being held for his attention upon his return early next week.

Very truly yours,

Dear Mr. Conklin:

Your letter of July 23 to Mr. Dyckes has arrived during his absence from the office on his vacation. It will be placed on his desk for attention when he returns next Monday, July 28.

Yours sincerely,

Dear Mr. McIntire:

Your letter of September 8 was received just a few hours after Mr. Henderson's departure for a business engagement in New York.

He is expected back in the office September 15, at which time your letter will be brought to his attention. I am sure you will hear from him within a few days after his return.

Yours sincerely,

Dear Mr. Pendleton:

Your letter of September 23 arrived the day after Mr. Tauber left on a two-week selling trip. Since it does not appear to require an immediate reply, I shall hold it for his attention upon his return.

Very truly yours,

Dear Mr. Inman:

Your letter of August 17 to Mr. John Avery arrived this morning.

Mr. Avery will be away from the office all this week attending a meeting in Los Angeles. I shall see that your letter reaches him on the morning of his return, Monday, August 27.

Sincerely yours,

Letters Granting Requests

Any letter granting a request constitutes a splendid opportunity to build good will. The letter conveys good news to the reader. If it does so with cordiality and enthusiasm, it is sure to stimulate a friendly reaction on the part of its recipient. By granting a request as if it were a pleasure, the writer places his reader at ease and makes him feel that the request was welcomed.

Because of the favorable effect of a gracious message granting a favor or other request, it is often advisable to write such a letter even when the situation does not require a written reply. For example, a request for a printed folder or booklet can be granted by simply mailing the article specified. But a friendly acknowledgment, expressing pleasure in granting the request, will personalize the contact and win a friend.

Specimen Letters Granting Requests

For information: [4]

Dear Mr. Lindstrom:

I am glad to give you the information requested in your note of March 3.

The chart I mentioned to you last week is known as the Correspondence Efficiency Chart. I am sure you can obtain one by writing to Amos & Bryant, Inc., 75 East Almer Street, New Orleans, Louisiana. The chart was apparently formulated by this concern, which uses it for advertising purposes.

The other day I saw a similar chart, which came to me in a promotional mailing from the Rulow Envelope Company. I am enclosing it with the thought that it may be of interest to you.

Sincerely yours,

Dear Mr. Dennis:

Your letter of May 15 was most welcome. Thank you for your interest in my recent talk on "Financing Higher Education in Private Colleges."

The figures on present tuition fees of twelve colleges, compared with those of the same institutions twenty years ago, are shown in the table on the attached sheet. It is a pleasure to send you this information.

Perhaps you have read John Hopwood's article, "Alumni Must Help Pay the Bills," in the September issue of *Modern Education*. If you have not seen this article, I believe you will be interested in looking it up.

Cordially yours,

---

[4] Letter specimens presented on pages 274 and 275 also grant requests for information, but explain that there will be some delay before it can be supplied.

Dear Mr. Dudley:

I have read with interest your letter of July 23. The problem you are facing is much like one that confronted us a year or so ago.

The distribution of territory among our sixteen traveling salesmen is shown on the enclosed chart map, which also lists each territory in terms of square miles and total population. Please do not bother to return this map; perhaps you will wish to place it in your file.

If there is any other aspect of our experience with territorial division that might be of interest to you, please let me know and I shall do my best to be of assistance.

Sincerely yours,

Dear Mr. McCarthy:

It is a pleasure to send you the information requested in your letter of October 11.

The enclosed promotional pieces outline the objectives of our annual-gift fund, which was established at the beginning of the current calendar year. Thus far 4,266 gifts have been recorded, and we hope to reach the 5,000 mark by the end of the year. Four solicitation pieces have been used to date; a fifth is planned for late November.

As your new program gets under way, feel free to call on us if we can co-operate in any way.

Sincerely yours,

Dear Mr. Boardman:

I am glad to send you the address of Barton & Green, Inc. Their central office is located at 314 Fifth Avenue, New York City; their warehouse address is 211 Varick Street, New York City.

If there is any other way in which I can co-operate as your project develops, by all means let me know.

Cordially yours,

Dear Mr. Warner:

You are most welcome to the information requested in your letter of April 2.

The tables on the attached page show the fund records of ten outstanding small colleges for the past calendar year. The first table indicates the number and percentage of alumni contributors to each fund. The second shows the total amount contributed to each institution.

It is a pleasure to supply these statistics, and I hope they will be helpful to you.

Sincerely yours,

For booklet, pamphlet, or magazine:

Dear Mr. Laughlin:

Thank you for your interest in the booklet entitled "The Direct-Mail Route to Better Business"—a road map to results by mail.

Your copy of this booklet is being mailed today. It will serve as a convenient reference whenever you have a direct-mail need.

We hope you'll enjoy reading it, and that it will be helpful in any direct-mail planning you may have to do.

Cordially yours,

Dear Mr. Stovall:

Enclosed is a copy of our pamphlet entitled "High Sales Records with Low-Pressure Selling." Thank you for requesting it.

This simplified approach to selling problems has attracted widespread attention and praise from sales experts. Thus far more than 200,000 copies have been distributed.

We are glad to send you this pamphlet, and we hope you will find it useful.

Sincerely yours,

Dear Mr. Vickers:

Thank you for your interesting letter of January 18.

It is a pleasure to add the name of your organization to the complimentary mailing list of *The Eagle Magazine.* We are happy to learn that members of your staff will find it helpful.

I am sending you copies of the two most recent issues of the magazine, so that you will have the complete set for 195-.

Cordially yours,

Dear Mr. Milliken:

We are glad to send you with our compliments the booklet, "A Dozen Ways to Build Business." Your copy is being mailed today in a separate folder.

Your interest in this publication is appreciated, and we hope the booklet will prove useful to you.

Cordially yours,

Dear Mr. Andrews:

It pleases us to learn that you have found helpful material in *The Credit Review*, and we are happy to grant your request for a copy of the July issue.

We believe you will also be interested in the content of the magazine for August. Two of its feature articles are "Scientific Credit Investigation Reduces Bad Debts" and "Taking the Sting out of Collection Letters."

Copies of *The Credit Review* for both July and August will be mailed to you today with our compliments. They should reach you in three or four days.

Sincerely yours,

Dear Bob:

It's a pleasure to send you the booklet containing our Annual Fund Report, as requested in your letter of January 12. I am mailing it to you today in a separate envelope, accompanied by the folder announcing our 195- campaign.

You have done so much to co-operate with me that I welcome the opportunity to reciprocate even in this small way.

Cordially,

For business appointment:

Dear Mr. Boyd:

I shall be happy to talk with you when you are in Minneapolis next week. Would it be convenient for you to come to my office at ten o'clock Thursday morning, November 5? I believe this hour would give us the best opportunity to discuss your project without interruption.

It will be a pleasure to see you again.

Cordially yours,

Dear Mr. Garrison:

I was glad to learn from your note today that you will be in Champaign next Wednesday morning, October 26.

Since your time here will be so short, perhaps you would prefer to come directly to my office upon your arrival in town at 9:45 A.M. Unless I hear further from you, I shall be looking for you about ten o'clock.

It will be a pleasure to talk with you about your Development Fund plans, and to be of assistance in any way possible.

Sincerely yours,

Dear Mr. Field:

Thank you for your letter of January 20, telling me that you are planning to be in Tulsa next Thursday morning, January 27.

I expect to be in the office throughout the morning, and shall be glad to see you at any time convenient for you.

Cordially yours,

Dear Mr. Simmons:

Thank you for your note of April 16.

The hour you suggest—3 P.M. on Monday, April 27—is an ideal time for our conference. Both the copy and art work will be ready, and I shall look forward to seeing you then.

Cordially yours,

Dear Mr. Needham:

Your letter of June 17 has just reached me.

It will be a pleasure to see you when you are in Seattle on Thursday, July 6. I expect to be in the office throughout the day. If it is equally convenient for you, perhaps the afternoon would give us the best opportunity to talk. A staff conference is scheduled for 10 A.M. on that day, and it will probably continue until noon.

If your afternoon hours are already committed to other appointments, however, I shall be glad to see you between 9 and 10 A.M.

Cordially yours,

Dear Mr. Hartnett:

Thank you for your letter of November 10, which reached me this morning.

I shall be in the office all afternoon Friday, November 28, and it will be a real pleasure to see you. Please come in at the time most convenient for you.

Cordially yours,

Dear Mr. Burton:

Thank you for your letter of October 14.

I shall be glad to see you when you are in Lincoln on November 8. If you will telephone me upon your arrival that morning, we can arrange a time for our visit.

Meeting you will be a real pleasure, and I shall be looking forward to it.

Cordially yours,

Dear John:

Your letter has just reached me, and I am glad to learn that you will be in Champaign on Thursday, September 16.

I shall be in the office that day, and it will be a pleasure to see you at two o'clock—the time you suggest. If your drive over here should take a little longer than you expect, don't be concerned about our appointment. I'll be at my desk all afternoon.

Cordially,

For permission to reprint material in book or article:

Dear Mr. Butler:

We are glad to grant permission for you to include in your new book on credit correspondence the three Burdine letters that you submitted to us with your letter of November 16. We feel highly complimented to be represented in this publication.

It will be a pleasure to co-operate with you further in this project or in any other endeavor in the future.

Cordially yours,

Dear Mr. Smithers:

I feel complimented that you consider some of my remarks before the retail merchants' meeting worthy of quotation in your forthcoming article.

Enclosed is a copy of my talk exactly as I gave it at the Milwaukee meeting. By all means feel free to use any excerpts that appeal to you.

I have enjoyed your series of articles in *Retail Store Management,* and I shall look forward to reading the one on which you are now working.

Cordially yours,

Dear Mr. Baker:

You are welcome to use the "Letter Analysis Check List" about which you wrote me June 6. Thank you for your courtesy in asking about it.

I hope you are making steady progress in preparing the correspondence handbook for your firm. It's a big job, but it will prove well worth the time and effort involved.

If I can co-operate in any other way, please let me know.

Sincerely yours,

Dear Mr. McDougal:

We are happy to grant you permission to reprint in your forthcoming book the excerpts from "Better Public-Relations Methods" that you recently submitted to us.

The credit acknowledgment you propose to use will be entirely satisfactory. We appreciate your mention of our booklet as the source of this material.

Sincere best wishes to you for the success of your book.

Cordially yours,

Dear Mr. Hillis:

When I returned to the office this morning from Chicago, your cordial letter of April 12 was waiting for me.

I am glad you have found something in *Credit and Collection Letters* that you think will be of interest to your readers.

You have my personal permission to reprint the items mentioned in your letter. I feel sure the National Retail Credit Association, publishers of the volume, will also welcome the chance to co-operate with you.

Cordially yours,

Dear Miss Doris:

Thank you for your letter of November 23, outlining plans for the new edition of the *Business Executive's Handbook*.

You have my permission to reprint from *Goodwill Letters That Build Business* the examples identified in your letter. I feel complimented that you wish to include them in your new edition. The type of credit line you suggest is quite satisfactory.

It is a pleasure to co-operate with you in this way.

Cordially yours,

For charge account:

Dear Mrs. Warner:

Thank you for your letter requesting a Forman charge account. Your account is now fully established, and we welcome most heartily this opportunity of broadening our service to you.

When you have a convenient moment, please fill out and return the enclosed card for our permanent files. A business-reply envelope is provided.

It will be a real pleasure to serve you as a charge patron. We shall try to make your account an avenue to greater enjoyment of Forman's.

Sincerely yours,

Dear Mrs. Cushman:

Thank you for giving us an opportunity to serve you as a charge patron. Your account is ready for use, bringing you the benefit and convenience of all charge privileges.

Your name is on our special announcement list, so you will receive style and sale notices from time to time.

Whenever there is any little extra service we may extend, please call on us. We want to do everything possible to make your shopping here a pleasure.

Sincerely yours,

Dear Mrs. Peters:

It is a pleasure to tell you that your Garland charge account is ready for use. We shall try to make it an ever-increasing convenience to you.

At the end of each month you will receive an itemized statement of your purchases. Payment is requested during the month following.

Perhaps you have already discovered that extra little distinctiveness and glamour about Garland fashions. That, combined with our personalized service, has made this store known as "St. Louis' Favorite Specialty Shop."

Just say "Charge it" the next time you visit us. And whenever you wish to shop by telephone, you'll enjoy the convenience of your account.

Cordially yours,

Dear Mrs. Elkins:

Thank you for requesting a Hillman charge account. We appreciate this expression of your friendship and confidence.

Your account is ready for use the next time you visit the store.

We'll do our best to make it a genuine satisfaction to you in shopping here.

Statements are mailed the last of each month, and payment will be appreciated during the month following.

As a credit patron you will receive advance notice of our sales and other special events. You will also find your account a frequent convenience in ordering by telephone.

It is a pleasure to welcome you as a charge customer. We hope for many opportunities to serve you through your account.

Sincerely yours,

Dear Mrs. Michaels:

Welcoming you as a charge customer of Kerr's is a real pleasure. Your account is ready for use at the Downtown Store, Uptown Store at 24th and Walker, and the Norman Store.

Statements are mailed under the cycle billing plan, which means that you will be billed about the tenth of the month. Your account is payable within fifteen days of that date.

You will find your charge account a real convenience and timesaver. Please use it often. We shall endeavor in every way to make you glad that you opened an account at Kerr's.

Sincerely yours,

Dear Mr. Wooster:

It's a pleasure to write you that your charge account has been opened and is ready for use.

Our accounts are carried on a thirty-day basis. Charges made during the month are payable as shown in the enclosed leaflet. Payment is appreciated within ten days after receipt of statement.

Your account will be a real convenience to you in making purchases at Boyd's, and you will find here complete selections of top-quality merchandise.

We shall try to serve you so well that all your visits to Boyd's will be enjoyable.

Sincerely yours,

Letters Declining Requests

Tact is extremely important in the letter declining a request. Care must be taken to avoid any suggestion or implication that the request is considered an imposition. The reader should be made to feel that his letter was welcomed, and that his request would be granted gladly if circumstances permitted. Often it is desirable to explain why the request cannot be granted—especially if the reason is simple and convincing.

Occasionally the writer can suggest some other means of being helpful, even though he is not in a position to grant the reader's request. Such an offer of co-operation shows a genuine desire to be accommodating.

In any case the letter should be sincere and friendly. A cordial tone goes a long way toward counteracting the reader's natural disappointment at the content of the message.

Specimen Letters Declining Requests

For information or material:

Dear Mr. Mason:

It would be a pleasure to send you a copy of the booklet, "Avoiding Traffic Fatalities," if the supply had not been completely exhausted by an unexpectedly heavy demand.

There is a definite possibility that we may reprint the booklet next month. If we do, I shall see that a copy is sent to you immediately.

Thank you for your interest in this publication. If we can be of service to you in any other way, please let us know.

Cordially yours,

Dear Mr. Mandell:

Thank you for your letter of November 14, and for your kind comments about our correspondence manual.

We wish it were possible to send you a copy of the manual with our compliments. When the revised edition was published, however, requests for it became so numerous that we were forced to adopt the policy of asking one dollar for each copy. This amount is just enough to meet the cost of printing and mailing.

Distribution of the manual on this basis serves to make it available to those who feel that it will be helpful, and at the same time relieves us of a cost item that would be prohibitive.

We feel sure you will understand and approve this policy, and we shall be glad to hear from you further if you feel that the manual justifies its non-profit price. It is always a pleasure to co-operate with those who share our interest in better methods of business correspondence.

Cordially yours,

Dear John:

I should be very glad to send you the Gordon Business Reports for the year 1949 if we had them. Our subscription to this service expired in 1948, and since we were no longer making very frequent use of it, we did not resubscribe.

It would be a real pleasure to assist you, and I regret that we are not in a position to do so. I believe, however, that our mutual friend Ralph Farnsley of Simpson & Company has the full series of Gordon Reports, and I am sure he would be glad to send you the 1949 releases. In case you do not have the address of his firm before you, it is 415 Geyer Avenue, Buffalo, New York.

Cordially,

Dear Mr. Alford:

Thank you for your note of June 17, and for your generous comments about the series of articles on "Better Public Relations by Mail."

If I had reprints of these articles, or even an extra copy of each one, sending them to you would be a pleasure. But it happens that I have only file copies, which I am now using in an effort to combine the articles into a book.

In all probability the *Public Relations Monthly* will be able to send you tear sheets covering the entire series if you will write them a note at 714 Fourth Avenue, New York City. I suggest that you address such an inquiry to Mr. Fred Stimson, Assistant Editor.

I hope you receive the material soon, and that it proves of some assistance in the work of your department.

Sincerely yours,

For business appointment:

Dear Mr. Holtman:

Your letter of September 12 reached me this morning.

It would be a pleasure to see you September 26 if I were to be in town at that time. But I must leave early next week on a business trip to the West Coast, from which I shall return October 1.

After that date I shall be in the office without interruption for a month or more. If you have occasion to be in Omaha any time in October, I shall be happy to see you.

Sincerely yours,

Dear Mr. Morrissey:

Thank you for your letter of March 28.

I regret that it will not be possible for us to arrange a visit during your stay in Cleveland next week, since I shall be in New York all week attending a meeting of our Advertising Division.

When you plan another trip to Cleveland, I hope you will let me know. It would be a real pleasure to meet you and talk with you.

Cordially yours,

Dear George:

Thanks for your cordial note of May 26.

It would be very good indeed to see you when you come through Des Moines next week. Unfortunately, however, I am scheduled to enter the Mayo Clinic the first of the week for a complete checkup, and I'll be away about ten days.

The next time Des Moines is on your itinerary, I hope we can get together. Meanwhile, if I can be of any help to you by mail or telephone, please feel free to call on me.

Best regards to you.

Sincerely,

Dear Mr. Dawson:

Your interesting letter of March 11 was on my desk this morning when I returned from Detroit.

It appears that we are going to miss connections when you are in St. Louis on April 3, since I am scheduled to be in Atlanta at that time. Otherwise it would be a pleasure to see you.

If your plans include another stop in St. Louis during the spring or summer months, I hope we can have lunch together. In the meantime, please let me know if this office can be helpful to you in planning your course in credit education.

Sincerely yours,

Dear Mr. Johns:

Your note of September 2 arrived this morning, telling me that you will be in Tulsa briefly on your way to Chicago next week.

I regret very much that a speaking engagement in Colorado Springs will deprive me of a visit with you on September 12. It happens that I am scheduled to address a bank conference there on that very day.

If you will be coming through Tulsa again on your way home from Chicago, perhaps we can arrange a meeting then. I shall be back in the office Monday, September 16, and shall not be away again until the first week in October.

Cordially yours,

For charge account:

Dear Miss Carberry:

Thank you for your recent request for a Keller & Lane charge account. Your confidence in this store is much appreciated.

Though we are not in a position to open the account just now, perhaps the situation later on will permit us to do so. We sincerely hope so.

Meanwhile, please visit the store often and enjoy the many conveniences of shopping here. Every effort will be made to serve you well, and we hope you'll give us frequent opportunities to do so.

Sincerely yours,

Dear Mrs. Wheelock: [5]

Thank you for requesting a Gilman Brothers charge account. We appreciate this expression of your good will.

As you probably know, a routine credit investigation is the usual business procedure before new accounts are opened. Since the available information in support of your credit application is incomplete, we shall appreciate your assistance.

When you find it convenient, will you please call at the Credit Office on the second floor? No doubt you can furnish the background of information we need in order to give further consideration to your request.

It will be a pleasure to talk with you, and we shall welcome the opportunity to meet you personally.

Sincerely yours,

Dear Mr. Dahlgren:

Thank you for your interest in arranging a charge account at Emery's.

The information received as a result of our usual investigation is incomplete, so we ask your assistance. No doubt you will be able to submit additional information to aid our decision in your behalf.

Will you please call at our office when you have a convenient moment? We'll be looking for you, and your co-operation will be appreciated.

Cordially yours,

For support of charitable organization, public-welfare institution, co-operative-advertising campaign, and so forth:

My dear Mr. Duval:

I have just received your letter of December 15, inviting me to participate in the fund-raising program of the Human Welfare Association, and I appreciate your thought in writing me.

---

[5] Although the following two letters do not actually decline the request for consumer credit, in most cases they serve the same purpose. Statistical surveys indicate that fewer than 10 per cent of the persons who receive such letters ever call at the credit office as requested.

There is no undertaking more deserving of financial aid, nor any to which I would more gladly contribute, than that which you represent. At the same time, I must tell you that all of the funds I have available for such purposes have already been earmarked, and that accordingly it just is not possible for me to do what you ask at this time. Later, perhaps—but just at the moment I do not feel free to make either a current or future commitment, and I hope you will hold me excused.

Though I am not in a position to lend active support just now, I send you my best wishes for success in the fine work you are doing.

Sincerely yours,

Gentlemen:

We appreciate your inviting us to join in the promotional activities of your association, and we wish we could participate in them; but to do so would really put us "on the spot."

It has always been our policy not to pay for co-operative advertising of any kind. This practice has long been necessary because hardly a day goes by that we do not receive two or three requests for some such form of co-operation. Since we cannot possibly comply with all, we believe the only fair way is to decline all.

Our idea of fairness is to spend our advertising money in such a manner that all grocers share, and share alike, in the results—rather than to tie up with any particular group, or with any one grocer.

We feel sure you will understand and appreciate this policy of trying to be fair to all. Thank you again for your courtesy in writing to us.

Sincerely yours,

Dear Mr. Jones:

Thank you for your letter of November 6.

The thought of pleasantly surprising our old customer greatly appeals to us—but a discomforting thought inevitably follows! There is a rule that hems us in.

We serve thousands of churches annually, and hundreds of special requests arrive in a steady stream. If we tried to grant them all, we should soon go bankrupt. If we arbitrarily granted some, but declined others, we should not only have a nervous collapse trying to decide where to draw the line, but we should be unhappy in knowing that we were discriminating unfairly against the rest of our customers.

So we have just had to adopt an iron-bound rule of putting all the value we can into our envelope systems, and asking to be excused from the "extras" that we can't give all our customers.

Sometimes rules make us unhappy, but we have to live by them, else we should all wind up in a permanently miserable state. In the face of this dilemma—wanting to surprise you with those letterheads and envelopes, but having a necessary rule that prohibits it—we ask for your understanding and your sympathy.

Sincerely yours,

Dear Mr. Claxton:

Thank you for your letter of August 16. I wish it were possible for us to accept your invitation to advertise in your coming program book.

Unfortunately, there seems to be no way in which we can work with you just now. Our advertising appropriations for all our books are studied, analyzed, and carefully prepared many months in advance. Detailed campaigns are planned, procedures and budgets are prepared, art work and production are studied. Everything is taken care of so that a long-range campaign can be carried through on each of our publications.

You can see that, on such a basis, it becomes impossible to break a schedule. Once that happens, there seems to be no end to the flood. Gradually we accumulate more exceptions than we have rules, and so finally the whole established procedure becomes upset. To avoid that, we have set a rigid rule that we cannot consider any extraordinary advertising venture after the original appropriation has once been determined. I am sure you will see the justice of this position and the logic underlying it.

I have gone rather into detail because I want you to know that we appreciate your courtesy in writing to us. Though we shall not be able to work with you in exactly the manner you contemplated, I should like to extend my personal best wishes and those of Prentice-Hall for a most successful affair.

Sincerely yours,

My dear Mr. Winstead:

Your letter of July 17 has been read with interest. I only wish we were in a position to make a donation to your college.

But here is our situation. We regularly sell to retailers in every city of 1,000 or more inhabitants, throughout the United States. Consequently, we receive a great many requests—from all parts of the country—for subscriptions and contributions for charitable, educational, religious, and other purposes. You can well see that it would be impossible for us to comply with all.

As we do not wish to discriminate, it has been necessary for us to formulate a rather strict policy as to subscriptions and contributions. We limit them to charitable, educational, and relief organizations within our own city, and to similar movements of a national or international character.

We feel sure you will understand our situation and approve our policy. Please accept our thanks for your letter and our sincere best wishes for the success of your Foundation Fund.

Yours very sincerely,

Dear Mr. Clemson:

I have just read your letter of August 14, outlining your plan for establishing an independent newspaper in this community. I appreciate your thought in writing me about it.

While your proposal is an interesting one, it is so far outside the scope of both my own activities and my business interests that I do not feel I can accept your invitation to become associated with it.

Nevertheless, I want to thank you for the opportunity of reviewing your project, and to wish you every success with it.

Sincerely yours,

TEN

Letters Soliciting Contributions to Charity

Organizations [1]

This chapter includes letter specimens made available through the courtesy of the following organizations: Boys Town, Omaha, Nebraska; The Dartnell Corporation, Chicago, Illinois; Glenwood Manual Training School, Glenwood, Illinois; Illinois Association for the Crippled, Inc., Chicago, Illinois; Infant Welfare Society of Chicago, Chicago, Illinois; Madison Square Boys' Club, New York City; Memorial Hospital for the Treatment of Cancer and Allied Diseases, New York City; Orthopaedic Hospital, Los Angeles, California; The Salvation Army, Philadelphia, Pennsylvania; Texas Scottish Rite Hospital for Crippled Children, Dallas, Texas; Travelers Aid Society of Chicago, Chicago, Illinois; United Charities of Chicago, Chicago, Illinois.

WHATEVER may be the nature of a public-welfare institution, the letter written to solicit contributions toward its maintenance should combine a strong human-interest element with a persuasive appeal to the reader's emotions. The average person will contribute funds to a hospital, orphanage, or other humanitarian organization only if he is convinced (1) that the institution is deserving of his support, (2) that his contribution will produce tangible results, and (3) that he will derive enough personal satisfaction from his generosity to compensate him for its cost.

To be effective, therefore, the letter of solicitation must describe the worthy functions performed by the organization,

[1] The following section is included in response to a survey conducted to ascertain the types of letters that businessmen have the greatest difficulty in composing. Though letters written in behalf of charity-supported institutions are not, strictly speaking, personal letters, they represent a type of correspondence that lies outside the usual routine of commercial offices, and that businessmen are frequently called upon to write in the interests of human-welfare organizations. The specimen examples presented in the following pages were selected upon the basis of their tested effectiveness in actual use.

the purpose for which the reader's contribution will be used, and the genuine service he will be rendering to humanity through his financial aid—however large or small his gift may be.

But before these points are made, the letter must gain the reader's interest through an opening that compels his attention. Use of the human-interest element at the outset is an effective device. A thought-provoking question or a concise statement of a significant fact will also serve to develop immediate interest in the message.

The following specimens of solicitation letters illustrate not only the technique of gaining reader interest, but also the integration of all elements essential to success in raising funds by mail.

Dear Mr. Farley: [2]

It's genuine—this U. S. Treasury note—ready to perform a mission of human kindness.

In effect it says to you: "When you'll let me, I will buy milk for a destitute family of four for almost a week, bread for three weeks, life-giving vegetables for days. With a few of my brothers I can multiply all of these things. I can help buy medical care and health-giving warmth for many in these bitter cold days of winter. When I am put into the treasury of the Salvation Army—that grand organization of unselfish devotion to humanity—I can often do more. Common obstacles are cleared away, profits on the things I buy are often sacrificed, my mission of helping the poor and the suffering is backed by kind co-operation on every side."

Yes, that's the true, simple appeal of this one-dollar bill. But it can't do any of these things while it is held captive. Were you in need of it more than the unfortunates it is intended to help, you would be welcome to it. To help someone is its only mission.

You see the point, I'm sure. Its first job is to enlist help—to go to those who have, in a sincere appeal for those who haven't. It needs company—lots of it—to see the good work of the Salvation Army blossom into worthy humanitarian deeds. No matter where it came from, it could carry with it no higher recommendation than that. So in behalf of the Salvation Army, I appeal to you not only

[2] The following message was accompanied by a genuine one-dollar bill.

to send back this emissary of good so that he can go to work, but also to add your personal check so that it may help, too.

The amount? Only you can determine that. Let it be in generous proportion to the amount of good you know the Salvation Army, from its past splendid record, will accomplish.

And please don't delay. The need is urgent. Hundreds of people have already died from intense cold this winter—many right in our own midst. By acting now you may save a human life, for your contribution will be used to buy fuel—one of life's prime necessities. Here is an envelope ready to carry the dollar and your contribution back to me. Please make your check payable to the Salvation Army.

Very sincerely yours,

My dear Mr. Carew: [3]

In December, 1917, when I borrowed $90 to pay the first month's rent on a building to house homeless and abandoned boys, I decided to spend my life saving boys from becoming misfits and recruits in the army of crime.

Our beginning was very humble. In fact, our first Christmas dinner consisted of sauerkraut and boiled potatoes—and we were grateful for it.

Now—28 years later—I wish it were possible for you to spend Christmas day with us. Here at Boys Town you would see hundreds of healthy, growing boys who, but a few months ago, were without hope, without a home, abandoned and utterly discouraged. You would see a fine rural community, with its own farm, schools, and workshops, made up of boys of every race and creed, from every corner of the United States. Here they live together, work together, learn together, and govern themselves in the American way. Here they have found opportunity and happiness.

Boys Town is non-sectarian, and receives no aid from church, state, Federal government, or Community Chest. It depends entirely on the voluntary contributions of its friends.

At this Christmas season, therefore, my boys join me in asking you to send us a contribution. Their hope is not for themselves alone, but for the thousands of homeless, neglected boys yet to come to Boys Town, whose wounds are yet to be healed and whose

[3] The following letter bore the personal signature of the late Father Flanagan, founder of Boys Town.

hearts are yet to be made glad. Think of them, later on, going out into the world with heads up and shoulders squared, and knowing that you helped to give them a chance.

Please don't think for a moment that "my bit won't help." It will! The cost of food, shelter, and clothing for each boy at Boys Town is only fifty cents a day, or less than $4 a week.

My boys will elect you an Honorary Citizen of Boys Town, and I will send your certificate with my acknowledgment.

A postpaid, addressed envelope is enclosed. You may provide for a boy for as many days or weeks as you wish. Regardless of the amount you send, it will be very much appreciated.

Sincerely,

My dear Mr. Reeves:

Yesterday it was I . . . tomorrow it may be you . . . the next day someone dear to you. Certain it is that one of us in eight, reaching middle age, will be delivered to Charon's ferry via the cancer route. No idle statement this, but cold statistics, medical records checked by cancer specialists.

I desire to serve, to save lives, if I can . . . to warn . . . to tell you what I know . . . to help you escape as I escaped. I have had cancer. It was cancer of the tonsil, a dangerous location and a bad type. I have heard the lapping of the waters of the Styx. That I did not cross is due to a devoted band of specialists, scientists, and nurses who retrieved me from death.

My story begins in Central Africa. A throat irritation, slight, not even painful, would not subside. Warned, I airplaned for seven days, flew across the Mediterranean, to France. Then a fast steamer to New York. In all, thirteen days from Central Africa, suspecting that the Grim Reaper was traveling with me. He was!

Inquiry led me to Memorial Hospital, for more than fifty years a fortress of scientists, battling, studying, standing bravely in the path of the world's greatest scourge—subtle, secretive, merciless, implacable in its ruthless advance. Their knowledge and skill saved my life, by methods which a few years ago were unknown.

My message to you is that *many stricken may be saved*—especially if discovered and treated promptly. Act immediately! Suspect every persistent irritation! Inform yourself of the early signs of the different forms of cancer. Avoid quacks as you would a rattlesnake. I owe my life to Memorial Hospital and to the promptness of my entrance there.

I ask you and your friends to do what no one person alone, in these times, is rich enough to do adequately. Reach out a helping hand to this institution. Dig deeply into your pockets. Memorial may sometime save your life or that of one you love.

The address is Memorial Hospital for the Treatment of Cancer and Allied Diseases, York Avenue at 68th Street, New York City. It was the first cancer hospital in America. It was founded more than fifty years ago by those whose loved ones died from cancer.

Today it is a broadly organized institution affiliated with Cornell University. It conducts undergraduate and post-graduate education. Visits to the institution number 100,000 annually. It is saving lives, studying the causes of cancer, and developing new methods of treatment. Will you help it?

Sincerely yours,

Dear Mrs. Edwards:

Nineteen years ago in Chicago a baby girl was born with a condition of the spine for which medical science has not yet found a cure.

Last week, with money she had earned herself, she bought her mother a wrist watch as a birthday gift. With shining eyes, she showed the watch to us with the remark: "All my life others have given to me; now I am able to give to others."

Barbara graduated two years ago from a special school for crippled children. Aptitude tests indicated that she would make an excellent stenographer, but the business college would accept her only after they had been assured they had no responsibility for finding her employment.

When she completed her stenographic course, Barbara again came for assistance to the Illinois Association for the Crippled. Because she is dependent on crutches the employer accepted her conditionally. After six months he reported that she was one of his most efficient workers and had been absent only ½ day—a record unequalled by any other employee.

There are several thousand crippled children such as Barbara in Illinois who need special help and attention. Many of them can become self-supporting if given that help. Others must always have help.

Your dollar—more, please, if you can spare it—for the enclosed Easter Seals will permit the Illinois Association for the Crippled to continue its work of helping other crippled children to a useful and happy life.

A return envelope is enclosed for your convenience in sending your remittance. We hope you will keep the Seals and use them on your letters and parcels as messages of Easter joy.

Sincerely yours,

Dear Mr. Forrest:

Even I was surprised and shocked when I asked our social workers how great the need for Christmas aid would be this year. All the ads pleading for workers and offering high wages had the same effect on me that I presume they have had on you—made me forget how many, many people in a big city like Chicago are still desperately poor.

Enclosed are descriptions of a few of the families they told me about—Mrs. Martin living on borrowed time so that her six children will have the memory of one more Christmas with her; old Mr. Kinsey who fainted from hunger when he asked for aid; six-year-old Donna Jean who tried to walk from Iowa to see her mother here; Private Dan Hill and the sisters he used to support.

They are a gallant crew, doing everything they can to help themselves, but fighting against odds that are just a little too big for them.

I know that living costs are high for everyone these days, but I can't reconcile myself to the idea that these folks and all of the 3,583 children in families now being helped by the United Charities shall be entirely forgotten.

Your Christmas check will tell the Martins, Donna Jean, and all the rest of them that there are still Men of Good Will who know about and care about home folks who are in trouble.

Will you send it today?

Yours very sincerely,

My dear Mr. Ryan: [4]

How big is your heart? Larger than the family circle? Expansive enough to help a bunch of "regular boys" like those here pictured— little victims of unfortunate circumstances?

We hope it is. For out at Glenwood Manual Training School are 300 fine youngsters who need care, training, and education right now—to prepare them for upright citizenship.

And we can't neglect our own!

If optimism and good will would buy bread and coal, pay teachers' salaries, and keep these youngsters in shoes and pants, we shouldn't have to ask your help—but MONEY is the only specie we know how to transform into a square deal for these lads who haven't had an even break in life.

We're leaving you a lot of leeway in the size of your check—

$1.00 to help 1 boy.
$5.00 to help 5 boys.
$25.00 to help 25 boys.
$300.00 to help the whole lot!

—a request elastic enough to fit any budget!

Please don't leave it for the next fellow to do—remember our most important line of defense is our boy-power of today—our man-power of tomorrow. And thanks a lot!

Yours sincerely,

———

Dear Mr. Burton:

I'm a firm believer in doing things the American Way; and I am sure you are, too. That's why I am writing you on behalf of the Texas Scottish Rite Hospital for Crippled Children.

During the past seventeen years 42,166 treatments and operations have been performed for all types of malformities, and the parents have never paid one single penny. That's the American Way . . . helping those who cannot help themselves! These children have come to this hospital from 896 different communities of Texas.

Lying there in bed or re-learning to walk with new braces and crutches, their laughter constantly ringing through the corridors,

[4] The following message was presented on a special letterhead that pictured four wholesome-looking teen-aged boys.

these unfortunate youngsters are happy and courageous. Each is filled with the determination to get well and "be like other children." True little Americans, they will be better citizens because of the mercy of generous Texas men and women.

Right now—today—hundreds more are on the Hospital waiting list . . . waiting patiently until their little bodies can be straightened or mended and braced back into more normal shapes. For these hundreds there is no other source of help, so the Hospital *must* operate at capacity.

If you could be at the Hospital and see this miraculous work being done, you'd probably think it was the greatest institution of its kind in the world. I *know* it is.

Will you join others of us again in providing the funds necessary for capacity operation during the coming year? Your check will bring you the greatest pleasure in the world—making crippled children into strong, useful, and happy citizens.

Sincerely yours,

———————

My dear Mr. Scott:

I hope you slept well last night—I didn't. I kept thinking about the youngsters who have been coming to us here at Travelers Aid ever since those first few warm days we had; boys of twelve—fourteen—sixteen—all of them bitten by the urge to travel.

I kept thinking, too, about the hundreds more of whom these are just the first harbingers—typical American boys, arriving here all hours of the day and night—hungry and dirty and weary.

Of course it's wrong for them to leave their homes—most of them, that is. I don't blame some of them; neither would you, if you knew what they left. It's an old story to us: family on relief, which means a mere subsistence diet; father not working or no longer at home; lots of brothers and sisters, the smaller ones invariably sick from malnourishment.

Is it any wonder that the teen-aged boys run away—believing that in so doing they will be leaving more for the younger ones to eat—hoping somewhere, somehow to find something better? A hundred years ago we'd have called them pioneers; but now they're just dependent non-resident juveniles, and somebody has to take care of them.

We feed them and house them temporarily and get in touch with the home community to find out why they ran away and what can be done to correct home conditions before they're returned. Sometimes, of course, it's pretty hopeless; and occasionally we even recommend that a boy be kept in Chicago where he may have a chance.

Whichever we do costs money—and it's money well spent. These boys are not pampered, but they are taken care of. We're not apologizing for them—we're sincerely trying to help them. That's a difficult job here in Chicago; and if you think it's worth while and would like to help by sending ten dollars, we'll surely be glad to have it.

Sincerely yours,

My dear Mr. Turner:

I want a better America for my children; so do you. We may not have all of the answers, but I can't conceive of disagreement on this—if we are to have a better world, we must give the children a better chance. If America is to be a better place for our children, we must make it a better place for children on the "other side of the tracks."

Does that seem too big to tackle? Not one of us can carry all of America's children, but each of us can see that one or two get the right start. The enclosed folder shows how you can help the Infant Welfare Society to give a child health and a foundation for living, from which we all will benefit.

Won't you make a place for Infant Welfare children in your Christmas budget? This will be a gift that will extend far beyond Christmas, 195-.

Very sincerely yours,

Dear Mr. Blanchard:

It's very hard to say "No" to a boy from the hot pavements of the east side when he asks "Can I go to Camp?" My answer to the boy depends upon you. The plentiful food, sunshine, and wholesome life of two weeks at Camp means everything in the world to these boys now, and to the future of America.

A contributor who has been helping boys go to Camp for years wrote the following letter:

"In this world that has gone cockeyed, it is up to you and me and our boys to do what we can toward preserving the ideals of America. So teach your boys something of the principles on which our country is based, give them an understanding of why these principles are sound and right, and give them such a love for these principles that they will be willing to go out and fight to defend them. If you can do that, you are accomplishing a man-sized job that should make you one of the happiest of men."

I am attaching an application that our boys fill out in order to go to Camp. So as not to disappoint a boy, I am sending this blank application to you with the hope that when a boy asks to go to Camp, I can say: "Yes, fill out this application and you can go because Mr. John Blanchard has sent a contribution to take care of you."

Your check for $7.00 will provide a boy with one week; or $14.00, with two weeks at Clear Pool Camp.

Sincerely yours,

———————

Dear Mr. Granville: [5]

Here's a dollar! Yes, it's a REAL dollar—nice and clean and new.

Keep it if you want to, after you've read this letter. But I don't believe you'll want to—then.

Here's what it's all about:

I've made an investment of a thousand dollars in human nature—human kindness. I've mailed a thousand dollars—in a thousand letters to a thousand people picked at random. I have done this because I believe that everyone is REALLY kind, way down inside—that no one is really heartless—and that the only reason why folks do not help where help is needed is just that these needs are not IMPRESSED upon them hard enough.

And that's the mission of each of my thousand dollars—to impress the importance of a need. This thousand dollars is my subscription to the Orthopaedic Hospital for crippled children—and I'm investing in the belief that EVERY ONE will come back in the stamped return envelopes I am enclosing—and that each dollar will bring back several more—at least another—with it. So our subscription, which I'm starting in this way, will be at least two thousand—maybe

[5] The following message was accompanied by a genuine one-dollar bill.

five—for there are going to be a lot of you who send a five or a ten—or more—when you mail my dollar back.

Remember—both my dollar and your dollars go to help crippled children.

Will EVERY ONE come back? Will every one bring something more? Are people really kind—or REALLY heartless? Have I made a good investment?

What is YOUR answer?

Sincerely yours,

My dear Mrs. Loomis: [6]

This is Boys Town's 28th Anniversary!

I established my home in 1917—during the first World War. Since that time about 5,000 homeless, deserted, and destitute boys have wended their way to our doors to be fed, clothed, and educated. They were boys from the cities, boys from the country, boys of all races and religious creeds. Some had been in trouble because they were too smart, too wild, and too eager. Others were downhearted, lazy, unkempt, slow to learn.

We first gave them a home and a parent's rightful attention, which they had been denied. I talked with them individually and discussed their problems, and then helped them to solve these problems. In the classrooms they were taught American history and the functions of our government. We put this training into practical application by allowing them to elect their own Mayor and City Commissioners. These boys worked in the shops and in the fields so they would learn to create something with their hands. They were given good, clean entertainment and a well-balanced athletic program.

The proof of the success of our work lies in the fact that all of these boys have become good citizens. There are hundreds of names on our Honor Roll of World War II, including a sizable group who have given their lives for their country.

As a result of the ravages of this war, many more boys have been left homeless. They are good boys, but they are the victims of vicious circumstances; and unless they are given a home and an

[6] The following letter bore the personal signature of the late Father Flanagan, founder of Boys Town.

opportunity to become good citizens, they will be easy prey to temptation and crime.

I am writing you because just a small contribution on your part will mean the difference between a life of usefulness and a life of crime for one of these homeless boys who should be with us here at Boys Town.

The cost of food, shelter, and clothing for each boy at Boys Town is only 50 cents a day, or less than $4 a week. You may provide for a boy for as many days or weeks as you wish, but *any gift* you send me will be of great assistance in getting my large family of boys through the coming year, and will surely bring a blessing on your own Holiday Season.

Enclosed is an addressed envelope that needs no postage. As an expression of their gratitude, my boys will elect you an Honorary Citizen of Boys Town, and I will send your certificate with my acknowledgment.

Sincerely,

APPENDICES

APPENDIX A

Trite Expressions to be Avoided in Letters

according to our records
acknowledge receipt of
acknowledge with pleasure
acknowledge with thanks
acknowledging yours
advise (meaning *inform* or *tell*)
advise me accordingly
along this line
and oblige
answering yours
as a matter of fact
as per
as stated above
assuring you of my interest
assuring you of our prompt
  attention
at all times
at an early date
at hand
at the earliest possible moment
at the present time
at the present writing
at this writing
at your convenience
at your earliest convenience
attached find
attached hereto
attached herewith
attached please find
avail yourself of this opportunity
await the pleasure of a reply
awaiting your further commands
awaiting your reply

balance (meaning *remainder* or
  rest)
beg to acknowledge

beg to advise
beg to announce
beg to assure
beg to call your attention
beg to inform
beg to inquire
beg to remain (immediately preceding complimentary close)
beg to request
beg to state
by return mail

carefully noted
communication (meaning *letter*)
complying with your request
concerning yours
contents carefully noted
contents duly noted
contents noted

deem it advisable
desire to state
drop me a line
due to the fact that
duly noted

enclosed find
enclosed herewith
enclosed please find
enclosed you will find
esteemed favor
even date

favor (meaning *letter*)
for your information

hand you herewith

has come to hand
has gone forward
have before me
herewith enclose
herewith hand you
herewith please find
hoping to be favored
hoping to hear from you

I am (immediately preceding
  complimentary close)
I have before me
I have your letter
I remain (immediately preceding
  complimentary close)
in accordance with
in answer to same
in connection therewith
in due course
in due time
in re
in receipt of
in regard to
in relation to
in reply to yours
in reply wish to state
in reply would say
in response to your favor
in the near future
in the not too distant future
in this connection
instant (*or* inst.)

kind favor
kindly advise
kindly be advised
kindly inform

let me call your attention

may I point out
may I say
may I suggest
meet your approval

note from your letter
note with interest
note with pleasure

of even date
of the above date
our Mr. ———
our records show
owing to the fact that

party (meaning an individual or
  group of individuals)
past favors
permit me to state
please advise
please be advised
please do not hesitate
please find enclosed
please let me hear from you
please note
please rest assured
pleasure of a reply
proximo (*or* prox.)
pursuant to

re
recent date
referring to your favor
referring to yours
regarding your communication
regarding yours
regret to advise
regret to state
replying to your favor
replying to yours

said (as an adjective)
same (as a pronoun)
state (as a verb)
submit herewith

take pleasure in announcing
take pleasure in presenting
take this opportunity

thank you kindly
thanking you in advance
the writer
this is to acknowledge
this is to advise you
this will inform you
to hand
trusting this will
trusting you will

ultimo (*or* ult.)
under separate cover
up to this writing
upon receipt of

valued favor
valued patronage

we are (immediately preceding
  complimentary close)
we are pleased to advise
we note
we remain (immediately preceding complimentary close)
we take pleasure
wherein you state
wish to acknowledge
wish to advise

wish to inform
wish to say
wish to state
with kindest regards
with reference to
with regard to
with your kind permission
would advise
would say
would state
would suggest

your esteemed communication
your esteemed favor
your favor to hand
your letter of even date
your letter of recent date
your letter received
your valued favor
your valued inquiry
your valued patronage
yours just to hand
yours of even date
yours of recent date
yours of the tenth (or other
  date)
yours received
yours to hand

APPENDIX B

Common Errors in English Usage [1]

DO NOT USE:

above for **foregoing** or **preceding.** *Above* is often misused in letters in such expressions as *the above material* and *the above details.* See also *the above. Examples:*

> INCORRECT: In view of the *above* explanation, I hope you will make an exception in this case.
>
> CORRECT: In view of the *foregoing* (or *preceding*) explanation, I hope you will make an exception in this case.

ad for **advertisement.** The abbreviated form *ad* is a colloquialism that should be avoided in correspondence. Its use suggests haste and carelessness. *Examples:*

> CARELESS: We plan to use the same *ad* in several well-known magazines.
>
> CORRECT: We plan to use the same *advertisement* in several well-known magazines.

adopt for **adapt.** *Adopt* means *to take over* or *to accept,* as: I shall *adopt* the policies of my predecessor. *Adapt* means *to adjust or make suitable to,* as: Perhaps we can *adapt* your plan to our circumstances. *Examples:*

> INCORRECT: We must *adopt* our advertising to our regular and prospective customers.
>
> CORRECT: We must *adapt* our advertising to our regular and prospective customers.

---

[1] The faults discussed and illustrated in this section are those that occur most frequently in letters. For a thorough review of the principles of correct expression and good usage, the following books are recommended:

Ewing, Rolfe, and Buell, *A Guide to Better Writing* (Prentice-Hall, Inc., New York).

Greever and Jones, *The Century Collegiate Handbook* (Appleton-Century-Crofts, Inc., New York).

Partridge, *Usage and Abusage* (Harper & Brothers, New York).

Perrin, *Writer's Guide and Index to English* (Scott, Foresman and Co., Chicago).

Stratton, *Guide to Correct English* (McGraw-Hill Book Co., Inc., New York).

Woolley and Scott, *New Handbook of Composition* (D. C. Heath and Co., Boston).

DO NOT USE:

advise for **inform.** *Advise* means *to give advice to. Inform* means *to convey information to.* The use of *advise* in the sense of *inform* is both trite and inaccurate. *Examples:*

INCORRECT: Within a week I shall *advise* you of my plans.
CORRECT: Within a week I shall *inform* you of my plans.

affect for **effect.** *Affect* is a verb meaning *to influence. Effect* is both a verb meaning *to bring about or accomplish* and a noun meaning *influence* or *result. Examples:*

INCORRECT: The new legislation will have a favorable *affect* on business.
CORRECT: The new legislation will have a favorable *effect* on business.
INCORRECT: I hope you will be able to *affect* a closer relationship between these departments.
CORRECT: I hope you will be able to *effect* a closer relationship between these departments.

afternoon with **p.m.** (or **P.M.**). Such a combination is repetitious, as in *this afternoon at 2 p.m.* or *at 4 p.m. Wednesday afternoon. Examples:*

REDUNDANT: The meeting is scheduled for tomorrow *afternoon* at 3 *p.m.*
CORRECT: The meeting is scheduled for tomorrow *afternoon* at three o'clock (or tomorrow at 3 *p.m.*).

all-around for **all-round.** Only the latter form is recognized as good usage. *Examples:*

INCORRECT: The man we select must be an *all-around* business-man.
CORRECT: The man we select must be an *all-round* business-man.

all of for **all** (except when the expression is followed by a pronoun). Ordinarily the preposition *of* is superfluous. *Examples:*

REDUNDANT: *All of* the salesmen attended the conference.
CORRECT: *All* the salesmen attended the conference.
CORRECT: *All of* us attended the conference.

all ready for **already.** *All ready* means *prepared* or *wholly ready. Already* means *beforehand* or *by or before a particular time. Examples:*

INCORRECT: Unfortunately, he has *all ready* accepted another invitation.
CORRECT: Unfortunately, he has *already* accepted another invitation.

DO NOT USE:

all together for **altogether.** *All together* means *gathered* or *assembled*. *Altogether* means *wholly, completely,* or *entirely. Examples:*

INCORRECT: The plan you suggest is *all together* satisfactory.
CORRECT: The plan you suggest is *altogether* satisfactory.

alright or **allright** for **all right.** Neither *alright* nor *allright* is recognized as a legitimate English word. *Examples:*

INCORRECT: This arrangement will be *alright* (or *allright*).
CORRECT: This arrangement will be *all right.*

amount for **number.** *Amount* applies to quantity, as: He has a surprising *amount* of endurance. *Number* applies to individual units, as: The *number* of automobiles sold during May exceeded even the most optimistic estimates. *Examples:*

INCORRECT: An unknown *amount* of persons died in the wreck.
CORRECT: An unknown *number* of persons died in the wreck.

angle for **aspect** or **point of view.** *Angle* is carelessly and inaccurately used by many letter writers. *Examples:*

CARELESS: Another *angle* of this arrangement must be considered.
CORRECT: Another *aspect* of this arrangement must be considered.
CARELESS: We must analyze the problem from every *angle.*
CORRECT: We must analyze the problem from every *point of view.*

anticipate for **expect.** *Anticipate* means *to foresee and forestall by prior action,* as: He *anticipated* his dismissal by resigning. This word is commonly misused in the sense of *expect* or *look forward to. Examples:*

INCORRECT: We *anticipate* a busy day at the store next Saturday.
CORRECT: We *expect* a busy day at the store next Saturday.

anxious for **eager.** *Anxious* should be used only when actual anxiety exists, as: An *anxious* group of relatives awaited news from the operating room. *Eager* should be used to denote enthusiastic desire, as: An *eager* crowd congregated in the street to congratulate the winner. *Examples:*

INCORRECT: I am *anxious* to attend the entertainment.
CORRECT: I am *eager* to attend the entertainment.

anyplace for **anywhere.** *Anyplace* is not recognized as good usage. *Examples:*

INCORRECT: He could not buy the necessary equipment *anyplace* in the state.
CORRECT: He could not buy the necessary equipment *anywhere* in the state.

DO NOT USE:

anytime for **any time.** The expression *any time* should be written as two words. *Examples:*

> INCORRECT: Please let me know *anytime* I can be of assistance.
> CORRECT: Please let me know *any time* I can be of assistance.
> INCORRECT: It will be a pleasure to co-operate with you *anytime.*
> CORRECT: It will be a pleasure to co-operate with you *any time.*

around for **about.** The use of *around* in the sense of *about* or *approximately* is incorrect. *Examples:*

> INCORRECT: We shall expect you *around* two o'clock.
> CORRECT: We shall expect you *about* two o'clock.

as for **that.** The use of *as* in place of *that* is a common grammatical error. *Examples:*

> INCORRECT: I am not sure *as* I shall be in the office next Friday.
> CORRECT: I am not sure *that* I shall be in the office next Friday.

as . . . as for **so . . . as.** *As . . . as* should be used only in affirmative statements. Good usage requires the use of *so . . . as* in negative statements and in questions implying a negative answer. *Examples:*

> INCORRECT: He is not *as* active *as* he was five years ago.
> CORRECT: He is not *so* active *as* he was five years ago.
> INCORRECT: Could any responsible editor be *as* careless *as* to make such a statement?
> CORRECT: Could any responsible editor be *so* careless *as* to make such a statement?

as yet for **yet.** The superfluous *as* should be omitted. *Examples:*

> REDUNDANT: We have not *as yet* learned the results of this experiment.
> CORRECT: We have not *yet* learned the results of this experiment.

at about for **at** or **about.** The expression *at about* is both inaccurate and awkward. Use *at* or *about,* depending upon the meaning intended. *Examples:*

> INCORRECT: The conference will be over *at about* five o'clock.
> CORRECT: The conference will be over *at* (or *about*) five o'clock.

awfully for **very** or **very much.** Since *awfully* means *in such a manner as to inspire awe,* its use in the sense of *very* or *very much* is incorrect. *Examples:*

> INCORRECT: He seemed *awfully* glad to see us.
> CORRECT: He seemed *very* glad to see us.

DO NOT USE:

> INCORRECT: They were *awfully* disappointed in his report.
> CORRECT: They were *very much* disappointed in his report.

badly for **very much.** Since *badly* means *poorly* or *inadequately,* its use in the sense of *a great deal* or *very much* is incorrect. *Examples:*

> INCORRECT: He wanted *badly* to attend the convention.
> CORRECT: He wanted *very much* to attend the convention.

balance for **remainder** or **rest** (except in referring to a bank balance, the only sense in which *balance* means *that which remains*). *Examples:*

> INCORRECT: He spent the *balance* of the afternoon interviewing applicants.
> CORRECT: He spent the *remainder* (or *rest*) of the afternoon interviewing applicants.

beside for **besides.** *Beside* means *by the side of* or *close to,* as: I sat *beside* him at the lecture. *Besides* means *additionally* or *in addition to,* as: *Besides* these questions, there are several other points that must be settled. *Examples:*

> INCORRECT: We have received these items, and several others *beside.*
> CORRECT: We have received these items, and several others *besides.*

best for **better.** As an adjective *best* is the superlative of *good.* As an adverb it is the superlative of *well.* In either case *best* should be used only when three or more persons or things have been considered. *Better* is the comparative of either the adjective *good* or the adverb *well.* It should be used instead of *best* when only two persons or things have been considered. *Examples:*

> INCORRECT: He is the *best* speaker of the two.
> CORRECT: He is the *better* speaker of the two.
> INCORRECT: If the choice lies between John and Paul, you should remember that Paul meets customers *best.*
> CORRECT: If the choice lies between John and Paul, you should remember that Paul meets customers *better.*

better for **more.** The use of *better* in the sense of *more* is not recognized as good usage. *Examples:*

> INCORRECT: He hopes to sell his equipment for $12,500 or *better.*
> CORRECT: He hopes to sell his equipment for $12,500 or *more.*
> INCORRECT: His share of the profit was *better* than $250.
> CORRECT: His share of the profit was *more* than $250.

DO NOT USE:

between for **among.** *Between* ordinarily applies to only two persons or things, whereas *among* applies to more than two. *Examples:*

INCORRECT: The work was divided *between* the three stenographers.

CORRECT: The work was divided *among* the three stenographers.

biannual for **biennial.** *Biannual* means *twice a year.* It is synonymous with *semiannual* and *half-yearly. Biennial* means *every two years.*

biennial for **biannual.** See *biannual.*

bimonthly for **semimonthly.** *Bimonthly* means *every two months. Semimonthly* means *twice a month.*

biweekly for **semiweekly.** *Biweekly* means *every two weeks. Semiweekly* means *twice a week.*

but I for **but me.** When *but* is used as a preposition, in the sense of *except,* it should be followed by the objective case. *Examples:*

INCORRECT: All the applicants *but I* had studied accounting.

CORRECT: All the applicants *but me* had studied accounting.

but that or **but what** for **that.** This error occurs most frequently after use of the word *doubt. Examples:*

INCORRECT: There is no doubt *but that* he will be back in time for the meeting.

INCORRECT: There is no doubt *but what* he will be back in time for the meeting.

CORRECT: There is no doubt *that* he will be back in time for the meeting.

can for **may.** *Can* carries the implication of being able or having the power to do something, as: He *can* manage the store in an emergency. *May* implies liberty or permission to do something, as: He *may* leave the office a day early if he wishes. *Examples:*

INCORRECT: You *can* inspect our plant whenever you wish.

CORRECT: You *may* inspect our plant whenever you wish.

can't hardly for **can hardly.** The expression *can't hardly* is a double negative—a violation of correct grammar. *Examples:*

INCORRECT: We *can't hardly* expect to equal such a splendid record.

CORRECT: We *can hardly* expect to equal such a splendid record.

DO NOT USE:

conscious for **aware.** A person is *conscious* of something within himself. He is *aware* of something outside himself. *Examples:*

> INCORRECT: He was not *conscious* of the financial problems that confronted the firm.
> CORRECT: He was not *aware* of the financial problems that confronted the firm.

consider . . . as for **consider.** The superfluous *as* should be omitted. *Examples:*

> REDUNDANT: We *consider* him *as* fully qualified for the position.
> CORRECT: We *consider* him fully qualified for the position.

considerable (as a noun or an adverb). This word should be used only as an adjective. *Examples:*

> INCORRECT: As an independent grocer he accumulated *considerable.* (Used as a noun.)
> CORRECT: As an independent grocer he accumulated *considerable* savings.
> INCORRECT: Your co-operation will help us *considerable.* (Used as an adverb.)
> CORRECT: Your co-operation will help us *considerably.*

continue on for **continue.** The superfluous *on* should be omitted. *Examples:*

> REDUNDANT: The program is scheduled to *continue on* into the evening.
> CORRECT: The program is scheduled to *continue* into the evening.

continuous for **continual.** These adjectives are not interchangeable. *Continuous* means *without stopping* or *without interruption. Continual* means *occurring in close succession* or *frequently repeated. Examples:*

> INCORRECT: *Continuous* interruptions have held up my work on this project.
> CORRECT: *Continual* interruptions have held up my work on this project.

contribute for **attribute.** *Contribute* means *to give,* as: We shall be glad to *contribute* to this fund. *Attribute* means *to ascribe,* as: I *attribute* his success to his perseverance. *Examples:*

> INCORRECT: We *contribute* our increase in sales to improved merchandising methods.
> CORRECT: We *attribute* our increase in sales to improved merchandising methods.

DO NOT USE:

co-operate together for **co-operate.** Since *co-operate* means *to work together,* the expression *co-operate together* is redundant. *Examples:*

REDUNDANT: We must all *co-operate together* to avert this common danger.

CORRECT: We must all *co-operate* to avert this common danger.

could of for **could have.** The use of *could of* is a crude grammatical error. (The expressions *should of, would of, must of, may of,* and *might of* are equally objectionable.) *Examples:*

INCORRECT: Under normal circumstances he *could of* attended the luncheon.

CORRECT: Under normal circumstances he *could have* attended the luncheon.

INCORRECT: Your letter *must of* been misplaced in our files.

CORRECT: Your letter *must have* been misplaced in our files.

count on for **depend on** or **rely on.** The expression *count on* is a colloquialism that is not recognized as good usage. *Examples:*

CARELESS: You may *count on* our co-operation.

CORRECT: You may *depend on* (or *rely on*) our co-operation.

credible for **creditable.** *Credible* means *believable,* whereas *creditable* means *deserving of credit. Examples:*

INCORRECT: His work as superintendent was *credible.*

CORRECT: His work as superintendent was *creditable.*

different (superfluously). The word *different* is often used superfluously for the purpose of showing separate identity that is already apparent. *Examples:*

REDUNDANT: Five *different* methods were discussed.

CORRECT: Five methods were discussed.

REDUNDANT: The three *different* low-priced cars were tested before the choice was made.

CORRECT: The three low-priced cars were tested before the choice was made.

different than for **different from.** The expression *different than* is not recognized as good usage. *Examples:*

INCORRECT: Your analysis of the situation is entirely *different than* mine.

CORRECT: Your analysis of the situation is entirely *different from* mine.

disorganized for **unorganized.** *Disorganized* implies that an earlier state of organization has been disturbed or destroyed. *Unorgan-*

DO NOT USE:

ized implies that a state of organization has never existed. *Examples:*

INCORRECT: Since the members of the committee had never worked together, they were completely *disorganized* at first.

CORRECT: Since the members of the committee had never worked together, they were completely *unorganized* at first.

don't for **doesn't.** *Doesn't* is the only correct contraction for *does not. Examples:*

INCORRECT: He *don't* expect to return until next week.

CORRECT: He *doesn't* expect to return until next week.

effect for **affect.** See also *affect. Examples:*

INCORRECT: The reorganization of the firm will not *effect* your department.

CORRECT: The reorganization of the firm will not *affect* your department.

either for **any.** *Either* is correct only when used to designate one of two persons or things; it is incorrect when used to designate one of three or more. *Examples:*

INCORRECT: The problem can be solved in *either* of three ways.

CORRECT: The problem can be solved in *any* of three ways.

INCORRECT: *Either* of these numerous difficulties would cause a delay.

CORRECT: *Any* of these numerous difficulties would cause a delay.

enthuse. This word has not attained a reputable status in the English language. *Examples:*

INCORRECT: He did not *enthuse* when he heard the report.

CORRECT: He did not *become enthusiastic* (or *show enthusiasm*) when he heard the report.

entirely complete for **complete.** The expression *entirely complete* is redundant, since completeness is absolute. *Examples:*

REDUNDANT: Our file of information about each employee is *entirely complete.*

CORRECT: Our file of information about each employee is *complete.*

equally as for **equally** or **as.** In the expression *equally as,* one or the other of the two words is superfluous, depending upon the construction. *Examples:*

DO NOT USE:

> REDUNDANT: The two machines are *equally as* good.
> CORRECT: The two machines are *equally* good.
> REDUNDANT: This machine is *equally as* good as any on the market.
> CORRECT: This machine is *as* good as any on the market.

every one (with a plural verb). Since the expression *every one* is singular in number, it requires a singular verb. *Examples:*

> INCORRECT: *Every one* of our salesmen *are* college graduates.
> CORRECT: *Every one* of our salesmen *is* a college graduate.

everybody . . . their for **everybody . . . his.** The pronoun *everybody* is singular in number. *Examples:*

> INCORRECT: *Everybody* should buy *their* clothing while prices are low.
> CORRECT: *Everybody* should buy *his* clothing while prices are low.

exactly identical for **identical.** The term *exactly identical* is redundant, since *identical* means *exactly alike*. *Examples:*

> REDUNDANT: The two devices are *exactly identical*.
> CORRECT: The two devices are *identical*.

except for **accept.** As a verb, *except* means *to exclude* or *to make an exception of*. The verb *accept* means *to receive with approval, to reply to affirmatively,* or *to agree to. Examples:*

> INCORRECT: I am happy to *except* your invitation.
> CORRECT: I am happy to *accept* your invitation.
> INCORRECT: The committee has decided to *except* your recommendation.
> CORRECT: The committee has decided to *accept* your recommendation.

expect for **suppose.** *Expect* should be used only when there is an element of expectation involved. Thus the word applies only to future events or developments. Its application to the present or to the past is illogical. *Examples:*

> INCORRECT: I *expect* he is on his way to Duluth.
> CORRECT: I *suppose* he is on his way to Duluth.
> INCORRECT: I *expect* he reached Denver yesterday.
> CORRECT: I *suppose* he reached Denver yesterday.

extra for **unusually** or **very.** The use of *extra* as a synonym for the adverbs *unusually* and *very* is not recognized as good usage. *Examples:*

> INCORRECT: We were *extra* busy at the store this morning.

DO NOT USE:

> CORRECT: We were *unusually* (or *very*) busy at the store this
> morning.

figure for **price.** The use of *figure* in the sense of *price* is a colloquialism that should be avoided in letter writing. *Examples:*

> CARELESS: This *figure* is the lowest for which our product has
> ever been sold.
> CORRECT: This *price* is the lowest for which our product has
> ever been sold.

fine (as an adverb). The use of *fine* in the sense of *well* is not
recognized as good usage. *Examples:*

> INCORRECT: You did *fine* with your part of the program.
> CORRECT: You did *well* (or *very well* or *splendidly*) with your
> part of the program.

finish up for **finish.** The superfluous *up* should be omitted. *Examples:*

> REDUNDANT: We shall *finish up* the repair work tomorrow.
> CORRECT: We shall *finish* the repair work tomorrow.

first and foremost for **first** or **foremost.** The constant use of *first
and foremost* has deprived the expression of whatever emphasis
value it may once have possessed. Today it is only a clumsy and
wordy substitute for *first* or *foremost. Examples:*

> WORDY: This possibility should be our *first and foremost*
> consideration.
> CORRECT: This possibility should be our *first* (or *foremost*)
> consideration.

first began for **began.** The expression *first began* is redundant,
since *first* adds nothing to the meaning of *began. Examples:*

> REDUNDANT: We *first began* to advertise five years ago.
> CORRECT: We *began* to advertise five years ago.

first-rate (as an adverb). The expression *first-rate* is acceptable as
an adjective, but its use as an adverb is not recognized as good
usage. *Examples:*

> INCORRECT: Our new adding machine works *first-rate.* (Used
> as an adverb.)
> CORRECT: Our new adding machine works *well* (or *splendidly*).
> CORRECT: Our new adding machine does *first-rate* work. (Used
> as an adjective.)

formally for **formerly.** *Formally* means *in a formal manner. Formerly* means *at some time in the past. Examples:*

DO NOT USE:

> INCORRECT: He was *formally* a member of our staff.
> CORRECT: He was *formerly* a member of our staff.

former for **first.** *Former* should be used when only two persons or things have been mentioned. *First* (or *first-mentioned*) should be used when more than two persons or things have been mentioned. *Examples:*

> INCORRECT: The *former* of the three methods is best suited to our needs.
> CORRECT: The *first* (or *first-mentioned*) of the three methods is best suited to our needs.

free gratis for **free** or **gratis.** The expression *free gratis* is redundant, since the words that compose it are synonymous. *Examples:*

> REDUNDANT: We shall gladly perform this service for you *free gratis.*
> CORRECT: We shall gladly perform this service for you *free* (or *gratis*).

further for **farther.** Careful writers do not use these words interchangeably. *Further* means *to a greater extent or degree,* as: I shall write you *further* in a day or two. *Farther* means *more distant,* as: New York City is *farther* from Boston than it is from Philadelphia. *Examples:*

> CARELESS: We are *further* from Omaha than we are from Denver.
> CORRECT: We are *farther* from Omaha than we are from Denver.

generally for **usually.** *Generally* means *in general* or *in a general sense,* as: The statement is *generally* true. *Usually* means *in most cases* or *as a usual practice,* as: He *usually* takes his vacation in August. *Examples:*

> INCORRECT: Our annual sales meeting is *generally* held in the early fall.
> CORRECT: Our annual sales meeting is *usually* held in the early fall.

good for **well.** The adjective *good* is incorrect in an adverbial sense, as a substitute for *well. Examples:*

> INCORRECT: He handled the transaction *good.*
> CORRECT: He handled the transaction *well.*

grand (as a substitute for an accurately descriptive adjective). The adjective *grand* is very much overworked and often used inaccu-

DO NOT USE:

rately as a substitute for *enjoyable, interesting, excellent, splendid,* and numerous other words. *Examples:*

CARELESS: Mr. Wheaton and I had a *grand* visit.
CORRECT: Mr. Wheaton and I had an *enjoyable* (or *interesting*) visit.
CARELESS: You have done a *grand* job.
CORRECT: You have done an *excellent* (or *splendid*) job.

greatly appreciate for **appreciate.** Since *appreciate* means *to esteem greatly* or *to value highly,* the adverb *greatly* is superfluous. *Examples:*

REDUNDANT: I shall *greatly appreciate* your co-operation.
CORRECT: I shall *appreciate* your co-operation.

greatly minimize for **minimize.** Since *minimize* means *to reduce to the minimum,* the adverb *greatly* is redundant. *Examples:*

REDUNDANT: The elimination of waste will *greatly minimize* the expense of operating our plant.
CORRECT: The elimination of waste will *minimize* the expense of operating our plant.

had of for **had.** This error is common in clauses introduced by *if.* The use of the superfluous *of* is a flagrant violation of good usage. *Examples:*

INCORRECT: Special arrangements could have been made if he *had of* made his request earlier.
CORRECT: Special arrangements could have been made if he *had* made his request earlier.

heighth for **height.** *Heighth* is not recognized as good usage. *Examples:*

INCORRECT: July should be the *heighth* of your selling season.
CORRECT: July should be the *height* of your selling season.

him for **his.** The use of *him* immediately preceding a gerund (verbal noun) is incorrect, since this construction requires the possessive form. *Examples:*

INCORRECT: There was no need of *him* apologizing for the misunderstanding.
CORRECT: There was no need of *his* apologizing for the misunderstanding.
INCORRECT: I was surprised at *him* seeking the appointment.
CORRECT: I was surprised at *his* seeking the appointment.

if for **whether.** These words are by no means interchangeable. The conjunction *if* means *in case,* as: Please let me know *if* you are going to Chicago. Such a request would require an answer from

DO NOT USE:

the recipient only in case he planned to go to Chicago. The conjunction *whether*, on the other hand, allows for either a positive or negative possibility, as: Please let me know *whether* you are going to Chicago. Such a request would require an answer from the recipient in any event; that is, whether he planned to go to Chicago or did not plan to go.

infer for **imply.** Writers and speakers *imply*, whereas readers and listeners *infer*. *Examples:*

> INCORRECT: Collection correspondents sometimes *infer* that legal action will soon be taken.
> CORRECT: Collection correspondents sometimes *imply* that legal action will soon be taken.

inside of for **within.** The use of *inside of* in the sense of *within* is a flagrant violation of good usage. *Examples:*

> INCORRECT: We shall complete the survey *inside of* a month.
> CORRECT: We shall complete the survey *within* a month.

irregardless for **regardless.** There is no such word as *irregardless*. The correct form is *regardless*. Misuse is perhaps caused by confusion with the word *irrespective*, which is somewhat similar in meaning. *Examples:*

> INCORRECT: I shall be glad to co-operate, *irregardless* of the plan you decide to follow.
> CORRECT: I shall be glad to co-operate, *regardless* of the plan you decide to follow.

it's for **its.** The contraction *it's* (for *it is*) should not be confused with *its*, which is the possessive form of the pronoun *it*. *Examples:*

> INCORRECT: The plan is still in *it's* infancy.
> CORRECT: The plan is still in *its* infancy.

just recently for **recently.** The superfluous *just* should be omitted. *Examples:*

> REDUNDANT: He called at the office *just recently*.
> CORRECT: He called at the office *recently*.

kind of for **rather** or **somewhat.** The expression *kind of* is not an acceptable substitute for an adverb. *Examples:*

> INCORRECT: The report on personnel policies was *kind of* interesting.
> CORRECT: The report on personnel policies was *rather* interesting.
> INCORRECT: He appeared *kind of* surprised at the announcement.
> CORRECT: He appeared *somewhat* surprised at the announcement.

DO NOT USE:

kind of a or **kind of an** for **kind of.** The superfluous article *a* or *an* should be omitted. *Examples:*

INCORRECT: This *kind of a* machine is well suited to our purpose.
CORRECT: This *kind of* machine is well suited to our purpose.
INCORRECT: This *kind of an* understanding is a big step forward.
CORRECT: This *kind of* understanding is a big step forward.

kindly for **please.** Since *kindly* means *in a kind or agreeable manner*, it is not a suitable substitute for *please. Examples:*

INCORRECT: *Kindly* let me know your decision.
CORRECT: *Please* let me know your decision.

know as for **know that.** The expression *know as* is a flagrant violation of good usage. *Examples:*

INCORRECT: I do not *know as* he will be interested.
CORRECT: I do not *know that* he will be interested.

last for **latest.** These words are not interchangeable. *Last* means *final*, whereas *latest* means *most recent*. Thus it is illogical to refer to an author's *last* book when he is still alive and may write others. *Examples:*

ILLOGICAL: His *last* business achievement was the sale of his factory at a profit. (Unless the person referred to is dead or has retired from business.)
CORRECT: His *latest* (or *most recent*) business achievement was the sale of his factory at a profit.

latter for **last.** *Latter* should be used when only two persons or things have been mentioned. *Last* (or *last-mentioned*) should be used when more than two persons or things have been mentioned. *Examples:*

INCORRECT: He considers the *latter* of the three methods the most effective.
CORRECT: He considers the *last* (or *last-mentioned*) of the three methods the most effective.

least for **less.** *Least* should be used when more than two persons or things have been mentioned. *Less* should be used when only two persons or things have been mentioned. *Examples:*

INCORRECT: This device is the *least* expensive of the two.
CORRECT: This device is the *less* expensive of the two.

less for **fewer.** *Less* applies to quantity, whereas *fewer* applies to number. *Examples:*

INCORRECT: We had *less* applicants this year than ever before.
CORRECT: We had *fewer* applicants this year than ever before.

DO NOT USE:

liable for **likely.** Although both words express probability, they are not interchangeable. *Liable* is correctly used only in referring to an unpleasant or undesirable probability, whereas *likely* is properly used when the probability referred to is either desirable or neutral in character. *Examples:*

> INCORRECT: He is considered the most *liable* to succeed.
> CORRECT: —He is considered the most *likely* to succeed.

like for **as** or **as if.** A subject followed by a verb should never be introduced by *like*. In such a construction *as* or *as if* should be used. *Examples:*

> INCORRECT: He misunderstood the directions just *like* I did.
> CORRECT: He misunderstood the directions just *as* I did.
> INCORRECT: He spoke *like* he planned to resign.
> CORRECT: He spoke *as if* he planned to resign.

likely for **liable.** See also *liable. Examples:*

> INCORRECT: The merchant who neglects his debts is *likely* to injure his credit standing.
> CORRECT: The merchant who neglects his debts is *liable* to injure his credit standing.

likely for **probably.** The adjective *likely* is a synonym for *probable,* but not for the adverb *probably. Examples:*

> INCORRECT: He will *likely* remain in Pittsburgh for two weeks.
> CORRECT: He will *probably* remain in Pittsburgh for two weeks.

line for **business.** The use of *line* as a substitute for *business* is both trite and inaccurate. *Examples:*

> CARELESS: He has been associated with the hardware *line* for several years.
> CORRECT: He has been associated with the hardware *business* for several years.

may of for **may have.** See *could of.*

may or may not for **may.** The expression *may or may not* is redundant, since the single word *may* implies the negative possibility. *Examples:*

> REDUNDANT: You *may or may not* be interested in a method that we have found successful.
> CORRECT: You *may* be interested in a method that we have found successful.

me for **my.** The use of *me* immediately preceding a gerund (verbal noun) is incorrect, since this construction requires the possessive form. *Examples:*

DO NOT USE:

> INCORRECT: I hope you will have no objection to *me* going.
> CORRECT: I hope you will have no objection to *my* going.
> INCORRECT: There is little chance of *me* winning.
> CORRECT: There is little chance of *my* winning.

might of for **might have.** See *could of.*

mighty for **extremely** or **very.** Since *mighty* means *powerful,* it is not a suitable substitute for *extremely* or *very. Examples:*

> INCORRECT: He was *mighty* upset over the error.
> CORRECT: He was *extremely* upset over the error.
> INCORRECT: I shall be *mighty* glad to see you.
> CORRECT: I shall be *very* glad to see you.

morning with **a.m.** (or **A.M.**). Such a combination is repetitious, as in *tomorrow morning at 10 a.m.* or *at 9 a.m. Friday morning. Examples:*

> REDUNDANT: Our fashion show will be held next Tuesday *morning* at 10 *a.m.*
> CORRECT: Our fashion show will be held next Tuesday *morning* at ten o'clock (or Tuesday at 10 *a.m.*).

most for **almost.** The colloquial use of *most* in the sense of *almost* can easily lead to misunderstanding. For example, *most confident* and *almost confident* have different meanings. *Most* should not be used as a substitute for *almost. Examples:*

> INCORRECT: The work of the committee is *most* finished.
> CORRECT: The work of the committee is *almost* finished.

most for **more.** *Most* should be used when more than two persons or things have been mentioned. *More* should be used when only two persons or things have been mentioned. *Examples:*

> INCORRECT: Which of the two methods do you consider *most* effective?
> CORRECT: Which of the two methods do you consider *more* effective?

must of for **must have.** See *could of.*

myself for **I** or **me.** *Myself* should be used only as an intensive or a reflexive. It is not a correct substitute for *I* or *me. Examples:*

> INCORRECT: Mr. Harris and *myself* will attend the convention.
> CORRECT: Mr. Harris and *I* will attend the convention.
> INCORRECT: Everyone was there except *myself.*
> CORRECT: Everyone was there except *me.*

nice (as a substitute for an accurately descriptive adjective). The adjective *nice* is one of the most abused words in the English

DO NOT USE:

language. It is constantly misused in such expressions as *nice* idea, *nice* profit, *nice* vacation, *nice* arrangement, *nice* building, and *nice* evening. *Examples:*

CARELESS: He did *nice* work as credit manager.

CORRECT: He did *good* (or *efficient* or *outstanding*) work as credit manager.

nothing else but for **nothing but.** The superfluous *else* should be omitted. *Examples:*

INCORRECT: *Nothing else but* the best of material was used.

CORRECT: *Nothing but* the best of material was used.

now (superfluously). *Now* often appears in sentences to which it contributes nothing. Avoid the superfluous use of this word. *Examples:*

REDUNDANT: For several years *now* we have advertised in popular magazines.

CORRECT: For several years we have advertised in popular magazines.

off of for **off.** The superfluous *of* should be omitted. *Examples:*

INCORRECT: His book will be *off of* the press next week.

CORRECT: His book will be *off* the press next week.

OK or **O.K.** (as a substitute for a correct adjective or verb). The expression *OK* or *O.K.* (sometimes written *okay* or *okeh*) is not recognized as good usage. *Examples:*

INCORRECT: We are sure the equipment will prove *O.K.*

CORRECT: We are sure the equipment will prove *satisfactory.*

INCORRECT: Please *O.K.* the arrangement if you consider it workable.

CORRECT: Please *approve* the arrangement if you consider it workable.

only for **but** or **except that.** The colloquial use of *only* in the sense of *but* or *except that* should be avoided in letters. *Examples:*

CARELESS: We should gladly send you a copy of our booklet, *only* the supply was exhausted several days ago.

CORRECT: We should gladly send you a copy of our booklet, *but* the supply was exhausted several days ago.

CARELESS: His qualifications for the position were excellent, *only* he lacked experience.

CORRECT: His qualifications for the position were excellent, *except that* he lacked experience.

over for **more than.** The use of *over* in the sense of *more than* or *in excess of* is avoided by careful writers. *Examples:*

DO NOT USE:

> CARELESS: The organization lost *over* $250,000 on the venture.
> CORRECT: The organization lost *more than* $250,000 on the venture.

over again for **again** or **over.** The expression *over again* is redundant, since the words that compose it have the same meaning. Use *again* or *over*. *Examples:*

> REDUNDANT: Several persons would like to see the film *over again*.
> CORRECT: Several persons would like to see the film *again*.
> REDUNDANT: Much of the work had to be done *over again*.
> CORRECT: Much of the work had to be done *over*.

over with for **over.** The preposition *with* is meaningless and therefore superfluous. *Examples:*

> INCORRECT: I shall return to Los Angeles when the meeting is *over with*.
> CORRECT: I shall return to Los Angeles when the meeting is *over*.

overly for **over.** *Overly* is not recognized as good usage. *Examples:*

> INCORRECT: He is not *overly* enthusiastic about the plan.
> CORRECT: He is not *over*enthusiastic about the plan.

party for **person.** Except in legal terminology (as in *party of the first part*), the use of *party* in referring to one person is a violation of good usage. *Examples:*

> INCORRECT: I know a *party* who is qualified for the position.
> CORRECT: I know a *person* who is qualified for the position.

people for **persons.** *People* is properly used in referring collectively to a group of individuals, as: The *people* of the United States want peace. *Persons* is properly used in referring to individuals as such, as: Five *persons* received promotions last week. *Examples:*

> INCORRECT: Several *people* are being considered for the position.
> CORRECT: Several *persons* are being considered for the position.

per cent for **percentage.** Use of the term *per cent* (also written *percent*) is correct only when it is preceded by a numeral. Otherwise *percentage* should be used. *Examples:*

> INCORRECT: A large *per cent* of our business is done with old customers.
> CORRECT: Seventy *per cent* of our business is done with old customers.
> CORRECT: A large *percentage* of our business is done with old customers.

DO NOT USE:

per year for **per annum** or **a year.** Either the Latin or the English term is correct, but a combination of the two is avoided by careful writers. *Examples:*

CARELESS: The cost of this service is $250 *per year*
CORRECT: The cost of this service is $250 *per annum.*
CORRECT: The cost of this service is $250 *a year.*

personal for **personnel.** This error is inexcusable. The word *personnel,* which is both a noun and an adjective, pertains to a group of persons engaged in some enterprise or activity. It might be applied to the staff of a business concern, the faculty of a college, or the membership of a civic organization. *Examples:*

INCORRECT: The *personal* of the film includes several very able men.
CORRECT: The *personnel* of the firm includes several very able men.
INCORRECT: He plans to study *personal* management.
CORRECT: He plans to study *personnel* management.

plan on for **plan.** The superfluous *on* should be omitted. *Examples:*

INCORRECT: We do not *plan on* an immediate revision of this book.
CORRECT: We do not *plan* an immediate revision of this book.

posted for **informed.** The use of *posted* as a synonym for *informed* is a colloquialism to be avoided in letter writing. *Examples:*

CARELESS: I agreed to keep him *posted* as to developments during his absence.
CORRECT: I agreed to keep him *informed* as to developments during his absence.
CARELESS: Relatively few persons are well *posted* on foreign affairs.
CORRECT: Relatively few persons are well *informed* on foreign affairs.

practical for **practicable.** These adjectives are not interchangeable. *Practical* (the opposite of *theoretical*) means *capable of being put to useful application.* *Practicable* (the opposite of *impracticable*) means *capable of being done or accomplished.* Thus flagpole sitting is *practicable* (since it can be done) but not *practical* (since it serves no good purpose). *Examples:*

INCORRECT: Gertrude Ederle proved that swimming the English Channel is *practical.*
CORRECT: Gertrude Ederle proved that swimming the English Channel is *practicable.*

DO NOT USE:

proposition (as a substitute for an accurate identifying noun). The word *proposition* is overworked and frequently misused as a substitute for *plan, arrangement, suggestion,* or *undertaking. Examples:*

> CARELESS: I hope this *proposition* will appeal to you.
> CORRECT: I hope this *plan* (or *arrangement*) will appeal to you.
> CARELESS: We believe you will find this *proposition* worthy of consideration.
> CORRECT: We believe you will find this *suggestion* (or *undertaking*) worthy of consideration.

proven for **proved.** *Proven* is no longer recognized as good usage. *Examples:*

> INCORRECT: This product is one of *proven* reliability.
> CORRECT: This product is one of *proved* reliability.
> INCORRECT: He has *proven* his right to the promotion.
> CORRECT: He has *proved* his right to the promotion.

providing for **provided.** Only *provided* is correct in the sense of *on condition that* or *with the provision that. Examples:*

> INCORRECT: We can complete the work on schedule, *providing* the material reaches us by June 15.
> CORRECT: We can complete the work on schedule, *provided* the material reaches us by June 15.

quantity for **number.** *Quantity* applies to amount, as: Each week we sell a large *quantity* of coal. *Number* applies to individual units, as: The *number* of applicants for the position increases each week. *Examples:*

> INCORRECT: Each year brings an increase in the *quantity* of trucks on the highways.
> CORRECT: Each year brings an increase in the *number* of trucks on the highways.

quite for **rather** or **somewhat.** Since *quite* means *completely* or *entirely,* it is not a synonym for *rather* or *somewhat. Examples:*

> INCORRECT: He was *quite* concerned over the decreased volume of sales.
> CORRECT: He was *rather* (or *somewhat*) concerned over the decreased volume of sales.

quite a few for **several.** Since *quite* means *completely* or *entirely,* the expression *quite a few* is self-contradictory. *Examples:*

> INCORRECT: *Quite a few* of our employees are married.
> CORRECT: *Several* of our employees are married.

DO NOT USE:

quite unique for **unusual.** Since *unique* means *without an equal or parallel,* the modifier *quite* is redundant. When this faulty expression is used, the intended meaning is *unusual. Examples:*

REDUNDANT: Some of his experiences were *quite unique.*
CORRECT: Some of his experiences were *unusual.*

rather unique for **unusual.** The adjective *unique* should not be qualified, since it means *without an equal or parallel. Examples:*

INCORRECT: His philosophy of business is *rather unique.*
CORRECT: His philosophy of business is *unusual.*

real for **very.** The adverbial use of *real* is not recognized as good usage. *Examples:*

INCORRECT: Their new office building is *real* impressive.
CORRECT: Their new office building is *very* impressive.
INCORRECT: Business conditions are improving *real* rapidly.
CORRECT: Business conditions are improving *very* rapidly.

reason . . . is (or **was**) **because** for **reason . . . is** (or **was**) **that.** The expression *the reason . . . is* (or *was*) should not be followed by a "because" clause or a "because of" phrase. *Examples:*

INCORRECT: The *reason* for the change *is because* Mr. Allaway is ill.
INCORRECT: The *reason* for the change *is because* of Mr. Allaway's illness.
CORRECT: The *reason* for the change *is that* Mr. Allaway is ill.
INCORRECT: The *reason* for the delay *was because* a breakdown occurred in our plant.
INCORRECT: The *reason* for the delay *was because* of a breakdown in our plant.
CORRECT: The *reason* for the delay *was that* a breakdown occurred in our plant.

refer back for **refer.** The superfluous *back* should be omitted. *Examples:*

INCORRECT: If you will *refer back* to the report of the committee, you will find several pages devoted to this question.
CORRECT: If you will *refer* to the report of the committee, you will find several pages devoted to this question.

remember of for **remember.** The superfluous *of* should be omitted. *Examples:*

INCORRECT: I *remember of* discussing this question with you last year.

DO NOT USE:

> CORRECT: I *remember* discussing this question with you last year.

repeat . . . again for **repeat.** The word *again* adds nothing to the meaning of *repeat*, which means *to do or say again. Examples:*

> REDUNDANT: We shall *repeat* this program *again* next week.
> CORRECT: We shall *repeat* this program next week.

run for **manage** or **operate.** This colloquial use of *run* should be avoided in letters. *Examples:*

> CARELESS: One of his assistants can *run* the business in his absence.
> CORRECT: One of his assistants can *manage* the business in his absence.
> CARELESS: We must continue to *run* the plant on the same financial basis.
> CORRECT: We must continue to *operate* the plant on the same financial basis.

saleslady for **saleswoman.** The term *saleslady* is no more appropriate than *salesgentleman.* The correct words are *saleswoman* and *salesman. Examples:*

> INCORRECT: An alert *saleslady* finds many opportunities to perform extra services.
> CORRECT: An alert *saleswoman* finds many opportunities to perform extra services.

see . . . where for **see . . . that.** This error usually occurs in references to newspaper items noticed by the writer. *Examples:*

> INCORRECT: I *see* in this morning's paper *where* you have been named Secretary of your firm.
> CORRECT: I *see* in this morning's paper *that* you have been named Secretary of your firm.

seldom ever for **seldom** or **hardly ever.** In the first expression *ever* is meaningless and therefore superfluous. *Examples:*

> INCORRECT: He *seldom ever* attends a meeting.
> CORRECT: He *seldom* (or *hardly ever*) attends a meeting.

semimonthly for **bimonthly.** See *bimonthly.*

semiweekly for **biweekly.** See *biweekly.*

shall for **will** or **will** for **shall.** Simple futurity or expectation is indicated by the use of *shall* in the first person and *will* in the second and third. Determination or promise is indicated by the use of *will* in the first person and *shall* in the second and third. The

DO NOT USE:

same distinction applies to *should* and *would* (*should* corresponds to *shall* and *would* corresponds to *will*). *Examples:*

INCORRECT: I *will* always be glad to hear from you. (Simple futurity.)

CORRECT: I *shall* always be glad to hear from you.

INCORRECT: I believe you *shall* enjoy a visit to our plant. (Simple futurity.)

CORRECT: I believe you *will* enjoy a visit to our plant.

INCORRECT: Though some may attempt to dissuade me, I *shall* continue to give you every possible assistance. (Both determination and promise.)

CORRECT: Though some may attempt to dissuade me, I *will* continue to give you every possible assistance.

shape for **condition.** The use of *shape* as a synonym for *condition* is a colloquialism to be avoided in letter writing. *Examples:*

INCORRECT: The entire plant is in good *shape.*

CORRECT: The entire plant is in good *condition.*

should for **would.** See *shall.*

should of for **should have.** See *could of.*

size for **sized.** *Size* should not be used as the latter word of a compound adjective. *Examples:*

INCORRECT: One of your medium-*size* banquet rooms would be suitable.

CORRECT: One of your medium-*sized* banquet rooms would be suitable.

size up for **appraise, evaluate, analyze,** or **estimate.** The expression *size up* is a colloquialism to be avoided in letter writing. *Examples:*

CARELESS: I hope you will soon have an opportunity to *size up* the equipment.

CORRECT: I hope you will soon have an opportunity to *appraise* (or *evaluate*) the equipment.

CARELESS: He will be able to *size up* our needs after he has visited the warehouse.

CORRECT: He will be able to *analyze* (or *estimate*) our needs after he has visited the warehouse.

so much for **very much.** The use of *so much* in the sense of *very much* or *to a great degree* is not recognized as good usage. *Examples:*

INCORRECT: Thank you *so much* for your letter.

CORRECT: Thank you *very much* for your letter.

DO NOT USE:

sooner for **rather.** The substitution of *sooner* for *rather* is a common violation of good usage. *Examples:*

INCORRECT: Probably you would *sooner* sell the property than rent it.

CORRECT: Probably you would *rather* sell the property than rent it.

sort of for **rather** or **somewhat.** The expression *sort of* is not an acceptable substitute for an adverb. *Examples:*

INCORRECT: He seemed *sort of* confident that the plan would be approved.

CORRECT: He seemed *rather* confident that the plan would be approved.

INCORRECT: We were *sort of* discouraged by the frequent delays.

CORRECT: We were *somewhat* discouraged by the frequent delays.

sort of a or **sort of an** for **sort of.** The superfluous article *a* or *an* should be omitted. *Examples:*

INCORRECT: This *sort of a* plan should produce good results.

CORRECT: This *sort of* plan should produce good results.

INCORRECT: This *sort of an* arrangement will assure efficiency.

CORRECT: This *sort of* arrangement will assure efficiency.

still remains for **remains.** The adverb *still* is superfluous, since it adds nothing to the meaning of *remains. Examples:*

REDUNDANT: One aspect of the problem *still remains* to be solved.

CORRECT: One aspect of the problem *remains* to be solved.

stop for **stay.** These words are not interchangeable. *Stop* means *to cease action or movement. Stay* means *to remain. Examples:*

INCORRECT: He will *stop* for a week at his ranch in Wyoming.

CORRECT: He will *stay* for a week at his ranch in Wyoming.

suspect for **suppose.** Since *suspect* means *to look upon with suspicion,* its use in the sense of *suppose* is incorrect. *Examples:*

INCORRECT: I *suspect* the meeting will be held in September.

CORRECT: I *suppose* the meeting will be held in September.

the above (as a substitute for an accurate identifying noun). This indefinite term should be avoided in letters. *Examples:*

INCORRECT: If *the above* does not answer your question, please write to me again.

CORRECT: If *the foregoing explanation* does not answer your question, please write to me again.

INCORRECT: I shall be glad if *the above* proves helpful to you.

DO NOT USE:

> CORRECT: I shall be glad if *the preceding information* proves helpful to you.

the fact that for **that.** In many constructions *the fact that* is both awkward and wordy as a substitute for *that. Examples:*

> WORDY: He realizes *the fact that* the delay was unavoidable.
> CORRECT: He realizes *that* the delay was unavoidable.

there for **their.** The incorrect use of *there* as a substitute for the possessive *their* is more frequently due to carelessness than to ignorance. *Examples:*

> INCORRECT: *There* credit rating is excellent.
> CORRECT: *Their* credit rating is excellent.

therefor for **therefore.** *Therefor* means *for that* or *for it,* as: He has made allowance *therefor. Therefore* means *consequently* or *for that reason,* as: We hope, *therefore,* that such an arrangement can be made. *Examples:*

> INCORRECT: He does not feel, *therefor,* that he can accept the position.
> CORRECT: He does not feel, *therefore,* that he can accept the position.

these kind are for **this kind is.** The noun *kind* is singular in number. *Examples:*

> INCORRECT: *These kind are* the best on the market.
> CORRECT: *This kind is* the best on the market.

thing (superfluously or as a substitute for an accurate identifying noun). The noun *thing* is overworked and often misused by letter writers. Either its superfluous use or its careless substitution for an accurate identifying noun indicates slovenliness of both thought and expression. *Examples:*

> WORDY: Care in selecting new agents is an important *thing.*
> CORRECT: Care in selecting new agents is important.
> CARELESS: This *thing* deserves careful consideration.
> CORRECT: This *problem* (or *question*) deserves careful consideration.

this data is for **these data are.** The noun *data* is the plural form of *datum. Examples:*

> INCORRECT: *This data is* at your disposal.
> CORRECT: *These data are* at your disposal.

to for **too.** This error is often due to carelessness rather than to ignorance, since the preposition *to* is used more frequently than the adverb *too. Examples:*

DO NOT USE:

> INCORRECT: His application arrived *to* late for consideration.
> CORRECT: His application arrived *too* late for consideration.
> INCORRECT: These problems, *to,* must be considered.
> CORRECT: These problems, *too,* must be considered.

transpire for **happen.** These words are not interchangeable. *Transpire* means *to become known,* whereas *happen* means *to occur. Examples:*

> INCORRECT: Such an accident could not *transpire* in a well-managed factory.
> CORRECT: Such an accident could not *happen* in a well-managed factory.

try and for **try to.** This common misuse of the conjunction *and* should be avoided. *Examples:*

> INCORRECT: Please *try and* complete your report by June 18.
> CORRECT: Please *try to* complete your report by June 18.

under for **less than.** The use of *under* in the sense of *less than* is avoided by careful writers. *Examples:*

> CARELESS: His expenses for the entire trip were *under* $250.
> CORRECT: His expenses for the entire trip were *less than* $250.

uninterested for **disinterested.** These adjectives are not interchangeable. *Uninterested* means *not interested, lacking interest,* or *indifferent. Disinterested* means *impartial, unprejudiced,* or *unbiased. Examples:*

> INCORRECT: Only an *uninterested* person could decide the issue fairly.
> CORRECT: Only a *disinterested* person could decide the issue fairly.

up to for **until.** The use of *up to* in the sense of *until* (as in the common expression *up to now*) is not recognized as good usage. *Examples:*

> INCORRECT: The store will be open *up to* six o'clock.
> CORRECT: The store will be open *until* six o'clock.
> INCORRECT: There was little demand for this merchandise *up to* this morning.
> CORRECT: There was little demand for this merchandise *until* this morning.

very for **very much** or **very well.** The use of *very* immediately before a past participle is incorrect. Such a construction requires the use of *very much* or *very well. Examples:*

> INCORRECT: He is *very* interested in the progress of your department.

DO NOT USE:

> CORRECT: He is *very much* interested in the progress of your department.
>
> INCORRECT: We are *very* satisfied with the results of your work.
>
> CORRECT: We are *very well* satisfied with the results of your work.

very complete for **complete.** The expression *very complete* is redundant, since completeness is absolute. *Examples:*

> REDUNDANT: Our records of this transaction are *very complete.*
>
> CORRECT: Our records of this transaction are *complete.*

wait on for **wait for.** The expression *wait on* is a violation of good usage when it is used in the sense of *wait for. Examples:*

> INCORRECT: We shall *wait on* you at the office.
>
> CORRECT: We shall *wait for* you at the office.

want to for **should.** This error is a flagrant violation of good usage. *Examples:*

> INCORRECT: You *want to* report the damage to the shipping department.
>
> CORRECT: You *should* report the damage to the shipping department.

will for **shall.** See *shall.*

with you and I for **with you and me.** The pronoun *I* is incorrect as the object of a preposition. (For this reason *with him and I, with John and I,* and *between you and I* are also ungrammatical.) *Examples:*

> INCORRECT: He may decide to go *with you and I.*
>
> CORRECT: He may decide to go *with you and me.*

would for **should.** See *shall.*

would have for **had.** This error, which is common after *if,* is a flagrant violation of English grammar. *Examples:*

> INCORRECT: If he *would have* reported the damage earlier, we could have duplicated the shipment promptly.
>
> CORRECT: If he *had* reported the damage earlier, we could have duplicated the shipment promptly.

would of for **would have.** See *could of.*

you for **your.** The use of *you* immediately preceding a gerund (verbal noun) is incorrect, since this construction requires the possessive form. *Examples:*

> INCORRECT: We appreciate *you* trying to help us.
>
> CORRECT: We appreciate *your* trying to help us.

DO NOT USE:

INCORRECT: Nothing will be gained by *you* going to New Orleans.
CORRECT: Nothing will be gained by *your* going to New Orleans.

yourself for **you.** *Yourself* should be used only as an intensive or a reflexive. It is not a correct substitute for *you. Examples:*

INCORRECT: Most of the credit belongs to *yourself.*
CORRECT: Most of the credit belongs to *you.*
INCORRECT: *Yourself* and your associates deserve most of the credit.
CORRECT: *You* and your associates deserve most of the credit.

APPENDIX C

Guides to Correct Punctuation [1]

The Comma (,)

The comma, since it is used most frequently, is the most important mark of punctuation. Compared with other marks, it indicates the smallest degree of separation between words and is used in a wide variety of cases. According to the following rules, we should separate or set apart by commas:

1. Members of a series. *Example:*

    You have done your work with vigor, enthusiasm, accuracy, and intelligence.

2. Parenthetical expressions, when the degree of separation is too slight to warrant the use of dashes or parentheses. The following may be considered parenthetical expressions:

    (a) A word in apposition with another word. *Example:*

    Our representative, Mr. Wallace, paid you a high compliment.

    (b) Explanatory expressions. *Example:*

    Mr. Hendricks, the man at the second window, will be glad to assist you. (*The man at the second window* is really in apposition with *Mr. Hendricks.*)

    (c) Nonrestrictive clauses. *Example:*

    The schedule is crowded just now, which accounts for the unavoidable delay.

    (d) Many adverbial expressions, like the one italicized below:

    I believe, *in the main,* that you are right.

[1] This section is adapted from *Business Writing—Theory and Practice,* by Parkhurst and Davis (Prentice-Hall, Inc., New York), by permission of the authors and publishers.

(e) Expressions coming between parts of a quotation. *Example:*

> "I will be there," he said, "if I can possibly arrange it."

3. Direct quotations. *Example:*

> He said, "I will be there if I can possibly arrange it."

4. Sometimes the clauses of a compound sentence when the clauses are simple and closely related in meaning (if the clauses are very short, the comma is usually omitted). *Example:*

> I shall be in the office all day March 8, and I shall look forward to seeing you.

5. Inverted or transposed expressions. *Example:*

> To make your shopping more enjoyable, we have installed air-conditioning throughout the store.

6. Direct address. *Example:*

> Mr. Jennings, I know you will understand the factors underlying this decision.

7. The absolute construction. *Example:*

> The river being choked with ice, it was impossible for us to proceed.

8. Sometimes words between which the verb is omitted. *Example:*

> Some delegates will arrive Friday evening; others, Saturday morning.

The Semicolon (;)

The semicolon is employed when it is desired to indicate a separation or break in the thought somewhat greater than that indicated by the comma. The semicolon is appropriate:

1. Between the members of a compound sentence not related closely enough to call for the comma. *Example:*

> It was the first step in the development of our public-relations program; and our present service department is the outgrowth of that early experiment.

2. Between the members of a compound sentence, especially when either or both contain commas. *Example:*

We try, whenever possible, to make helpful suggestions; and often, we are told, these suggestions are of value to our patrons.

3. When, in order to indicate a closer relation, several simple sentences are regarded as clauses of a single sentence. *Example:*

There are the sales executives; there are the credit managers; there are the public-relations experts.

4. Before the expressions *namely, as, to wit, i.e., e.g.,* and *viz.,* when used to introduce an example or illustration. *Examples:*

Mr. Fisher was the father of the plan; *i.e.,* he was the chief author of its original outline.

He has contributed much to our selling efficiency; *e.g.,* he planned the best direct-mail campaign we have ever conducted.

The Colon (:)

The colon is employed to indicate a degree of separation or break in the thought somewhat greater than that indicated by the semicolon, but not so great as that indicated by the period. The colon is appropriate:

1. Between members of a compound sentence either or both of which are punctuated by semicolons. *Example:*

Be sure your methods are efficient; your decisions, fair; your policies, sound: thus will you lay the foundation stones of lasting success.

2. After an expression that formally introduces a series or quotation, whether or not there are present the words *as follows, the following, thus,* or some similar introductory expression. *Examples:*

The following qualities are essential to good business correspondence: clearness, correctness, conciseness, completeness, and courtesy.

Mr. Wellman spoke on two subjects: first, "How to Plan Effective Sales Campaigns"; and second, "Sales Letters That Get Results."

3. After the salutation in a business letter.[2] *Examples:*

My dear Mrs. Gifford:
Dear Mr. Martin:
Gentlemen:

[2] An informal salutation, as in a personal letter to an intimate friend, may be followed by a comma. *Example:* Dear Jim,

4. Usually between the hours and minutes in expressions denoting time. *Examples:*

7:30 A.M.
5:45 P.M.

The Period (.)

The comma, the semicolon, the colon, and the period perform almost the same function—separation—the difference being that of degree. The comma indicates the smallest degree of separation; the period, the largest; with smaller and larger intermediate degrees indicated by the semicolon and the colon, respectively. The period is used:

1. After a declarative sentence. *Example:*

The contract will be signed next week.

2. After almost every abbreviation. *Examples:*

Mr.
Calif.
W. Algonquin St.

Other Punctuation Marks

The other punctuation marks in general use are the interrogation mark, the exclamation mark, the quotation marks, the hyphen, marks of parentheses, and the dash.

The interrogation point (?) not only is used at the end of a direct question, but also is enclosed within marks of parentheses to indicate that a word or statement is doubtful.

The exclamation point (!) is intended primarily to show that a word or sentence expresses some strong emotion. It is also used in advertising as a means of placing special emphasis upon some important feature.

Quotation marks (" "), which are usually employed to indicate the exact words of another writer or speaker, are also frequently used to indicate an expression or thought for which the writer wishes to disclaim responsibility.

The hyphen (-) is used as a means of drawing together two separate words into a compound word with some new or special significance. After the word becomes established, however, the hyphen is likely to disappear, and the word is thence-forth written as a unit. The hyphen is also used to separate parts of words divided at the ends of lines.

Marks of parentheses, ( ), are used to enclose some expression introduced gratuitously and regarded by the writer as not strictly essential. An expression so written is not attractive, however, and it is often possible to avoid it by using commas instead of the marks of parentheses.

The dash ($-$) is legitimately used to indicate a sudden break in the continuity of thought, as: "I could tell you about a—but I must bring my letter to a close." In general, however, one should beware of overusing this mark. Its excessive use usually indicates that a writer does not know how to use correctly other punctuation marks.

APPENDIX D

Guides to Correct Capitalization [1]

1. Capitalize points of the compass when they are used to designate specific geographical sections of the country. *Examples:*

   Seattle is an important city of the *Northwest.*
   Texas is the largest state in the *Southwest.*

   Do not capitalize points of the compass or their derivatives when they are used merely to indicate direction. *Example:*

   After visiting several cities in *southern* Oklahoma, he traveled *south* to Dallas and then *east* to Shreveport.

2. Capitalize a common noun:

   (a) when it is particularized by use as part of a proper name. *Example:*

   During our motor trip we saw Pike's *Peak, Lake* Michigan, the Mississippi *River,* Concord *Bridge,* and Dartmouth *College.*

   (b) when it is used to represent a proper noun. *Examples:*

   The *University* was founded in 1740. (*University* refers specifically to the University of Pennsylvania.)

   The expansion of the *Company* has been both sound and rapid. (*Company* refers specifically to the Phillips Petroleum Company.)

   Do not capitalize a common noun used as such—that is, a noun used to designate a general class of persons or things. *Examples:*

   Many large *universities* have been handicapped by financial limitations.

   The experience he gained as a *bookkeeper* and *stenographer* proved valuable to him in later life.

---

[1] This section deals only with common points of confusion in the use of capital letters. No attempt is made to set forth all the rules of capitalization, most of which are clearly understood and consistently applied by business correspondents. An exhaustive treatment of the rules of capitalization may be found in any of the books on English usage listed on page 314.

3. Capitalize a designation of rank or position:

  (a) when it is particularized by use in connection with the name of a person. *Examples:*

> The principal speaker was *Professor* James Ward of Purdue University.

> The guest of honor was Mr. Warren D. Black, *President* of Marshall & Black, Inc.

  (b) when it refers to a specific person. *Examples:*

> In 1939 the *King* of England visited the *President* of the United States at the White House.

> Yesterday he called on the *Vice President* of Prentice-Hall, Inc.

> The *Governor* will officiate at the cornerstone laying.

Do not capitalize a designation of rank or position when it is used as a common noun—that is, in a general rather than a specific sense. *Examples:*

> Hard work and ability are required of anyone who would become *managing editor* of a metropolitan newspaper.

> The *presidents* of several large universities are both thorough scholars and capable administrators.

> Conscientious devotion to duty has impaired the health of many *governors.*

4. Capitalize the names of months and days of the week, but not the names of seasons. *Examples:*

> Our *spring* advertising campaign will begin next *Wednesday, March* 24.

> At the *April* meeting we voted to hold another conference in the *fall.*

5. Capitalize the names of the various fields of learning:

  (a) when they are used to designate specific courses of study. *Example:*

> His course schedule included *Mathematics* 6, *Physics* 30, and *Economics* 10.

  (b) when they are proper nouns. *Example:*

> Many universities require the study of *French, German,* or *Spanish.*

Do not capitalize the names of the various fields of learning when they are used as common nouns—that is, in a general rather than a specific sense. (It should be noted, however, that when the name of a field of learning is a proper noun, such as *English,* the word retains its capital letter even when used in a general sense.) *Example:*

> His preparation for newspaper work included the study of *journalism, English, economics,* and *history.*

6. Capitalize the principal words (usually all except prepositions, conjunctions, and articles) in the title of a book, magazine, pamphlet, chapter, article, address, or report. Capitalize the first word of such a title even when it is a preposition, conjunction, or article. *Examples:*

> He will speak on "A Plan for World Peace."

> He is the author of a recent article entitled "The Origin and Growth of the Oklahoma Highway Patrol System."

> His new book, *How to Write Effective Letters,* has just been published.

APPENDIX E

Titles Commonly Used in Addressing Individuals

Both custom and courtesy in letter writing dictate the use of an appropriate title in connection with the reader's name. Correct form in the use of common titles is discussed in the following paragraphs.

1. *Mr.* (abbreviation of *Mister*) is probably the title most frequently used in letter writing. It is employed in addressing a man who has no other title, or whose special title is unknown to the writer. It is always abbreviated.

In the salutation the title *Mr.* should be accompanied by the surname of the addressee.[1] *Examples:*

> INCORRECT: Dear Mr.:
> CORRECT: Dear Mr. McKeever:

2. *Mrs.* (abbreviation of *Mistress*) is the title used in addressing a married woman, a widow, or a divorcee (unless she assumes the title *Miss* after the divorce). It is always abbreviated. When the title is employed in addressing a married woman, it is followed by the name of her husband. *Example:*

> CORRECT: Mrs. Raymond G. Barber

When the title is used in addressing a widow, it may be followed either by the name of her late husband or by her own name. When it is possible to ascertain which form she prefers, this should be done. *Examples:*

> CORRECT: Mrs. John G. Lindsey
> CORRECT: Mrs. Grace D. Lindsey

When the title is used in addressing a divorcee, it should be followed by her own name. *Example:*

> CORRECT: Mrs. Helen B. Young

[1] A few exceptions occur in special forms of address for persons of rank (pages 356-370), in which an official designation is used instead of the surname. *Examples: My dear Mr. Attorney General, My dear Mr. Chief Justice, My dear Mr. Secretary.*

In the salutation the title *Mrs.* should be accompanied by the surname of the addressee. *Examples:*

> INCORRECT:　My dear Mrs.:
> CORRECT:　　My dear Mrs. Bowman:

3. *Miss* is the title employed in addressing a girl or an unmarried woman. Since it is not an abbreviation, it should not be followed by a period. When the writer is unable to ascertain whether the title of the addressee is *Miss* or *Mrs.*, the form *Miss* should be employed.

In the salutation the title *Miss* should be accompanied by the surname of the addressee. *Examples:*

> INCORRECT:　Dear Miss:
> CORRECT:　　Dear Miss Milburn:

4. *Dr.* (abbreviation of *Doctor*) is the title used in addressing a man or woman who holds a doctor's degree from a university. The degree may represent any of several fields of learning, such as medicine (*M.D.*), philosophy (*Ph.D.*), science (*D.Sc.*), law (*LL.D.*), divinity (*D.D.*), or literature (*Lit.D.*). The title *Dr.* is correctly abbreviated.

In the inside address, if the writer prefers to use the abbreviation of the specific doctor's degree held by the reader, this abbreviation should follow the person's name, separated from it by a comma. In this case no title should precede the name.[2] *Examples:*

> CORRECT:　Dr. James H. Sheldon
> CORRECT:　James H. Sheldon, M.D.
> CORRECT:　Dr. Roger L. Porter
> CORRECT:　Roger L. Porter, Ph.D.

In the salutation the abbreviation of a specific doctor's degree should never be substituted for the title *Dr. Examples:*

> INCORRECT:　Dear Colvert, M.D.:
> INCORRECT:　Dear Colvert, Ph.D.:
> CORRECT:　　Dear Dr. Colvert:

The title *Dr.* in the salutation should be accompanied by the surname of the addressee. *Examples:*

> INCORRECT:　Dear Dr.:
> CORRECT:　　Dear Dr. Robertson:

---

[2] There is one exception to this rule. The title *Reverend* may precede the name of a clergyman even when the abbreviation *D.D.* follows it (see page 354).

5. *Professor* is the title used in addressing a member of a college or university faculty, either man or woman, who holds the rank of *professor, associate professor,* or *assistant professor.* The title is preferably written in full, although the abbreviation *Prof.* is frequently used. The latter form is permissible in the inside address when its use is necessary in order to reduce a long line to a satisfactory length. *Examples:*

> PREFERABLE: Professor John R. Dunn
> PERMISSIBLE: Prof. Alexander H. Richardson

When the title *Professor* is used in the inside address, it should also be used (instead of *Mr.* or *Dr.*) in the salutation. The abbreviation *Prof.* is not considered good form in the salutation. *Examples:*

> POOR FORM: Dear Prof. Wharton:
> CORRECT: Dear Professor Wharton:

The title *Professor* in the salutation should be accompanied by the surname of the addressee. *Examples:*

> INCORRECT: My dear Professor:
> CORRECT: My dear Professor Morgan:

Further illustrations of correct form in addressing a college or university professor are shown on page 366.

6. *Honorable* is the title frequently employed in addressing persons prominent in affairs of government. (For specific examples, see *Forms of Address for Persons of Rank,* pages 356-370.) The title is preferably written in full and preceded by *The,* although the omission of the prefix is permissible. The abbreviation *Hon.* is permissible when its use is necessary in order to reduce a long line to a satisfactory length. When the abbreviated form is used, the prefix *The* should be omitted. *Examples:*

> PREFERABLE: The Honorable John G. Clark
> PERMISSIBLE: Honorable Walter J. Clifton
> PERMISSIBLE: Hon. Mortimer G. Dillingsworth
> INCORRECT: The Hon. Percy E. Dodson

When the title *Honorable* is used in the inside address, the group of appropriate salutations varies according to the official position held by the addressee (see pages 356-370). Under no circumstances, however, should the word *Honorable* appear in the salutation.

7. *Reverend* is the title employed in addressing a clergyman. This title, like *Honorable,* is preferably written in full and preceded by *The,* although the omission of the prefix is permissible. The abbreviation *Rev.* is permissible when its use is necessary in order to reduce a long line to a satisfactory length. When the abbreviated form is used, the prefix *The* should be omitted. *Examples:*

PREFERABLE: The Reverend James D. Finch
PERMISSIBLE: Reverend Charles B. Williams
PERMISSIBLE: Rev. Hamilton H. Sollenberger
INCORRECT: The Rev. Walter L. Peters

The title *Reverend* (written in full and preceded by *The*) may be combined with *Mr.* in addressing a clergyman, provided neither his given name nor his initials appear. *Examples:*

CORRECT: The Reverend Mr. Franklin
INCORRECT: Rev. Mr. Franklin
INCORRECT: The Reverend Mr. J. R. Franklin
INCORRECT: The Reverend Mr. James Franklin

When a clergyman holds a doctor's degree, the title *Reverend* (written in full and preceded by *The*) may be combined with the title *Dr.* in addressing him, provided neither his given name nor his initials appear. *Examples:*

CORRECT: The Reverend Dr. Andrews
INCORRECT: Rev. Dr. Andrews
INCORRECT: The Reverend Dr. H. J. Andrews
INCORRECT: The Reverend Dr. Homer Andrews

Another form is also correct in addressing a clergyman who holds a doctor's degree. The title *Reverend* (preferably preceded by *The*) may appear before the name, which is followed by the abbreviation of his doctor's degree. *Examples:*

PREFERABLE: The Reverend John Kellogg, D.D.
PERMISSIBLE: Reverend John Kellogg, D.D.

When the title *Reverend* is used in the inside address, the title *Mr.* (or *Dr.*, if the addressee holds a doctor's degree) should ordinarily be used in the salutation. Except in special forms of address, the word *Reverend* should not appear in the salutation.[3] *Examples:*

CORRECT: My dear Mr. (*or* Dr.) Wheeler:
INCORRECT: My dear Reverend Wheeler:
CORRECT: Dear Mr. (*or* Dr.) Mathews:
INCORRECT: Dear Reverend Mathews:

8. *Esq.* (abbreviation of *Esquire*) is the equivalent of *Mr.* in American usage. It is used mainly in addressing professional men.

[3] One exception is a special form appropriate in greeting a Roman Catholic priest (see page 366); another is a special form appropriate in greeting a Jewish rabbi (see page 366).

The title *Esq.* is correctly abbreviated. It should follow the name of the addressee, separated from it by a comma, and should be preceded by no other title. *Examples:*

CORRECT: Mr. George L. Whitman
CORRECT: George L. Whitman, Esq.
INCORRECT: Mr. George L. Whitman, Esq.

When the title *Esq.* is used in the inside address, the title **Mr.** should be substituted for it in the salutation. *Examples:*

INCORRECT: Dear Phillips, Esq.:
INCORRECT: Dear Esq. Phillips:
CORRECT: Dear Mr. Phillips:

APPENDIX F

Forms of Address for Persons of Rank

Special forms are used in addressing and greeting persons of rank. In each case the inside address should be identical in content with the envelope address. Letters to persons of rank are frequently written in the official form, an example of which is shown on page 376.

When the extremely formal salutation *Sir* is employed, consistency requires the use of a complimentary close that includes the word *respectfully* (such as *Respectfully yours* or *Yours respectfully*). Such a close may also be used with a salutation of a less formal character when the writer wishes to show special deference to rank or authority. Otherwise one of the complimentary closes including the word *truly* (such as *Very truly yours* or *Yours very truly*) is appropriate for use with any salutation (except *Sir*) that appears in the following lists. If the writer is well acquainted with the addressee, a salutation and a complimentary close of less formality may be employed.

The following special forms are correct in addressing and greeting the officials designated: [1]

[1] Forms that apply to government officials may be used in addressing and greeting women as well as men, provided the word *Madam* is substituted wherever *Sir* or *Mr.* appears. The words *Assemblywoman* and *Congresswoman* should be avoided in favor of alternative forms.

Examples:

Men	Women
Sir:	Madam:
Dear Sir:	Dear Madam:
My dear Mr. Secretary:	My dear Madam Secretary:
My dear Mr. Mayor:	My dear Madam Mayor:

AMBASSADOR

American:

Inside address	*Salutation*
His Excellency The American Ambassador to Great Britain The American Embassy London, England	Sir: Your Excellency: My dear Mr. Ambassador:

The Honorable Walter D. Morrison
American Ambassador to Great Britain
The American Embassy
London, England

British (same general form used in addressing ambassador of other foreign country):

Inside address	*Salutation*
His Excellency The Ambassador of Great Britain British Embassy Washington, D. C.	Sir: Excellency: Your Excellency: My dear Mr. Ambassador: Dear Mr. Ambassador:

His Excellency
George Dillingham
Ambassador of Great Britain
British Embassy
Washington, D. C.

ARMY OFFICER

See *Correct Form in Writing to Army and Naval Officers,* pages 371-372.

ASSEMBLYMAN (MEMBER OF THE ASSEMBLY OF A STATE LEGISLATURE)

Inside address	*Salutation*
The Honorable John B. Rogers Member of Assembly Albany, New York	Sir: Dear Sir: My dear Mr. Rogers: Dear Mr. Rogers:

Assemblyman John B. Rogers
The State Capitol
Albany, New York

Associate Judge of a Court of Appeals

Inside address	*Salutation*
The Honorable Eugene P. Clements Associate Judge of the Court of Appeals Albany, New York	Sir: Dear Sir:

Associate Justice of a State Supreme Court

Inside address	*Salutation*
The Honorable Allen R. Forrester Associate Justice of the Supreme Court Albany, New York	Sir: Dear Sir:

Associate Justice of the Supreme Court of the United States

Inside address	*Salutation*
The Honorable James S. Randall Associate Justice of the Supreme Court Washington, D. C.	Sir: Dear Sir: My dear Mr. Justice: Dear Mr. Justice:
The Honorable James S. Randall Justice, Supreme Court of the United States Washington, D. C.	My dear Mr. Justice Randall: Dear Mr. Justice Randall:

Attorney General

Inside address	*Salutation*
The Honorable The Attorney General Washington, D. C.	Sir: Dear Sir: My dear Mr. Attorney General:
The Honorable Wayne D. Parker The Attorney General Washington, D. C.	

Cabinet Officer

See *Attorney General, Postmaster General, Secretary of Agriculture, Secretary of Commerce, Secretary of Defense, Secretary of Labor, Secretary of State, Secretary of the Interior, Secretary of the Treasury.*

CHANCELLOR OF A UNIVERSITY

Inside address [2]	*Salutation*
Robert Grimes Harlowe, LL.D.	Dear Sir:
(*or* Lit.D., D.Sc., etc.)	My dear Chancellor Harlowe:
Chancellor of Syracuse University	My dear Dr. Harlowe:
Syracuse, New York	(if he holds the degree)
	Dear Chancellor Harlowe:
Dr. Robert Grimes Harlowe	Dear Dr. Harlowe:
Chancellor of Syracuse University	(if he holds the degree)
Syracuse, New York	
Chancellor Robert Grimes Harlowe	
Syracuse University	
Syracuse, New York	

CHIEF JUDGE OF A COURT OF APPEALS

Inside address	*Salutation*
The Chief Judge of the Court of Appeals	Sir:
Albany, New York	Dear Sir:
	My dear Judge Milton:
The Honorable Clifford D. Milton	
Chief Judge of the Court of Appeals	
Albany, New York	

CHIEF JUSTICE OF A STATE SUPREME COURT

Inside address	*Salutation*
The Chief Justice	Sir:
Supreme Court of the State of New York	Dear Sir:
Albany, New York	My dear Mr. Chief Justice:
	Dear Mr. Chief Justice:
The Honorable Warren F. Gilmore	My dear Mr. Justice Gilmore:
Chief Justice of the Supreme Court	Dear Mr. Justice Gilmore:
Albany, New York	

CHIEF JUSTICE OF THE UNITED STATES

Inside address	*Salutation*
The Chief Justice of the United States	Sir:
Washington, D. C.	Dear Sir:
	My dear Mr. Chief Justice:
The Chief Justice of the Supreme Court	Dear Mr. Chief Justice:
Washington, D. C.	My dear Mr. Justice
	Thornton:
The Honorable Howard M. Thornton	Dear Mr. Justice Thornton:
Chief Justice of the Supreme Court of	
the United States	
Washington, D. C.	

[2] The third form should be used when the addressee does not hold a doctor's degree, or when the writer is not certain that he does.

CLERGYMAN

See *Reverend,* pages 353-354. For special forms appropriate in addressing a Roman Catholic priest, see page 366. For special forms appropriate in addressing a Jewish rabbi, see page 366.

COMMISSIONER OF A GOVERNMENT BUREAU

Inside address	*Salutation*
The Commissioner of the Bureau of Education	Sir:
	Dear Sir:
Department of the Interior	My dear Mr. Commissioner:
Washington, D. C.	Dear Mr. Commissioner:
	My dear Mr. Foster:

The Honorable Dwight L. Foster
Commissioner of the Bureau of Education
Department of the Interior
Washington, D. C.

CONGRESSMAN

See *Representative in Congress* and *Senator (United States).*

CONSUL

Inside address [3]	*Salutation*
To the American Consul at London	Sir:
London, England	My dear Sir:
	Dear Sir:
Mr. Arthur Whittington	My dear Mr. Whittington:
American Consul at London	
London, England	

DEAN OF A COLLEGE FOR WOMEN

Inside address	*Salutation*
Dean Elizabeth Ames Jackson	My dear Dean Jackson:
Wellesley College	My dear Dr. Jackson:
Wellesley, Massachusetts	(if she holds the degree)
	Dear Dean Jackson:
Dean Jackson	Dear Dr. Jackson:
Wellesley College	(if she holds the degree)
Wellesley, Massachusetts	

[3] In addressing a Consul in Central or South America, substitute *United States* for *American* in the following forms.

DEAN OF A COLLEGE OR UNIVERSITY

Inside address [4]	*Salutation*
Dean Albert S. Gardner School of Business Columbia University New York, New York	Dear Sir: My dear Dean Gardner: My dear Dr. Gardner: (if he holds the degree) Dear Dean Gardner:
Albert S. Gardner, Ph.D. Dean of the School of Business Columbia University New York, New York	Dear Dr. Gardner: (if he holds the degree)
Dr. Albert S. Gardner Dean of the School of Business Columbia University New York, New York	

DELEGATE (MEMBER OF THE HOUSE OF DELEGATES OF A STATE LEGISLATURE)

Inside address	*Salutation*
The Honorable Donald H. Gregory The House of Delegates Charleston, West Virginia	Sir: Dear Sir: My dear Mr. Gregory: Dear Mr. Gregory:

GOVERNOR OF A STATE

Inside address	*Salutation*
The Honorable The Governor of Michigan Lansing, Michigan	Sir: Dear Sir: Your Excellency: My dear Governor Wood:
His Excellency The Governor of Michigan Lansing, Michigan	Dear Governor Wood:
His Excellency, Robert E. Wood Governor of Michigan Lansing, Michigan	
The Honorable Robert E. Wood Governor of Michigan Lansing, Michigan	

[4] The first form should be used when the addressee does not hold a doctor's degree, or when the writer is not certain that he does.

HEAD OF A STATE DEPARTMENT

Inside address [5]	*Salutation*
The Secretary of State	Sir:
or	Dear Sir:
The State Treasurer	My dear Mr. McIntire:
or	
The Attorney General	
The State Capitol	
Topeka, Kansas	
The Secretary of State	
State of Kansas	
Topeka, Kansas	
The Honorable Carl R. McIntire	
Secretary of State	
The State Capitol	
Topeka, Kansas	

INSTRUCTOR IN A COLLEGE OR UNIVERSITY

Inside address [6]	*Salutation*
Ira B. Thompson, Ph.D.	Dear Sir:
Department of Economics	My dear Dr. (*or* Mr.)
Harvard University	Thompson:
Cambridge, Massachusetts	Dear Dr. (*or* Mr.)
	Thompson:
Dr. Ira B. Thompson	
Department of Economics	
Harvard University	
Cambridge, Massachusetts	
Mr. Ira B. Thompson	
Department of Economics	
Harvard University	
Cambridge, Massachusetts	

[5] In states that employ the term *commonwealth* (Pennsylvania and Massachusetts, for example), this term should be used instead of *state*. *Examples:* The Secretary of the Commonwealth, The Treasurer of the Commonwealth.

[6] The third form should be used when the addressee does not hold a doctor's degree, or when the writer is not certain that he does. The designation of the addressee's official position may be substituted for the name of the department in any of the forms that follow. In this case the word *Instructor* is followed by *in*, not *of*. *Examples:*

CORRECT:	Instructor in Economics
INCORRECT:	Instructor of Economics

JUDGE OF A FEDERAL DISTRICT COURT

Inside address	*Salutation*
The Honorable Edward J. Kendall United States District Judge Eastern District of New York Brooklyn, New York	Sir: Dear Sir: My dear Judge Kendall:

LEGISLATOR (MEMBER OF A UNICAMERAL LEGISLATURE)

Inside address	*Salutation*
The Honorable Harold E. Tompkins The State Legislature Lincoln, Nebraska	Sir: Dear Sir: My dear Mr. Tompkins: Dear Mr. Tompkins:
The Honorable Harold E. Tompkins Member of Legislature The State Capitol Lincoln, Nebraska	

LIEUTENANT GOVERNOR OF A STATE

Inside address	*Salutation*
The Lieutenant Governor State of Wisconsin Madison, Wisconsin	Sir: My dear Sir: Dear Sir: My dear Mr. Campbell:
The Honorable Ralph D. Campbell Lieutenant Governor of Wisconsin Madison, Wisconsin	

MAYOR OF A CITY

Inside address	*Salutation*
The Mayor of the City of Chicago City Hall Chicago, Illinois	Sir: Dear Sir: My dear Mr. Mayor: My dear Mayor Sherman: Dear Mayor Sherman:
The Honorable Paul V. Sherman Mayor of the City of Chicago City Hall Chicago, Illinois	

MILITARY OFFICER

See *Correct Form in Writing to Army and Naval Officers*, pages 371-372.

MINISTER (DIPLOMATIC)

American:

Inside address [7]	*Salutation*
His Excellency	Sir:
The American Minister	Your Excellency:
Stockholm, Sweden	My dear Mr. Minister:

His Excellency John N. Grayson
American Minister
Stockholm, Sweden

The Honorable John N. Grayson
American Minister
Stockholm, Sweden

Foreign:

Inside address	*Salutation*
His Excellency	Sir:
The Swedish Minister	Your Excellency:
The Swedish Legation	My dear Mr. Minister:
Washington, D. C.	

The Swedish Minister
The Swedish Legation
Washington, D. C.

NAVAL OFFICER

See *Correct Form in Writing to Army and Naval Officers,* pages 371-372.

POSTMASTER GENERAL

Inside address	*Salutation*
The Honorable	Sir:
The Postmaster General	Dear Sir:
Washington, D. C.	My dear Mr. Postmaster General:
The Honorable Charles T. Corley	
The Postmaster General	
Washington, D. C.	

[7] For American Minister resident in Central or South America, substitute *United States* for *American* in the following forms.

PRESIDENT OF A COLLEGE OR UNIVERSITY

Inside address [8]	*Salutation*
James Allison Carter, LL.D.	Dear Sir:
(*or* Lit.D., D.Sc., etc.)	My dear President Carter:
President of Dartmouth College	My dear Dr. Carter:
Hanover, New Hampshire	(if he holds the degree)
	Dear President Carter:
Dr. James Allison Carter	Dear Dr. Carter:
President of Dartmouth College	(if he holds the degree)
Hanover, New Hampshire	

President James Allison Carter
Dartmouth College
Hanover, New Hampshire

PRESIDENT OF STATE SENATE

Inside address	*Salutation*
The Honorable Henry C. Jennings	Sir:
President of the Senate of Kansas	
The State Capitol	
Topeka, Kansas	

PRESIDENT OF THE SENATE OF THE UNITED STATES

Inside address	*Salutation*
The Honorable	Sir:
The President of the Senate	
of the United States	
Washington, D. C.	

The Honorable George F. Conley
President of the Senate
Washington, D. C.

PRESIDENT OF THE UNITED STATES

Inside address	*Salutation*
The President	Sir:
The White House	To the President:
Washington, D. C.	My dear Mr. President:
	Dear Mr. President:
The President of the United States	
The White House	
Washington, D. C.	

The President
Washington, D. C.

[8] The third form should be used when the addressee does not hold a doctor's degree, or when the writer is not certain that he does.

Priest (Roman Catholic)

Inside address	*Salutation*
The Reverend Father John G. Donahue (followed by specific postal address)	Reverend dear Father: My dear Father Donahue: Dear Father Donahue:
The Reverend John G. Donahue (followed by specific postal address)	

Professor in a College or University

Inside address [9]	*Salutation*
Professor Morris A. Brinkman Department of English Northwestern University Evanston, Illinois	Dear Sir: My dear Professor Brinkman: My dear Dr. Brinkman: (if he holds the degree) Dear Professor Brinkman: Dear Dr. Brinkman: (if he holds the degree)
Morris A. Brinkman, Ph.D. Professor (*or* Associate Professor, *or* Assistant Professor) of English Northwestern University Evanston, Illinois	
Dr. Morris A. Brinkman Professor (*or* Associate Professor, *or* Assistant Professor) of English Northwestern University Evanston, Illinois	

Rabbi

Inside address	*Salutation*
Rabbi Isaac S. Bernstein (followed by specific postal address)	Reverend Sir: Dear Sir: My dear Rabbi Bernstein: Dear Rabbi Bernstein:
The Reverend Isaac S. Bernstein (followed by specific postal address)	

Representative in Congress

Inside address	*Salutation*
The Honorable Kenneth A. Marshall The House of Representatives Washington, D. C.	Sir: My dear Sir: Dear Sir: My dear Congressman Marshall: My dear Mr. Marshall: Dear Mr. Marshall:
For letter directed to home address: The Honorable Kenneth A. Marshall Representative in Congress (followed by specific postal address)	

[9] The first form should be used when the addressee does not hold a doctor's degree, or when the writer is not certain that he does.

SECRETARY OF AGRICULTURE

Inside address	*Salutation*
The Honorable The Secretary of Agriculture Washington, D. C.	Sir: Dear Sir: My dear Mr. Secretary:

The Honorable Ralph G. Davidson
Secretary of Agriculture
Washington, D. C.

SECRETARY OF COMMERCE

Inside address	*Salutation*
The Honorable The Secretary of Commerce Washington, D. C.	Sir: Dear Sir: My dear Mr. Secretary:

The Honorable Walter A. Hill
Secretary of Commerce
Washington, D. C.

SECRETARY OF DEFENSE

Inside address	*Salutation*
The Honorable The Secretary of Defense Washington, D. C.	Sir: Dear Sir: My dear Mr. Secretary:

The Honorable Roger C. Barton
Secretary of Defense
Washington, D. C.

SECRETARY OF LABOR

Inside address	*Salutation*
The Honorable The Secretary of Labor Washington, D. C.	Sir: Dear Sir: My dear Mr. Secretary:

The Honorable Paul B. Grant
Secretary of Labor
Washington, D. C.

SECRETARY OF STATE

Inside address	*Salutation*
The Honorable The Secretary of State Washington, D. C.	Sir: Dear Sir: My dear Mr. Secretary:

The Honorable Robert E. Collins
Secretary of State
Washington, D. C.

SECRETARY OF THE AIR FORCE

Inside address	*Salutation*
The Honorable	Sir:
The Secretary of the Air Force	Dear Sir:
Washington, D. C.	My dear Mr. Secretary:

The Honorable James E. Dillard
Secretary of the Air Force
Washington, D. C.

SECRETARY OF THE ARMY

Inside address	*Salutation*
The Honorable	Sir:
The Secretary of the Army	Dear Sir:
Washington, D. C.	My dear Mr. Secretary:

The Honorable Albert D. Marsten
Secretary of the Army
Washington, D. C.

SECRETARY OF THE INTERIOR

Inside address	*Salutation*
The Honorable	Sir:
The Secretary of the Interior	Dear Sir:
Washington, D. C.	My dear Mr. Secretary:

The Honorable Arthur J. Wingate
Secretary of the Interior
Washington, D. C.

SECRETARY OF THE NAVY

Inside address	*Salutation*
The Honorable	Sir:
The Secretary of the Navy	Dear Sir:
Washington, D. C.	My dear Mr. Secretary:

The Honorable William C. Hargrove
Secretary of the Navy
Washington, D. C.

SECRETARY OF THE TREASURY

Inside address	*Salutation*
The Honorable	Sir:
The Secretary of the Treasury	Dear Sir:
Washington, D. C.	My dear Mr. Secretary:

The Honorable John F. Salisbury
Secretary of the Treasury
Washington, D. C.

SENATOR (UNITED STATES)

Inside address	*Salutation*
The Honorable Martin L. Stevens The United States Senate Washington, D. C.	Sir: My dear Sir: Dear Sir: My dear Senator Stevens:
Senator Martin L. Stevens The United States Senate Washington, D. C.	Dear Senator Stevens:

For letter directed to home address:
The Honorable Martin L. Stevens
United States Senator
(followed by specific postal address)

SPEAKER OF THE HOUSE OF REPRESENTATIVES

Inside address	*Salutation*
The Honorable The Speaker of the House of Representatives Washington, D. C.	Sir: My dear Sir: Dear Sir: My dear Mr. Speaker: Dear Mr. Speaker:
The Speaker of the House of Representatives Washington, D. C.	My dear Mr. Robbins:

The Honorable William D. Robbins
Speaker of the House of Representatives
Washington, D. C.

STATE REPRESENTATIVE

Inside address	*Salutation*
The Honorable Lee W. Sanderson The House of Representatives The State Capitol Jefferson City, Missouri	Sir: Dear Sir: My dear Mr. Sanderson: Dear Mr. Sanderson:

STATE SENATOR

Inside address	*Salutation*
The Honorable Philip J. Bentley The State Senate Trenton, New Jersey	Sir: Dear Sir: My dear Senator Bentley: Dear Senator Bentley:
Senator Philip J. Bentley The State Capitol Trenton, New Jersey	

VICE PRESIDENT OF THE UNITED STATES

Inside address	*Salutation*
The Honorable The Vice President of the United States Washington, D. C.	Sir: Dear Sir: My dear Mr. Vice President: Dear Mr. Vice President:
The Vice President The United States Senate Washington, D. C.	
The Honorable Richard C. Claypool Vice President of the United States Washington, D. C.	

APPENDIX G

Correct Form in Writing to Army and Naval Officers

When the addressee holds a military or naval title, this should be substituted for the usual form *Mr.* in the inside address. Such a title may be abbreviated in the inside address when space limitation necessitates (with the exceptions noted below), although it is preferably written in full. The following military and naval titles, with their abbreviations, are arranged in the order of descending rank:

Military titles	*Naval titles*
General (no abbreviation)	Admiral (no abbreviation)
Lieutenant General (Lt. Gen.)	Vice Admiral (Vice Adm.)
Major General (Maj. Gen.)	Rear Admiral (Rear Adm.)
Brigadier General (Brig. Gen.)	Commodore (Como.)
Colonel (Col.)	Captain (Capt.)
Lieutenant Colonel (Lt. Col.)	Commander (Comdr.)
Major (Maj.)	Lieutenant Commander
Captain (Capt.)	(Lt. Comdr.)
First Lieutenant (1st Lieut.)	Lieutenant (Lieut.)
Second Lieutenant (2d Lieut.)	Lieutenant (junior grade)
Cadet (no abbreviation)	Lieut. (j.g.)
Sergeant (Sgt.)	Ensign (Ens.)
	Midshipman (Midn.)

The highest-ranking officer of the Marine Corps is the Lieutenant General Commandant. All ranks below that of the Lieutenant General are the same as observed by the Army. The lowest commissioned rank, of course, is that of Second Lieutenant. Marine Corps officers wear the same insignia of rank as Army officers.

The appropriate designation—U.S.A. (United States Army),

U.S.N. (United States Navy), or U.S.M.C. (United States Marine Corps)—should follow the branch of the service in which the addressee is engaged. *Examples:*

Captain James B. Randall	Lieut. Roy Adams
Field Artillery, U.S.A.	Medical Corps, U.S.N.

The most formal of salutations, *Sir,* is sometimes used in greeting an officer of extremely high rank (such as one whose title includes the word *General* or *Admiral*), although the form *Dear Sir* is more frequently employed. The latter form is the standard business salutation and is always correct, regardless of the rank of the addressee. When the writer desires to personalize his greeting, the salutation may include the surname of the recipient. In this case the title *Mr.* (or *Dr.,* if the addressee is a member of the medical personnel) is customarily employed when the rank of the recipient is below that of *Captain* in the *Army* or that of *Commander* in the *Navy.* Otherwise the appropriate military or naval title should be used. If this title consists of two words, the first or qualifying word should be omitted from the salutation. For example, a *Lieutenant General, Major General,* or *Brigadier General* should be greeted as *My dear General Summers* or *Dear General Summers,* and a *Vice Admiral* or *Rear Admiral* should be greeted as *My dear Admiral Winters* or *Dear Admiral Winters.* A military or naval title should not be abbreviated when it is used in the salutation.

The standard complimentary closes arc used in letters addressed to army and naval officers. When the extremely formal salutation *Sir* is employed, consistency requires the use of a complimentary close that includes the word *respectfully.* Such a close may also be used with a salutation of a less formal character when the writer wishes to show special deference to rank or authority. Otherwise one of the complimentary closes including the word *truly* represents an appropriate degree of formality.

APPENDIX H

Standard Forms of Letter Layout

NATIONAL RETAIL CREDIT ASSOCIATION

national in name — *International in scope*

EXECUTIVE OFFICES   SHELL BUILDING

LINDLEY S. CROWDER
GENERAL MANAGER-TREASURER

ST LOUIS 3. MO

October 15, 195-

Mr. Robert A. Jackson
750 Allerton Street
Jamestown, New York

Dear Mr. Jackson:

This letter illustrates the block or straight-edge form.
The date line may be placed as shown in this example, or
it may be centered beneath the letterhead.

The lines of the inside address are blocked, and paragraph
beginnings align with the left-hand margin of the page.
The complimentary close begins a little to the right of
the vertical center of the sheet. When the date line is
arranged as shown in this letter, the complimentary close
and signature usually align with this preceding item.

Many business and professional men prefer the block form
because of its neat, clean-cut appearance. Several correspondence supervisors also recommend this form because its
marginal uniformity makes for rapid typing.

Sincerely yours,

L. S. Crowder

LSC:MR

Block or Straight-Edge Form

⤳SHIPPING UTILITIES⤳

SHIPPING ROOM SUPPLIES...MATERIALS HANDLING EQUIPMENT
STAPLING DEVICES...SCALES.. TAPING MACHINES ...STENCIL MACHINES

J. G. BUETTNER
President

3107 PINE STREET
ST. LOUIS 3, MISSOURI

TELEPHONE
NEWSTEAD 5800

OFFICES
ST. LOUIS, MO.
KANSAS CITY, MO.

October 15, 195-

Mr. Robert A. Jackson
750 Allerton Street
Jamestown, New York

Dear Mr. Jackson:

          This letter is an example of the combination or semi-block form. It differs from the block form only in the indention of paragraph openings. Lines that begin new paragraphs should be uniformly indented either five or ten spaces. This letter employs ten-space indentions.

          Many correspondents feel that indented paragraph openings add to the attractiveness of a letter and make it easier to read. Consequently, the combination form is preferred by a large number of business and professional men.

Sincerely yours,

J. G. Buettner

J. G. Buettner
President

JGB:MS

Combination or Semi-Block Form

NATIONAL RETAIL CREDIT ASSOCIATION

national in name — *International in scope*

EXECUTIVE OFFICES   SHELL BUILDING

LINDLEY S. CROWDER
GENERAL MANAGER-TREASURER

ST. LOUIS 3. MO

October 15, 195-

Mr. Robert A. Jackson
   750 Allerton Street
      Jamestown, New York

Dear Mr. Jackson:

     This letter is an example of the indented or stepped-in form. The date line is arranged in the upper right-hand portion of the sheet. The first line of the inside address sets the left-hand margin of the page. Each additional line of the inside address is uniformly indented either three or five spaces more than the preceding line.

     Paragraph beginnings are usually indented the same amount as the last line of the inside address, although they may coincide with the indention of the next to the last line of the inside address. The complimentary close ordinarily aligns with the date line. The signature is written two or three spaces to the right of the point at which the complimentary close begins.

     The indented form is frequently employed by conservative organizations, which often prefer the long-established method to its newer variations. This form is entirely proper, however, for the correspondence of any business or professional man.

             Sincerely yours,

             L. S. Crowder

LSC:MR

Indented or Stepped-in Form

Prentice-Hall, Inc.

EXECUTIVE OFFICES

70 Fifth Avenue, New York 11

October 15, 195–

Dear Mr. Jackson:

This letter is an example of the official form, which differs from the standard arrangement of structural units only in the position of the inside address. The official form is employed not only in letters to government officials, but also in many of the personal letters written by business and professional men.

Although the date line may be centered beneath the letterhead, it is preferably arranged as illustrated in this letter. The salutation may be placed from two to five spaces below the date line, according to the length of the message.

The inside address should begin flush with the left-hand margin, from two to five spaces below the final item of the signature, the exact position depending upon the length of the letter. The identification line should be placed two or three spaces below the last item of the inside address.

Sincerely yours,

Richard P. Ettinger
President

Mr. Robert A. Jackson
750 Allerton Street
Jamestown, New York

RPE:HA

Official Form

APPENDIX I

Mechanics of Envelope Address

THE ENVELOPE ADDRESS is double-spaced when it contains either two or three lines, and single-spaced when it consists of more than three lines. Its indention form corresponds with that employed in the inside address of the letter.

The first line of the address is usually placed just below the horizontal center of the envelope. The address as a whole should be attractively arranged with respect to the left- and right-hand edges. It may be centered upon the envelope, or placed somewhat to the right of the center, so that the margin on the right is approximately two-thirds as wide as that on the left. In no case, however, should the right-hand margin be the greater of the two.

Instructions to postal employees, such as AIR MAIL or SPECIAL DELIVERY, are written in capital letters above the address in the upper right-hand portion of the envelope. Care must be taken that such instructions are placed at least $1\frac{1}{8}$ inches below the top edge of the envelope, to allow sufficient space for the stamps and postmark. Special directions pertaining to the addressee, intended for notice after delivery—such as *Personal* or *Please Forward*—may be placed in the lower left-hand corner of the envelope.

In addition to the name and address of the intended recipient, the envelope should bear the name and return address of the sender. When a No. $6\frac{3}{4}$ envelope ($3\frac{5}{8}$ by $6\frac{1}{2}$ inches) is used, the information concerning the sender should appear in the upper left-hand corner. The same position is preferable when a No. 10 envelope ($4\frac{1}{8}$ by $9\frac{1}{2}$ inches) or No. 9 envelope ($3\frac{7}{8}$ by $8\frac{7}{8}$ inches) is used, although in either case the sender's name and address may be placed on the flap. A No. 6 baronial envelope (5 by 6 inches) should carry these details on the flap.

377

The envelopes of business establishments, professional organizations, and institutions—as well as the personal envelopes of many individuals—are imprinted with the name and address of the sender. When the envelope does not bear these items in printed form, they should be typewritten in the proper position. Single spacing is recommended in all cases to conserve space. The block form is preferable even when the envelope address is indented.

APPENDIX J

Proper Folding and Insertion of Letters in Envelopes

A LETTER must be properly folded and inserted in the envelope if it is later to be removed in the right position for immediate inspection by the reader. The correct method of folding and inserting the letter is determined by the size of the sheet, and by the dimensions of the envelope that is to contain it.

The following paragraphs list several types of envelopes that may be used to accommodate a letter written upon a sheet of standard size (8½ by 11 inches), and outline the proper method of folding and inserting the letter in each type of envelope.

(1) The No. 6¾ envelope (standard business size), 3⅝ by 6½ inches. This type is widely used in business correspondence.

Method of procedure for folding and inserting the letter:

(a) Place the sheet face up on a flat surface.

(b) Turn the bottom edge upward until it rests about a quarter of an inch below the top edge, exactly parallel to it, and crease the fold.

(c) Turn the right edges over one-third of the distance toward the left edges, and crease the fold.

(d) Turn the left edges over toward the right until they rest about a quarter of an inch short of the previous fold, and crease the fold. If the letter contains an enclosure, place it in this fold.

(e) Insert the letter so that the last fold rests against the bottom of the envelope, with the free edges turned upward against the back (sealed side) of the envelope.

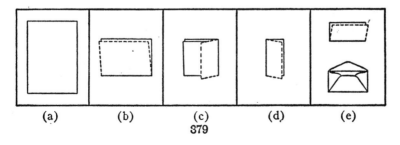

(a)   (b)   (c)   (d)   (e)

(2) The No. 10 envelope (official size), 4⅛ by 9½ inches. This type is also used extensively in business correspondence. It should be used in preference to the No. 6¾ size when a letter consists of more than one page, or when an enclosure is too large for convenient insertion in the smaller envelope.

Method of procedure for folding and inserting the letter:

(a) Place the sheet face up on a flat surface.

(b) Turn the bottom edge upward one-third of the distance toward the top edge, with the side edges even, and crease the fold.

(c) Turn the top edge downward until it rests about a quarter of an inch above the previous fold, exactly parallel to it, and crease the fold. If the letter contains an enclosure, place it in this fold.

(d) Insert the letter so that the last fold rests against the bottom of the envelope, with the free edge turned upward against the back (sealed side) of the envelope.

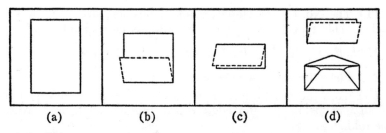

| (a) | (b) | (c) | (d) |

(3) The No. 9 envelope, 3⅞ by 8⅞ inches. This type is frequently used instead of the No. 10 size. The method of procedure for folding and inserting the letter is exactly the same as that employed when the No. 10 envelope is used.

(4) The No. 6 baronial envelope, 5 by 6 inches. This type is used occasionally to accommodate a sheet of standard size.

Method of procedure for folding and inserting the letter:

(a) Place the sheet face up on a flat surface.

(b) Turn the bottom edge upward until it rests exactly even with the top edge, and crease the fold.

(c) Turn the right edges over toward the left until they rest exactly even with the left edges, and crease the fold. If the letter contains an enclosure, place it in this fold.

(d) Insert the letter so that the last fold (the vertical fold) rests against the bottom of the envelope, with the two halves of the first fold (the horizontal fold) at the right side of the envelope, with respect to the back (sealed side).

Any of the so-called two-fold sheets, 7½ by 10½ inches, 7¼ by 10½ inches, or 7 by 10 inches, may be accommodated by the No. 9 envelope, which is better adapted to the size of these sheets than the larger No. 10 envelope. Many correspondents who use these smaller two-fold sheets employ envelopes somewhat smaller than the No. 9 size that are specially proportioned to the dimensions of the letter page. A sheet 7¼ by 10½ inches (monarch size) or 7 by 10 inches may be nicely accommodated by the No. 7½ envelope (3⅞ by 7½ inches). This envelope is known as the monarch or bifold size.

The baronial sheet, 5½ by 8½ inches, is best accommodated by the No. 6 baronial envelope. When this type of envelope is used, the sheet should be folded so that the top and bottom edges are exactly even, with the face of the letter concealed within the fold. The sheet should be inserted so that the fold rests against the bottom of the envelope, with the upper half of the letter against the face (addressed side) of the envelope. The baronial sheet may also be enclosed in an envelope of the No. 6¾ size, or in one of the slightly smaller No. 6 size (3⅜ by 6 inches). When either of these types is used, the sheet should be folded and inserted exactly as a page of standard size is folded and inserted in a No. 10 envelope (see page 380).

Index

A

Acceptance, letters of, 236–249
  of hospitality of home or club on overnight visit, 239–241
  of invitation to attend meeting or convention, 243–244
  of invitation to banquet, club luncheon, lecture, or entertainment, 237–238
  of invitation to serve on civic or professional committee or board, 245–246
  of luncheon or dinner invitation, 238–239
  of membership in professional or civic organization, 244–245
  of resignation from club or association, 248–249
  of resignation from position, board, or committee, 246–248
  of speaking invitation, 241–242
Address, envelope, 377–378
  forms of, for persons of rank, 356–370
Agriculture, Secretary of, forms of address for, 367
Air Force, Secretary of, forms of address for, 368
Ambassador, American, forms of address for, 357
  British, forms of address for, 357
Apology, letters of, 261–268
  for absence from meeting, 266–267
  for delay in acknowledging favor or courtesy, 262–264
  for delay in returning borrowed property, 261–262
  for delay in sending promised material, 264–266
  for inability to keep appointment, 267–268
Appreciation, letters of, 46–117
  to business and professional associates:
    for assistance to firm, club, or association, 54–59
    for favorable mention in speech, article, or book, 77–79

Appreciation, letters of, to business and professional associates (*cont.*)
    for luncheon or dinner at home or club, 59–62
    for message of condolence or sympathy, 71–73
    for message of congratulation, 66–70
    for overnight visit at home or club, 62–64
    for personal favor or service, 48–54
    for speaking before club or association, 73–77
    for theater, sports event, or other entertainment, 64–66
  to consumers:
    for co-operation in correcting error, 111–112
    for first use of charge account, 99–102
    for opening charge account, 96–99
    for prompt payment of bills, 107–111
    for recommending firm to others, 112–114
    for regular patronage, 102–107
    for renewed patronage, 115–117
  to dealers:
    for act of special service or courtesy, 93–96
    for loyal patronage over period of years, 85–87
    for outstanding success in sale of product, 87–90
    for promptness in meeting obligations, 90–93
  to employees:
    for loyal or outstanding service, 79–82
    for valuable suggestion, 82–85
Army, Secretary of, forms of address for, 368
Army officers, correct form in writing to, 371–372
Assemblyman, forms of address for, 357
Associate Judge, of court of appeals, forms of address for, 358

Associate Justice, of state supreme court, forms of address for, 358

of Supreme Court of United States, forms of address for, 358

Attorney General, forms of address for, 358

B

Block form, of letter layout, 373

Business and professional associates, letters to:

of appreciation:

for assistance to firm, club, or association, 54–59

for favorable mention in speech, article, or book, 77–79

for luncheon or dinner at home or club, 59–62

for message of condolence or sympathy, 71–73

for message of congratulation, 66–70

for overnight visit at home or club, 62–64

for personal favor or service, 48–54

for speaking before club or association, 73–77

for theater, sports event, or other entertainment, 64–66

of condolence and sympathy:

upon a death in family, 151–155

upon death of a company officer, 161–163

upon injury or illness of a member of family, 159–161

upon material loss or damage, 163–167

upon personal injury or illness, 155–159

of congratulation and good wishes:

upon accomplishment of son or daughter, 28–30

upon business anniversary or special business achievement, 30–34

upon new business or professional connection, 9–12

upon outstanding community service, 25–28

upon professional or civic honor, 2–9

Business and professional associates, letters of congratulation and good wishes (*cont.*)

upon promotion, 12–17

upon retirement from business, 17–19

upon speech, article, pamphlet, or book, 19–25

of invitation:

to attend banquet, club luncheon, lecture, or entertainment, 208–210

to be luncheon or dinner guest, 211–214

to be overnight guest at home or club, 214–216

to give address or informal talk, 217–220

of seasonal good wishes, 119–121

of welcome, 132–134

Business or professional associate, letters introducing, 199–202

letters recommending, 185–189

C

Cabinet officer, forms of address for (*see* Agriculture, Secretary of; Attorney General; Commerce, Secretary of; Defense, Secretary of; Interior, Secretary of; Labor, Secretary of; Postmaster General; State, Secretary of; Treasury, Secretary of)

Capitalization, guides to correct, 348–350

Chancellor, of university, forms of address for, 359

Charity organizations, letters soliciting funds for, 296–307

Chief Judge, of court of appeals, forms of address for, 359

Chief Justice, of state supreme court, forms of address for, 359

of Supreme Court of United States, forms of address for, 359

Clergyman, forms of address for (*see* Priest, Roman Catholic; Rabbi; *Reverend,* use of)

College officials, forms of address for (*see* Chancellor, of university; Dean, of college for

College officials, forms of address for (*cont.*)
women; Dean, of college or university; Instructor, in college or university; President, of college or university; Professor, in college or university)

Combination form, of letter layout, 374

Commendation, letters of (*see* Congratulation and good wishes, letters of)

Commerce, Secretary of, forms of address for, 367

Commissioner, of government bureau, forms of address for, 360

Complimentary close, in letters to military and naval personnel, 372
in letters to persons of rank, 356

Condolence and sympathy, letters of, 150–179
to business and professional associates:
upon a death in family, 151–155
upon death of a company officer, 161–163
upon injury or illness of a member of family, 159–161
upon material loss or damage, 163–167
upon personal injury or illness, 155–159
to dealers, 151 (footnote)
to employees:
upon a death in family, 167–169
upon personal injury or illness, 169–173
to relatives of business associates taken by death, 173–176
to relatives of employees taken by death, 177–179

Congratulation and good wishes, letters of, 1–45
to business and professional associates:
upon accomplishment of son or daughter, 28–30
upon business anniversary or special business achievement, 30–34
upon new business or professional connection, 9–12
upon outstanding community

Congratulation and good wishes, letters of, to business and professional associates (*cont.*)
service, 25–28
upon professional or civic honor, 2–9
upon promotion, 12–17
upon retirement from business, 17–19
upon speech, article, pamphlet, or book, 19–25
to dealers, 2 (footnote)
to employees:
upon outstanding work for firm, 39–43
upon professional honor **or** achievement, 43–45
upon promotion or other business advancement, 34–37
upon significant personal occasion, 37–39

Congressman, forms of address for (*see* Representative, in Congress; Senator, United States)

Consul, forms of address for, 360

Consumers, letters to:
of appreciation:
for co-operation in correcting error, 111–112
for first use of charge account, 99–102
for opening charge account, 96–99
for prompt payment of bills, 107–111
for recommending firm to others, 112–114
for regular patronage, 102–107
for renewed patronage, 115–117
of invitation:
to attend special event, 232–235
to open charge account, 224–228
to renew use of account, 228–232
of seasonal good wishes, 128–130
of welcome, 142–145

Contributions, letters soliciting, 296–307

D

Dealers, letters to:
of appreciation:
for act of special service **or** courtesy, 93–96

Dealers, letters of appreciation (*cont.*)
for loyal patronage over period of years, 85–87
for outstanding success in sale of product, 87–90
for promptness in meeting obligations, 90–93
of condolence and sympathy, 151 (footnote)
of congratulation and good wishes, 2 (footnote)
of invitation, 208 (footnote)
of seasonal good wishes, 124–128
of welcome, 138–142
Dean, of college for women, forms of address for, 360
of college or university, forms of address for, 361
Declination, letters of, 249–261 (*see also* Requests, letters declining)
of hospitality of home or club on overnight visit, 253–254
of invitation to attend meeting or convention, 257–258
of invitation to banquet, club luncheon, lecture, or entertainment, 250–251
of invitation to serve on civic or professional committee or board, 259–261
of luncheon or dinner invitation, 251–253
of membership in professional or civic organization, 258–259
of speaking invitation, 254–257
Defense, Secretary of, forms of address for, 367
Delayed action, letters explaining, 273–277
acknowledgment by secretary in absence of addressee, 276–277
requesting additional time in which to make final reply, 274–276
Delegate (member of state legislative body), forms of address for, 361
Dr., use of, 352

E

Employee or former employee, letters recommending, 189–194

Employees, letters to:
of appreciation:
for loyal or outstanding service, 79–82
for valuable suggestion, 82–85
of condolence and sympathy:
upon a death in family, 167–169
upon personal injury or illness, 169–173
of congratulation and good wishes:
upon outstanding work for firm, 39–43
upon professional honor or achievement, 43–45
upon promotion or other business advancement, 34–37
upon significant personal occasion, 37–39
of invitation, to attend company social event, 220–224
of seasonal good wishes, 122–124
of welcome, 134–138
English usage, common errors in, 314–342
Envelope address, in letters to persons of rank, 356
mechanics of, 377–378
Envelopes, folding and insertion of letters in, 379–381
Esq., use of, 354–355

F

Folding, of letter, 379–381
Forms of address, for persons of rank, 356–370
Forms of letter layout, 373–376

G

Good usage, common errors in, 314–342
Good wishes, letters of (*see* Congratulation and good wishes, letters of; Seasonal good wishes, letters of)
Governor, forms of address for, 361
Greeting (*see* Salutation)

H

Hackneyed expressions, 311–313

Honorable, use of, 353

I

Indented form, of letter layout, 375
Indention, forms of, 373–376
Insertion, of letter in envelope, 379–381
Inside address, in letters to military and naval personnel, 371–372
in letters to persons of rank, 356–370
Instructor, in college or university, forms of address for, 362
Interior, Secretary of, forms of address for, 368
Introduction, letters of, 195–206
of business or professional associate, 199–202
of new sales representative, 203–206
of personal friend, 196–199
Invitation, letters of, 207–235
to business and professional associates:
to attend banquet, club luncheon, lecture, or entertainment, 208–210
to be luncheon or dinner guest, 211–214
to be overnight guest at home or club, 214–216
to give address or informal talk, 217–220
to consumers:
to attend special event, 232–235
to open charge account, 224–228
to renew use of account, 228–232
to dealers, 208 (footnote)
to employees, to attend company social event, 220–224
to prospective consumers, 224 (footnote)
Invitations, letters accepting (*see* Acceptance, letters of)
letters declining (*see* Declination, letters of)

J

Judge, of Federal district court, forms of address for, 363

L

Labor, Secretary of, forms of address for, 367
Layout, of letter, 373–376
Legislator (member of unicameral body), forms of address for, 363
Letter mechanics:
envelope address, 377–378
folding, 379–381
forms of layout, 373–376
insertion in envelope, 379–381
Lieutenant Governor, forms of address for, 363

M

Madam, use of, in writing to government officials, 356
Marine Corps officers, correct form in writing to, 371–372
Mayor, forms of address for, 363
Military officers (*see* Army officers)
Minister (diplomatic), American, forms of address for, 364
foreign, forms of address for, 364
Miss, use of, 352
Mr., use of, 351
Mrs., use of, 351–352

N

Naval officers, correct form in writing to, 371–372
Navy, Secretary of, forms of address for, 368

O

Official form, of letter layout, 376

P

Personal friend, letters introducing, 196–199
letters recommending, 181–185
Postmaster General, forms of address for, 364
President, of college or university, forms of address for, 365
of state senate, forms of address for, 365

President (*cont.*)
of United States, forms of address for, 365
of United States Senate, forms of address for, 365
Priest, Roman Catholic, forms of address for, 366
Professional associate, letters introducing, 199–202
letters recommending, 185–189
Professional associates, letters to (*see* Business and professional associates, letters to)
Professor, in college or university, forms of address for, 366
Professor, use of, 353
Public-welfare institutions, letters soliciting funds for, 296–307
Punctuation, guides to correct, 343–347

R

Rabbi, forms of address for, 366
Recommendation, letters of, 180–194
of business or professional associate, 185–189
of employee or former employee, 189–194
of personal friend, 181–185
Regret, letters of, 268–273 (*see also* Declination, letters of)
for absence during call of out-of-town visitor, 269–270
for absence of associate from meeting or convention, 272–273
for inability of associate to call at office as planned, 271–272
for inability to call upon associate during visit to his city, 270–271
Representative, in Congress, forms of address for, 366
state, forms of address for, 369
Requests, letters declining, 288–295
for business appointment, 290–291
for charge account, 291–292
for information or material, 288–289
for support of charitable organization, public-welfare institution, co-operative-advertising campaign, etc., 292–295

Requests (*cont.*)
letters granting, 277–287
for booklet, pamphlet, or magazine, 280–281
for business appointment, 282–283
for charge account, 285–287
for information, 278–280
for permission to reprint material in book or article, 284–285
Reverend, use of, 353–354

S

Sales representative, letters introducing, 203–206
Salutation, in letters to military and naval personnel, 372
in letters to persons of rank, 353, 354, 356–370
Seasonal good wishes, letters of, 118–130
to business and professional associates, 119–121
to consumers, 128–130
to dealers, 124–128
to employees, 122–124
Semi-block form, of letter layout, 374
Senator, state, forms of address for, 369
United States, forms of address for, 369
Solicitation, letters of, 296–307
Speaker, of House of Representatives, forms of address for, 369
State, Secretary of, forms of address for, 367
State department, head of a, forms of address for, 362
Stepped-in form, of letter layout, 375
Stock expressions, 311–313
Straight-edge form, of letter layout, 373
Sympathy, letters of (*see* Condolence and sympathy, letters of)

T

Thanks, letters of (*see* Appreciation, letters of)
Titles, commonly used, 351–355
military and naval, 371–372

Treasury, Secretary of, forms of address for, 368

Trite expressions, 311–313

U

University officials, forms of address for (*see* Chancellor, of university; Dean, of college for women; Dean, of college or university; Instructor, in college or university; President, of college or university; Professor, in college or university)

V

Vice President, of United States, forms of address for, 370

W

Welcome, letters of, 131–149
to business and professional associates, 132–134
to consumers, 142–145
to dealers, 138–142
to employees, 134–138
to prospective consumers, 145–149